# POLICING HUMANITARIANISM

*Policing Humanitarianism* examines the ways in which European Union policies aimed at countering the phenomenon of migrant smuggling affects civil society actors' activities in the provision of humanitarian assistance, access to rights for irregular immigrants and asylum seekers. It explores the effects of EU policies, laws and agencies' operations in anti-migrant smuggling actions and their implementation in the following EU Member States: Italy, Greece, Hungary and the UK. The book critically studies policies designed and implemented since 2015, during the so called 'European refugee humanitarian crisis'.

# Policing Humanitarianism

## *EU Policies Against Human Smuggling and their Impact on Civil Society*

Sergio Carrera
Valsamis Mitsilegas
Jennifer Allsopp
and
Lina Vosyliūtė

• HART •
OXFORD • LONDON • NEW YORK • NEW DELHI • SYDNEY

HART PUBLISHING

Bloomsbury Publishing Plc

Kemp House, Chawley Park, Cumnor Hill, Oxford, OX2 9PH, UK

HART PUBLISHING, the Hart/Stag logo, BLOOMSBURY and the Diana logo are trademarks of Bloomsbury Publishing Plc

First published in Great Britain 2019



A catalogue record for this book is available from the British Library.

Library of Congress Cataloging-in-Publication data

Names: Carrera, Sergio (Political scientist), author. | Mitsilegas, Valsamis, author. | Allsopp, Jennifer, author. | Vosyliūte, Lina, author.

Title: Policing humanitarianism : EU policies against human smuggling and their impact on civil society / Sergio Carrera, Valsamis Mitsilegas, Jennifer Allsopp and Lina Vosyliūte.

Description: Oxford, UK ; Portland, Oregon : Hart Publishing, 2019. | Includes bibliographical references.

Identifiers: LCCN 2018040273 (print) | LCCN 2018041417 (ebook) | ISBN 9781509923007 (Epub) | ISBN 9781509922994 (hardback : alk. paper)

Subjects: LCSH: Emigration and immigration law—European Union countries. | Human smuggling—Law and legislation—European Union countries.

Classification: LCC KJE6044 (ebook) | LCC KJE6044 .C37 2019 (print) | DDC 345.24/0237—dc23

LC record available at https://lccn.loc.gov/2018040273

ISBN: HB: 978-1-50992-299-4
ePDF: 978-1-50992-301-4
ePub: 978-1-50992-300-7

Typeset by Compuscript Ltd, Shannon
Printed and bound in Great Britain by TJ International Ltd, Padstow,Cornwall

MIX
Paper from responsible sources
FSC® C013056

To find out more about our authors and books visit www.hartpublishing.co.uk. Here you will find extracts, author information, details of forthcoming events and the option to sign up for our newsletters.

# ACKNOWLEDGEMENTS

This book presents the findings of the research project Anti-Smuggling Policies and their Intersection with Humanitarian Assistance and Social Trust, which was funded by the UK's Economic and Social Research Council (ESRC) and coordinated by the School of Law of Queen Mary University London. The authors would like to express their gratitude to the project partners, the Platform for International Cooperation on Undocumented Migrants (PICUM) and the Centre for European Policy Studies (CEPS).

Professor Sergio Carrera acted as scientific coordinator and principal investigator of the project, managing the overall direction and coordination of the research team and project activities. He participated in research field visits and interviews conducted across Italy, Greece and Hungary, contributed to the writing of chapters one, two, three, eight and nine, and oversaw the writing of this manuscript.

Professor Valsamis Mitsilegas provided scientific advice over the course of the project and facilitated reaching out to key stakeholders in Italy and Greece. He also contributed to the writing of chapters two and three and reviewed the manuscript.

Dr. Jennifer Allsopp was responsible for organising the field trips to Hungary, Serbia, the UK and France. She also carried out fieldwork in Italy. She co-authored chapters one, four, five, seven and eight and nine, and co-designed the research methodology and research project framework for analysis.

Lina Vosyliūtė was responsible for the organisation of the field trips to Italy and Greece, and provided the contacts in Hungary. She organised the closed-door meeting with law enforcement authorities and judicial actors in Brussels and the final event at the European Parliament. She contributed to the writing of chapters one, two and three and co-authored chapters four, five, seven and eight. Ms Allsopp and Ms Vosyliūtė together planned, organised and analysed data from the focus group with civil society actors and NGOs in Brussels, and disseminated the online survey.

The authors of this book thank Francesca Galleli for contributing background research to the Italian and Hungarian country case studies and to Professor Elspeth Guild (Queen Mary University London) for her insights and guidance. Ms Allsopp would also like to thank Professor Matthew Gibney (Refugee Studies Centre, University of Oxford) for supporting her early work on this topic, and George Gabriel for his assistance.

The authors are grateful to all interviewees for their cooperation and for contributing insights during a busy period in which the needs of migrants and refugees within EU Member States remained a key priority. Special thanks also go to the participants of the civil society focus group discussion which took place in Brussels on 11 May 2017, and to participants at the closed-door meeting with EU and national law enforcement and judicial actors and coastguards which took place on 21 September 2017. The project's main research findings and PICUM's website of testimonies were launched at the European Parliament on 22 November 2017. The authors would like to thank MEP Jean Lambert and her office for this opportunity, and all the participants who joined this important discussion, particularly MEP Elly Schlein for her commitment to following these issues, as well as Salam Aldeen, Founder of Team Humanity, for sharing his personal testimony.

Finally, the authors also would like to thank editor Lee Gillette for careful proofreading as well as to Hart editors for this opportunity to share the research findings with wider readership.

# CONTENTS

# TABLE OF FIGURES

# TABLE OF ABBREVIATIONS

| Abbreviation | Meaning |
|---|---|
| CJEU | Court of Justice of the European Union |
| CSA | Civil Society Actor |
| CSO | Civil Society Organisation |
| DG HOME | Directorate General for Migration and Home Affairs |
| DG JUSTICE | Directorate General for Justice and Consumers |
| EASO | European Asylum Support Office |
| EC | European Commission |
| ECGFF | European Coast Guard Functions Forum |
| ECtHR | European Court of Human Rights (CoE) |
| EEAS | European External Action Service |
| EMPACT | European Multidisciplinary Platform against Criminal Threats (Europol) |
| EPMT | European Monitoring Team (Europol) |
| EMSC | European Migrant Smuggling Centre (Europol) |
| EP | European Parliament |
| EUNAVFOR MED | European Union's Naval Force in the Mediterranean – Operation Sophia (EEAS) |
| Eurojust | The European Union's Judicial Cooperation Unit |
| Europol | European Union Agency for Law Enforcement Cooperation |
| EUROSUR | European Border Surveillance System |
| FRA | European Union Agency for Fundamental Rights |
| Frontex | European Border and Coast Guard Agency |
| IO | International Organisation (such as the UNHCR or IOM) |

| | |
|---|---|
| IOM | International Organisation for Migration |
| JIT | Joint Investigation Team (Europol and/or Eurojust) |
| JO | Joint Operation |
| MRCC | Maritime Rescue Coordination Centre |
| NGO | Non-Governmental Organisation |
| OMN | Operation Mare Nostrum |
| PICUM | Platform for International Cooperation on Undocumented Migrants |
| SAR | Search and Rescue |
| SIENA | Secure Information Exchange Network Application (Europol) |
| SOCTA | Serious Organised Crime Threat Assessment |
| UN | United Nations |
| UN OHCHR | The Office of the United Nations High Commissioner for Human Rights |
| UNHCR | United Nations High Commissioner for Refugees |
| UNODC | United Nations Office on Drugs and Crime |

# 1

# Introduction

Countering migrant-smuggling has been framed as one of the top political priorities of the European Union (EU) in responding to the so-called European humanitarian refugee crisis which emerged in 2015. Significantly, this phenomenon is also known as the European migration *management* crisis (Carrera et al 2015), or crisis of the EU's values and solidarity (Allen et al 2018). As a consequence of conflict and violence in North Africa and the Middle East, the number of first asylum applications rose dramatically, from 563,000 in 2014 to roughly double (1.2 million) in 2015.[1] The 2015 European Agenda on Migration identified as a key area of policy intervention the targeting of criminal networks of smugglers (European Commission 2015a). A wide range of EU policies, laws and agencies were consequently redesigned or tailored with the political aim of preventing, investigating and prosecuting migrant smugglers. The 2015 EU Action Plan against Migrant Smuggling (European Commission 2015b) acknowledged a challenge inherent to such policies: the risk of criminalising those who provide humanitarian assistance and fundamental rights to migrants in distress, ie, civil society actors and non-governmental organisations.

Academic literature has shown how the progressive development of common EU migration and border policies since the mid-1980s has contributed to what has become known as the 'criminalisation of migration' (Guild 2010; Mitsilegas 2015; Parkin 2013; Provera 2015). This has taken the shape of an increasing use of substantive criminal law and traditional criminal law-like approaches in the management of migration; and the use of preventive policing instruments in addressing the phenomenon of irregular immigration. The obstacles and adverse consequences that these policies present to third-country nationals seeking to access their fundamental rights when irregularly entering or residing in the EU have been amply documented (Guild 2010; EU Agency for Fundamental Rights 2014; Baird and van Liempt 2016; Triandafyllidou 2017; Fekete, Webber and Edmond-Pettitt 2017).

Previous scholarly research has illustrated that among these effects there are cases where civil society actors and individuals such as family members who are suspected of facilitating the entry or residence of irregular immigrants have been

[1] See Eurostat, Asylum statistics explained: http://ec.europa.eu/eurostat/statistics-explained/index.php/Asylum_statistics.

brought to criminal proceedings before relevant courts, leading to prosecutions and even criminal convictions (Aliverti 2012, 2013; Allsopp 2012; Carrera et al 2015; Fekete, Webber and Edmond-Pettitt 2017). Importantly, international and regional instruments designed to counter the smuggling of human beings – chiefly the UN Protocol against the Smuggling of Migrants by Land, Sea and Air (UN Smuggling Protocol 2000) – stipulate that the facilitation of entry and stay for non-profit purposes, including therefore for humanitarian assistance, should be exempted from criminalisation. Less attention has been given, however, to the actual effects that the implementation of these anti-smuggling policies have on civil society actors and whether these differ depending on their actual manifestations and roles, ie, formalised and non-formalised groups; service-providers or human rights organisations monitoring states' policies engaged in strategic litigation; and/or those engaged in political mobilisation or activism.

The EU's adoption of the so-called Facilitators' Package (composed of Council Directive 2002/90/EC defining the facilitation of unauthorised entry, transit and residence and Council Framework Decision 2002/946/JHA on the strengthening of the penal framework to prevent the facilitation of unauthorised entry, transit and residence) left it optional for EU Member States to exempt individuals or civil society groups which provide humanitarian assistance to irregular immigrants from criminal penalties. This has led to significant variation in how each EU Member State has incorporated or transposed the package into its national legislation and administrative practices (Carrera et al 2016; Fekete, Webber and Edmond-Pettitt 2017). It has also taken away the initial requirement for criminalisation of financial or material gain in the case of facilitation of entry for the act to constitute a criminal offence. Article 27 of the Convention implementing the 1985 Schengen Agreement explicitly included such a requirement:

> The Contracting Parties undertake to impose appropriate penalties on any person who, *for financial gain*, assists or tries to assist an alien to enter or reside within the territory of one of the Contracting Parties in breach of that Contracting Party's laws on the entry and residence of aliens.[2]

A recent report published by the Institute of Race Relations describes this shift as the 'EU's obsession with controlling borders and stopping "disorderly movements" and spontaneous migration of refugees and migrants to Europe from elsewhere' (Fekete, Webber and Edmond-Pettitt 2017). This shift has led to the emergence of legal uncertainty regarding which activities fall precisely within the scope of criminal offence or illegality and which ones do not; and who may or may not be considered a 'smuggler' or 'complicit' with smuggling activities.

The 2015 European humanitarian refugee crisis prompted a wide-ranging response by civil society organisations and volunteers who were among the first responders to the humanitarian emergency both at the EU's external borders and within the EU. Diverse actors, ranging from activists, individual

[2] Schengen acquis 2000: Art 27 para 1 (emphasis added).

volunteers and citizen movements to well-established national and international non-governmental organisations (NGOs) addressed the visible gaps in search and rescue (SAR) in the Mediterranean Sea and provided shelter and assistance to those in need, irrespective of their immigration status. Local communities, citizens and individual volunteers were the first – and for a while the main – actors who received migrants and asylum-seekers and provided life-saving and reception services. Examples included the civil society actors involved in SAR close to Libyan territorial waters in the Central Mediterranean; those who saved lives in the Aegean Sea; those who assisted people transiting through Greece, Italy and Hungary, where they felt conditions to be unsafe and inhumane; or those who helped people trapped in the Calais 'Jungle' camp and attempting to enter the UK. Whereas our own research focuses on Italy, Greece, Hungary and the UK, there are many more instances documented across the EU (Fekete, Webber and Edmond-Pettitt 2017; PICUM 2017; Ataç et al 2016). These instances of solidarity are the subject of an emerging European scholarship. A range of ethnographic studies of civil society groups have been published in recent years which document and analyse the dynamics of this assistance. They have mostly focused on the local and national levels and framed debates in terms of access to and transformation of citizenship (see, eg Stock 2017 and the 2016 Special Issue 5(20) of Citizenship Studies on 'The Contentious Politics of Refugee and Migrant Protest and Solidarity Movements: Remaking Citizenship from the Margins'). Another body of academic scholarship has explored how, in recent tensions between civil society actors responding to the refugee crisis and the increasingly centralised and non-transparent EU anti-smuggling apparatus, we may be witnessing a relatively new and poorly studied phenomenon of pan-national European citizen mobilisation (Ataç et al 2016; Allsopp 2017a).

The relationship between these acts of humanitarian assistance on the one hand and anti migrant smuggling policies that govern and criminalise the facilitation of entry, transit and stay within the scope of EU and national policies on the other, has become increasingly tense and contested (Gkliati 2016). A major controversy has been the extent to which actions by civil society groups and individuals involved in SAR at sea or delivering access to social services and access to human rights and justice (in hotspots, transit and destination) are exempted from criminalisation. Some EU Member States and EU agencies (such as the Frontex Agency) have criticised or expressed concerns about the work of civil society actors and NGOs. Among the accusations are that civil society may be assisting and even collaborating with smuggling networks; and that their very existence and operations constitute a 'pull factor' for irregular immigration across the Mediterranean and across internal EU borders (Bellezza and Calandrino 2017). Civil society actors have also faced increasing demands and pressures for registration, coordination and financial transparency, which have profound repercussions for their independence and impartiality from government interference.

This book addresses the effects of the EU's approach to countering migrant-smuggling and the wider set of dynamics affecting civil society actors (CSAs) in selected EU Member States. Building upon the existing academic literature covering the 'criminalisation of migration' in the EU, the book examines the wider set of punitive, coercive or control-oriented dynamics affecting CSAs' work and activities through the lens of the notion of 'policing the mobility society'. This concept seeks to provide a framework of analysis that allows for an examination of a wider set of practices, mechanisms and tools driven by a logic of *policing* in the context of the EU Schengen border framework: those which affect not only people who *move* (qualified as third-country nationals for the purposes of EU law), but also people who *mobilise* in a rights-claiming capacity on behalf of and with immigrants and asylum-seekers.

The academic literature has highlighted the central role played by CSAs in shaping and contributing to public policies and administration of public services and creating a sense of community and social trust (Edwards 2004; van der Ploeg 2017), however, as van der Ploeg concludes, a generally accepted and consensual definition of 'civil society' does not exist (2017: 3). The term 'mobility society' includes those traditionally falling under the label of NGOs,[3] but also more informal civil society groups which play a crucial role in service provision through EU or nationally funded programmes and projects. We also include more loosely structured social movements of activists and individual volunteers, who constitute civic movements and activist initiatives (Edwards 2010; Held 2006).

We use the term civil society actors (CSAs) broadly, encompassing both civil society organisations (CSOs) and non-formal groups as well as engaged individuals (who may or may not be 'citizens'). Our analysis encompasses CSAs which assist in the implementation or effective delivery of state migration and asylum policies, but especially those which mobilise beyond this by maintaining accountability, presenting to the judiciary the effects of national and regional migration management policies on the fundamental rights of irregular immigrants and asylum-seekers, and playing a crucial monitoring role in upholding fundamental rights and social trust in liberal democracies as well as in countries falling short of liberal values and rule of law standards.

The conception of 'policing' relates not only to the traditional control/surveillance and preventative practices used by police officers or border authorities for migration management purposes, or traditional criminal law or other pre-emptive criminal law-like approaches and cases of criminal prosecution and sentencing before competent courts. Rather, this book analyses the wider set of practices and policies employed by the EU and Member States which directly or indirectly impact CSAs' activities and are aimed at (or have the effect of) limiting

[3] The main features of NGOs have been said to be: self-governing, private, not-for-profit and with an explicit social mission. NGOs are seen to be embedded into a wider 'civil society'. See A Vakil 'Confronting the Classification Problem: Toward a Taxonomy of NGOs' (1997) 25(12) *World Development*, 2057.

dissent, monitoring, judicial litigation or political mobilisation. 'Policing' here includes three different modalities or 'faces' which we use to structure our analysis: (i) suspicion/intimidation; (ii) disciplining; and (iii) formal criminalisation. This framework is developed in more detail in chapter eight.

The book draws on primary research conducted with statutory and non-statutory actors operating in sites of entry, residence and transit in Italy, Greece, Hungary and the UK between 2015 and 2017. These countries have been chosen because of the presence of significant – and qualitatively different – public debates and legislation concerning the criminalisation of assistance to immigrants and asylum-seekers. All four countries have been influential actors in directing the course of EU responses to the European humanitarian refugee crisis.

The data collected for this research covered the practical, day-to-day manifestations of the implementation of EU policies on countering migrant-smuggling and their effects on the provision by CSAs of humanitarian assistance and access to justice and fundamental rights for irregular immigrants, asylum-seekers and refugees. While the data do not claim to be representative, efforts were successfully made to ensure a broad sample representing a diversity of stakeholders. The methodology was the following:

— Field visits to Italy, Greece, the UK and Hungary were carried out between November 2016 and September 2017. A total of 89 semi-structured interviews were carried out during the visits and follow-up (see Annex 1 for the full list of anonymised interviewees).
— Qualitative and quantitative data were collected via an online survey of CSAs providing humanitarian assistance (total number of responses: 114).
— Two focus group discussions were used to add nuances to the research from the view point of CSAs (number of participants: 25, 11 May 2017) and of the EU and national actors representing coastguards, law enforcement and judiciary (number of participants: 25, 21 September 2017).

This research is also informed by previous work conducted by the authors on the topic which was commissioned by the European Parliament's Committee on Civil Liberties, Justice and Home Affairs (LIBE) in 2015, in light of growing concerns among Member States about the policing of humanitarian assistance to migrants and asylum-seekers and the lack of protections for those assisting them in EU law (Carrera et al 2016a).

The map shown in Figure 1.1 indicates the countries and localities covered during the field visits in the four countries under investigation. During the field trip to Italy, 16 face-to-face interviews were carried out in Rome and Catania from 7–12 November 2016. In Greece, 14 face-to-face interviews were conducted in Athens and Lesvos from 6–12 June 2017. In Hungary, 16 face-to-face interviews were conducted in Budapest and Szeged from 28 August–1 September, 2017, and two additional interviews were conducted across the border in Subotica (Serbia).

In the UK, 15 face-to-face interviews were carried out in London from 3 July–16 August 2017.

Skype interviews were used to supplement data collected via the field trips. Because of the changing circumstances – owing to the demolition of the Calais Jungle camp in October 2016 – while research was being conducted, interviews with actors previously (and in some cases continually) present in the Calais region were conducted either in London or via Skype (see Annex 1 for an anonymised list of interviewees). In addition to the field trips, a visit to the EU's Justice and Home Affairs agencies in The Hague (the Netherlands) was conducted on 24 August 2017 to record the opinions and input of six interviewees. Finally, follow-up interviews were organised via Skype so as to provide information and context on the latest developments. In all four countries, the Platform for International Cooperation on Undocumented Migrants (PICUM) collected testimonies from CSAs and monitored relevant news to provide evidence of the phenomenon of policing CSAs engaging with undocumented migrants and asylum-seekers in the EU (PICUM 2017).

**Figure 1.1** Map of the countries covered in this study and their neighbours

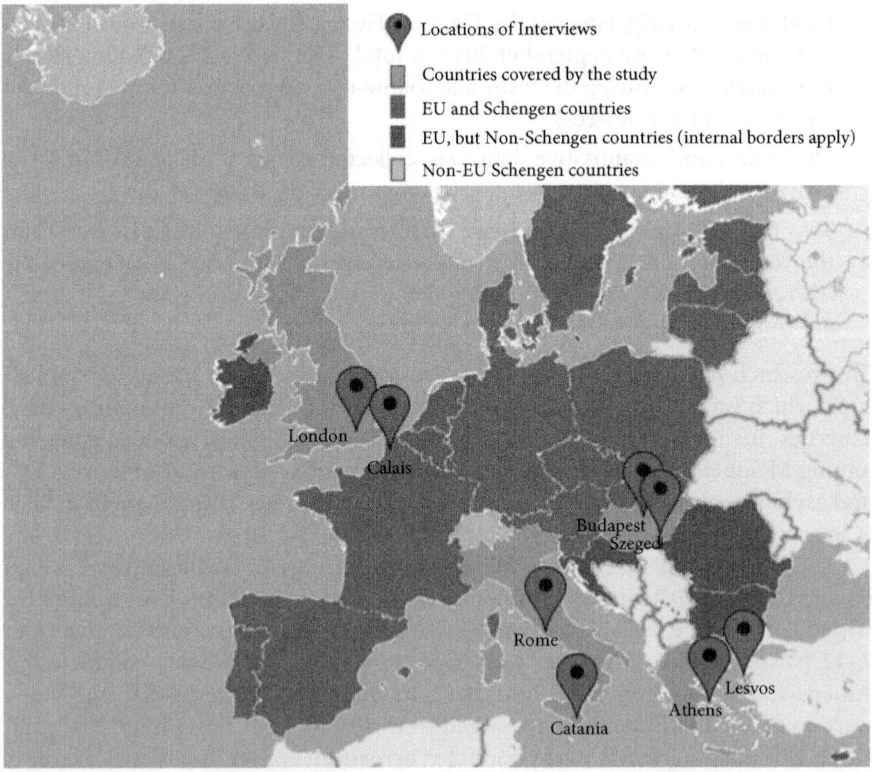


Source: Authors 2017.

Throughout this book we classify interviewees as belonging to one of the following categories:

(i) EU officials, including representatives from the European Commission, and EU agencies such as Frontex, the European Asylum Support Office (EASO), Europol and Eurojust;
(ii) national authorities, which are further divided into the sub-categories a) domestic border/coastguard and b) law enforcement and judicial actors;
(iii) UN actors, including the United Nations High Commissioner for Refugees (UNHCR) and the International Organisation for Migration (IOM);
(iv) formal civil society organisations (CSOs) (including registered local and national NGOs, larger international NGOs and formal organisations registered abroad);
(v) non-formal groups, covering small-scale initiatives and large movements of volunteers and/or activists comprised of locals and/or foreigners.

We use the term civil society actors (CSAs) to include both CSOs (iv) and non-formal groups (v).

The online survey was carried out between April and August 2017 in cooperation with PICUM. In total, 114 respondents representing diverse CSAs answered the survey. Of these, 84 respondents represented the four countries covered in this research – Italy, Greece, Hungary and the UK (see Figure 1.2). Only seven respondents from Hungary participated in the survey, which was thereafter complemented with semi-structured interviews during the field trip. Keeping in mind this limitation, numbers for the Hungarian survey are provided in percentages with the aim of cross-comparison, but it should be noted that the data in Hungary and the other

**Figure 1.2** Number of survey respondents by country where they work

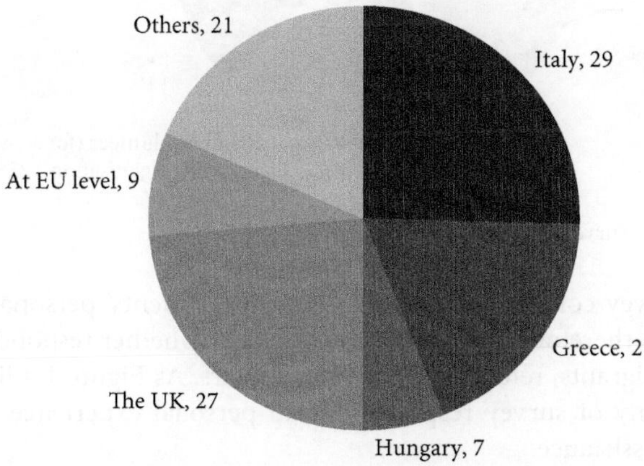


Source: CSA Online Survey (2017).

countries are not in any way systematic or representative of the national context as a whole. Efforts were nevertheless made to maximise the diversity of participants. The survey also received answers from nine respondents working at the EU level and 21 respondents working in other countries. Among the latter, seven respondents worked in France (at the Calais camp), two in Germany and a range of singular responses scattered across Western Europe (Belgium, Netherlands, Ireland and Switzerland), Eastern Europe (Belarus, Czech Republic and Romania) and Southern Europe (Malta and Portugal).

Survey respondents represented a wide spectrum of civil society actors (CSAs) – from service providers to activists (see Figure 1.3) – though approximately half of all respondents were employees or volunteers of formally established CSOs. One-fifth of all respondents were individual volunteers, usually from another EU Member State, who felt an obligation to come to the assistance of refugees, asylum-seekers and migrants during their journey to (presumed) safety in Europe. Among the 'Other respondents' were a few researchers, people working in the community, one person representing a UN actor and a self-identified 'refugee helping other refugees and asylum-seekers'.

**Figure 1.3** Distribution of survey respondents by type of CSAs they represent

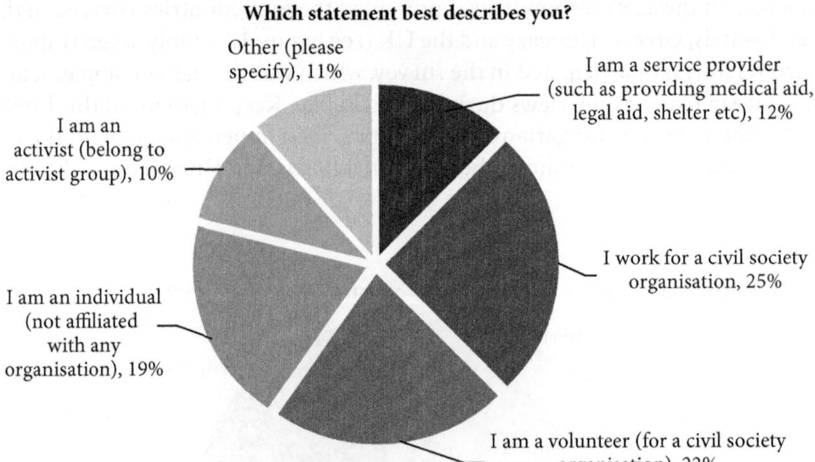


Source: CSA Online Survey (2017).

The online survey contained questions about respondents' personal and practical experiences, therefore it was important to verify whether respondents actually worked with migrants, refugees and asylum seekers. As Figure 1.4 illustrates, the absolute majority of survey respondents had personal experience of providing humanitarian assistance.

**Figure 1.4** Distribution of survey respondents by experience in providing humanitarian assistance

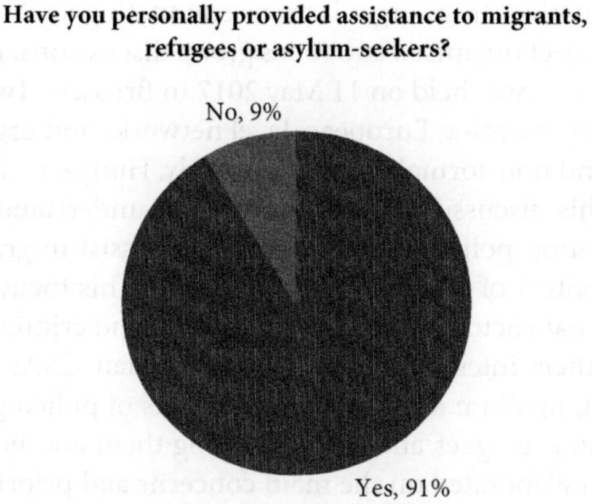


Source: CSA Online Survey (2017).

Figure 1.5 indicates that among the sites where humanitarian assistance was provided, the non-formal and community setting constituted one-third of all options chosen, followed by reception centres. Among the other sites, informal settlements were prevalent, including at the borders as well as in squats and informal gathering spaces, such as streets and squares. Several respondents also mentioned their homes as sites of humanitarian assistance. A very small fraction

**Figure 1.5** Distribution of survey respondents by sites of humanitarian assistance

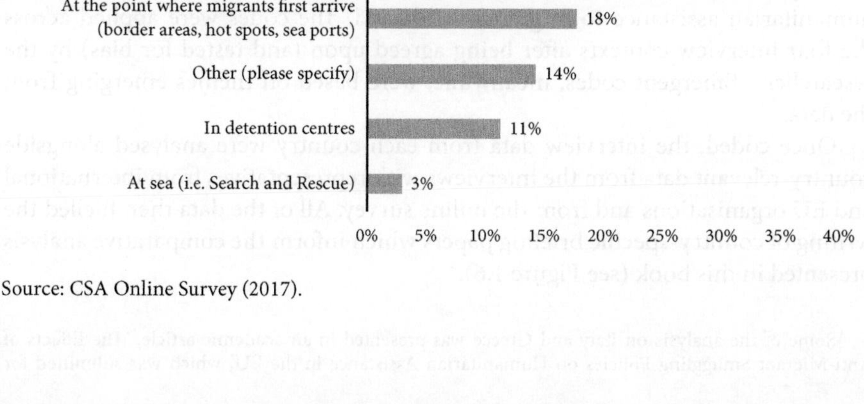


Source: CSA Online Survey (2017).

of online survey interviewees represented CSAs conducting search and rescue (SAR) activities. Nevertheless, this deficit was compensated during interviews, in which five representatives from organisations conducting SAR were interviewed.

The research project organised two focus group discussions. A first focus group with civil society actors was held on 11 May 2017 in Brussels. Twenty-five individuals participated, representing European-level networks and organisations as well as national CSOs and non-formal groups from Italy, Hungary, Greece and the UK. The main aim of this discussion was to get a better understanding of how policing and criminalisation policies affect CSAs which assist migrants and refugees, especially in the context of search and rescue at sea. This focus group discussion helped to map the main actors in the field of policing and criminalisation in different contexts and their interactions with humanitarian CSAs. Participants also discussed the short, medium and long-term impacts of policing and criminalisation on migrants and refugees and those assisting them and how CSAs respond. Participants further elaborated on the main concerns and priorities of individuals and organisations going forward as regards this phenomenon, especially in terms of advocacy and policy.

The second focus group discussion with 25 representatives of EU agencies and national coastguards, law enforcement and judicial actors, took the form of a high-level closed-door meeting. The event was held on 21 September 2017 in Brussels. The discussion, which was carried out under Chatham House rules, provided a coherent picture of migrant-smuggling, covering topics including the EU's operations at sea, the policing of 'hotspots', police investigations and the (lack of) prosecutions in national courts. It gave a critical account of the important role of coastguards, police and immigration officers and prosecutors at the national level in saving lives, fighting abuses of the vulnerable position of refugees and other migrants, and ensuring their access to justice and protection of their rights. The discussion focused on the actual and desired role of civil society actors in the highly politicised context of migrant-smuggling, and of possibilities for cooperating while simultaneously preserving and respecting different mandates.

Interviews and focus group notes were coded using a framework combining a priori and emergent codes (see Annex 2). A priori codes were based on desk-based, primary research conducted by the authors on the topic of the criminalisation of humanitarian assistance to migrants conducted. The codes were applied across the four interview contexts after being agreed upon (and tested for bias) by the researchers. Emergent codes, meanwhile, were based on themes emerging from the data.

Once coded, the interview data from each country were analysed alongside country-relevant data from the interviews with representatives from international and EU organisations and from the online survey. All of the data then fuelled the writing of country-specific briefing papers which inform the comparative analysis presented in this book (see Figure 1.6).[4]

[4] Some of the analysis on Italy and Greece was presented in an academic article, 'The Effects of Anti-Migrant Smuggling Policies on Humanitarian Assistance in the EU', which was submitted for

**Figure 1.6** Research methods and outputs

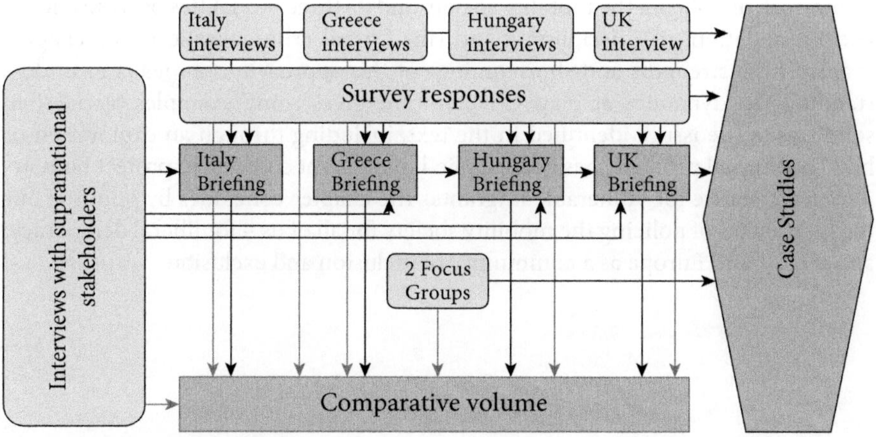


Legend: ▭ – inputs/data; ▭ – outputs;

Source: Authors 2017.

After this introductory chapter, Part I considers the EU's policy approach to countering migrant-smuggling, including both legal and EU Home Affairs agencies-based components. Chapter two begins by analysing the EU Facilitators Package and related critical perspectives. Chapter three considers the role of EU Home Affairs agencies and elaborates on the increasing employment of predictive policing approaches. It also highlights best practices in the field of co-operation.

Part II draws on new evidence to consider how the anti-smuggling framework laid out in Part I affects the work of those who move and those who mobilise to help migrants (what we call 'the mobility society'). Chapter four begins with an outline of anti-smuggling laws in the national law of the four Member States of interest. Subsequently, chapters five to seven examine the evidence of how these laws and political pressures have played out in three settings. Chapter five examines the effects of countering the facilitation of entry on the work of CSOs involved at external EU sea and land borders, as well as at the Calais–UK Schengen border. Chapter six explores in detail how the new EU hotspots approach intersects with the provision of humanitarian assistance and policing CSOs. Chapter seven addresses the effects of anti-smuggling policies on the provision of services and access to rights for irregular migrants and asylum-seekers who reside in the four Member States in question.

Part III offers more detailed analysis of the state of play outlined in Parts I and II, proposing a theoretical framework to analyse the outlined phenomena and

peer-review to a Special Issue of the *International Journal of Migration and Border Studies* (IJMBS) in 2017. Meanwhile, some of the analysis on Hungary and the UK was presented in J Allsopp (2017a), which is expanded and enriched in this book with additional findings from the interviews, focus group discussions and online survey results.

ways forward in terms of policy solutions. Chapter eight outlines the theoretical framework of policing the mobility society and its three modalities of (i) suspicion and intimidation, (ii) disciplining and (iii) formal criminalisation. The chapter evaluates the strengths and shortcomings of this approach as a means to understanding the dynamics at play. Chapter nine gives some examples of possible solutions to the issues identified in the text, including through an exploration of how the firewall principle has been applied in different contexts to protect humanitarian assistance for vulnerable migrants. The chapter concludes by pointing out the high stakes of policing the mobility society for all of us – for liberal democracy, social trust and Europe as a community of inclusion and exclusion.

# PART I

# Countering Migrant-Smuggling: EU Policies and Actors

# 2

# Countering Migrant-Smuggling: The EU's Policy Approach

The EU has played an increasingly active role in developing policies to counter migrant-smuggling, and criminalising the facilitation of entry and residence of irregular immigrants (Carrera and Guild 2016; Cholewinski 2012). This chapter examines two main components of the EU's policy approach to countering migrant-smuggling: the EU Facilitators Package (section I); the ways in which it has been transposed and implemented at domestic level in the four EU Member States under examination (section II); and the remaining gaps and challenges (section III).

## I. The EU Facilitators Package in Light of UN Standards

The EU has a common legal framework on migrant-smuggling embodied in the 2002 Facilitators Package. The package is composed of Directive 2002/90 of 28 November 2002 defining the facilitation of unauthorised entry, transit and residence; and Framework Decision 2002/946 of 28 November 2002 on the strengthening of the penal framework to prevent the facilitation of unauthorised entry, transit and residence.

There are three key issues of contention regarding the current legislation in the EU. First, it requires EU Member States to provide criminal sanctions for migrant-smuggling and for the provision of assistance to irregular immigrants, including in cases when no illicit financial gain or other material benefit is obtained. Secondly, the actual decision on whether to use criminal sanctions against people and organisations facilitating access to humanitarian assistance has been left to the discretion of each Member State. Thirdly, criminal and preventative justice measures are applied systematically as migration management tools in highly controversial and politicised national and EU contexts.

### A. Financial and Material Benefit Requirement and Criminal Intent

The UN standards in the area of organised crime contain a clear reference to 'financial or other material benefit' as a criterion for migrant-smuggling to be considered a crime. Article 3 of the UN Migrant Smuggling Protocol (United Nations 2000a) is intended to exclude family members or support groups such as religious or non-governmental organisations from punishment (UNODC: ix). Therefore, drafters included 'financial or other material benefit' in Article 6 as a basic requirement for criminalising migrant-smuggling.

The EU's Facilitators Package allows law enforcers to target 'any intentional assistance' for any person who is undocumented, lacking documentation or cannot yet prove to be seeking asylum. Article 1 para 1 of Directive 2002/90 of 28 November 2002 provides two options for criminalisation:

> Each Member State shall adopt appropriate sanctions on: (a) any person who intentionally assists a person who is not a national of a Member State to enter, or transit across, the territory of a Member State in breach of the laws of the State concerned on the entry or transit of aliens; (b) any person who, for financial gain, intentionally assists a person who is not a national of a Member State to reside within the territory of a Member State in breach of the laws of the State concerned on the residence of aliens.

Clause (a) above is clearly not consistent with the above-mentioned UN standards, yet it is the preferred option of Member States for criminalising the facilitation of entry. At the moment, facilitation of entry even when the 'smuggler' does not receive financial gain or profit is a criminal offence in most EU countries, punishable by imprisonment or/and a fine. This includes all four countries covered in this research – Italy, Greece, Hungary and the UK (European Union Agency for Fundamental Rights (FRA) 2014: 9).[1] Financial or other material benefit in these countries is considered merely an aggravating circumstance, not the very proof of criminal intent (see chapter four for further discussion). In addition, EU Member States are divided regarding the facilitation of stay if there is no financial gain motive (United Nations Office on Drugs and Crime 2017). In Greece and the UK, and in half of the EU Member States, for the facilitation of stay, a profit factor is not needed in order to establish a crime/offence; in Italy, Hungary and the remaining half of the EU,[2] some financial or other material benefit motive is necessary to constitute a crime (FRA 2014: 11).

The closed-door discussion with practitioners which took place in the scope of this research confirmed that due to political pressures, practitioners have to investigate and prosecute cases without clear criminal intent, including acts of solidarity and compassion by family, friends or volunteers. Thus, what is criminal per se is helping someone to cross the national border without proper documents, often including people who seek to apply for asylum.

[1] Austria, Belgium, Bulgaria, Croatia, Cyprus, Czech Republic, Denmark, Estonia, Finland, France, Greece, Hungary, Italy, Latvia, Lithuania, Malta, the Netherlands, Poland, Romania, Slovakia, Slovenia, Spain, Sweden and the United Kingdom.

[2] Austria, Bulgaria, the Czech Republic, Cyprus, Germany, Hungary, Italy, Luxembourg, the Netherlands, Poland, Portugal, Slovakia, Spain and Sweden.

At the UN level, migrant-smuggling is defined quite differently from 'human trafficking' in two separate Protocols of the United Nations Transnational Organized Crime Convention. According to the separate UN Protocol to Prevent, Suppress and Punish Trafficking in Persons, the base crime of human trafficking requires the establishing of a certain level of violence:

> [Persons are recruited, transported, harboured and/or received] by means of the threat or use of force or other forms of coercion, of abduction, of fraud, of deception, of the abuse of power or of a position of vulnerability or of the giving or receiving of payments or benefits to achieve the consent of a person having control over another person, for the purpose of exploitation.[3]

The definition of migrant-smuggling, however, does not contain any of the abuse elements; the smuggler simply requires the migrant to pay for the 'facilitation of entry/stay'. Draft Council Conclusions on Migrant Smuggling (Council of the EU 2016b) issued in January 2016 acknowledged the difference between the two phenomena but then concluded that they essentially constitute a similar crime:

> Both forms of crime [migrant-smuggling and human trafficking] can be often interlinked, and … migrant smuggling has become an increasingly violent form of crime, often involving serious physical or psychological violence and human rights abuse.

This raises serious questions as to why these two different phenomena are conflated in EU policymaking (Statewatch 2016). UN standards quite clearly state that migrant-smuggling is based on an informal consensual agreement between a migrant and his/her smuggler to pay for getting to a destination country while bypassing the border controls. If a smuggler were to use threat, force, coercion and abduction or fraud, then this informal agreement would be violated, as the migrant did not agree to those conditions. Thus, the situation could qualify as an attempt at human trafficking or another type of crime in addition to migrant-smuggling. EU policymakers and agencies seem to continue to broaden the image of migrant-smuggling as a 'violent crime', whereas there is no such requirement for it to be the subject of criminalisation by current EU legislation; rather, it need only involve 'intentional assistance'. The fact that makes such assistance a 'crime' from the EU's viewpoint is the mere lack of documentation on the side of migrants and asylum-seekers. Recently conducted empiric studies have substantiated that relationships between migrants and their smugglers have many faces, and rarely conform to the mainstream notion of helpless migrant and ruthless smuggler (Zhang, Sanchez and Achilli 2018).

[3] United Nations 2000: Art 3 para A.

## B. Optional Clause to Exempt Humanitarian Actors

Article 1 para 2 of Directive 2002/90 provides only an optional clause for Member States to exclude humanitarian actors from criminal sanctions and only in cases where there was no financial or other material benefit:

> Any Member State *may* decide *not to impose sanctions* with regard to the behaviour defined in paragraph 1(a) by applying its national law and practice for cases where the aim of the behaviour is to provide humanitarian assistance to the person concerned (emphasis added).

This option has been invoked, for example, by Greece and France, among other countries (see EU FRA 2014; Provera 2015). In countries such as France, the humanitarian exemption clause was revised following national debate led in part by civil society (Allsopp 2012). Such a wide margin for Member States to decide whether to prosecute humanitarian actors potentially allows the goals and objectives of humanitarian aid to be undermined. Article 214 of the TFEU defines the principles of the humanitarian aid (TFEU Art 214 para 2) as those of 'international law and … impartiality, neutrality and non-discrimination'. Article 214 para 3 contains the provision that EU legislators have an explicit role to inject more legal certainty into this area:

> The European Parliament and the Council, acting in accordance with the ordinary legislative procedure, shall establish the measures defining the framework within which the Union's humanitarian aid operations shall be implemented.

Even though the article is aimed at EU humanitarian aid operations in third (and mainly developing) countries, it is logical that such standards should apply internally. UN standards are clear on the issue of humanitarian exemption. Article 19 of the UN Protocol against Migrant Smuggling has an explicit 'saving clause' exempting humanitarian assistance (United Nations 2000a: Art 19 para 1):

> Nothing in this Protocol shall affect the other rights, obligations and responsibilities of States and individuals under international law, including international humanitarian law and international human rights law and, in particular, where applicable, the 1951 Convention and the 1967 Protocol relating to the Status of Refugees and the principle of non-refoulement as contained therein.

The drafters of the UN Protocol against Migrant Smuggling had a well-founded fear of such anti-smuggling laws being applied to humanitarian workers as well as to refugees and asylum-seekers. The UNODC Legislative Guide on the protocol's application reiterates the drafters' concern that 'the Protocol should not require States to criminalize or take other action against groups that smuggle migrants for charitable or altruistic reasons, as sometimes occurs with the smuggling of asylum-seekers' (United Nations Office on Drugs and Crime 2004).

## C. Criminal Law as a Migration Management Tool

Whereas the UN's Protocol to Prevent, Suppress and Punish Trafficking in Persons (United Nations 2000b) regards the consent of the victim as irrelevant, the question of consent is left entirely out of the UN Protocol against Migrant Smuggling (United Nations 2000a). The protocol tries to account for migrants who are themselves willing to leave their country of residence or transit, thus smugglers are rather providing a 'service' which aims to trespass/deceive border controls. On the other hand, Article 5 of the UN Protocol against the Smuggling of Migrants explicitly exempts criminalisation of 'complicity' of the undocumented migrant or asylum-seeker for the irregular entry, transit or stay:

> Migrants shall not become liable to criminal prosecution under this Protocol for the fact of having been the object of conduct set forth in article 6 of this Protocol.

The United Nations Office on Drugs and Crime (UNODC) warns against the use of criminal justice tools when the intent is not criminal but rather aims to prevent and control migration as such. UNODC highlights that: 'Migration-focused measures risk not fully addressing the challenges presented by migrant-smuggling as a form of serious organized crime, to the potential benefit of criminals and to the detriment of migrants' (2017: iii). A study by the EU Fundament Rights Agency (FRA) has problematised such efforts by some EU Member States which, in trying to manage migration by criminalising irregular entry, put suspicion on migrants and makes them easy targets for criminals and pushes into human trafficking (EU FRA 2014: 2):

> The use of criminal sanctions and imprisonment to fight irregular migration harms not only the persons concerned, but also casts a negative light on how society as a whole perceives them [undocumented migrants]. Migrants lacking permits to stay may be committing an offence and are, therefore, often unfairly seen as criminals, which makes them more vulnerable to exploitation and abuse.

Politically motivated use of criminal law is not only doomed to fail in effectively dismantling migrant-smuggling, it also risks fuelling the phenomenon of migrant trafficking, and various other abuses of migrants, including slave markets in Libya (Elbagir et al 2017). UN High Commissioner for Human Rights Zeid Ra'ad Al Hussein was among the first to criticise the EU's irregular migration policies as worsening the situation:

> The increasing interventions of the EU and its member states have done nothing so far to reduce the level of abuses suffered by migrants ... Our monitoring, in fact, shows a fast deterioration in their situation in Libya ... We cannot be a silent witness to modern day slavery, rape and other sexual violence, and unlawful killings in the name of managing migration and preventing desperate and traumatized people from reaching Europe's shores.[4]

Nevertheless, the road to addressing migration challenges with criminal measures is further strengthened by making migrant-smuggling a top policy priority in both

[4] UN High Commissioner for Human Rights (2017).

the European Agenda for Migration and, as will be examined in chapter three, in the work of EU Justice and Home Affairs agencies.

# II. Assessing the Impact of the EU's Facilitators Package on Civil Society Actors

This chapter elaborates on the various existing assessments of the Facilitators Package, including the Commission's own REFIT Evaluation (sub-section IIA). It then moves into the discussion of how civil society actors across the EU perceive the Facilitators' package's effects (sub-section IIB). The 'perceptions' are further evidenced in Part II.

## A. Commission REFIT Evaluation

In 2017, the European Commission published a REFIT Evaluation of the Facilitators Package (European Commission 2017d), which concluded:

> As of today there appears to be rather limited evidence that social workers, family members or citizens acting out of compassion have been prosecuted and convicted for facilitation of unauthorised entry, transit and residence.

However, it acknowledged that the package has not been effective in creating clarity and legal certainty. This has been particularly due to the absence of a provision explicitly exempting civil society actors from criminalisation and the lack of a definition of humanitarian assistance. The Commission highlighted that the optional nature of Article 1.2 leaves too much margin of appreciation to Member States and national authorities. It also underlined the existence of 'unintended consequences' in deterring service provision and limiting civil society spaces.

The Commission's evaluation emphasised, however, that these fears or any 'chilling effect' of the Facilitators Package do not seem to be so prominently linked to the legal framework in place as to its understanding and actual application. It claimed that to date, there is still limited intelligence available on the nature and extent of illicit financial flows associated with migrant-smuggling, noting that:

> the cash intensive nature of the payment methods linked to smuggling makes it difficult to trace illicit financial flows and in turn to conduct investigations on the financial nature of the crime … [S]ince the time of the adoption of the Facilitators Package and still today, the risks that such difficulties in tracing financial flows connected to migrant smuggling would disproportionately hamper the investigation and prosecution of this crime, affecting states' legitimate interest to control borders and regulate migration flows, have been raised as a reason to avoid including a constituent financial gain element in the offence of facilitating irregular border crossing.[5]

[5] European Commission (2017d: 9).

The Commission adds that it is 'difficult to disentangle the effects of the legal framework from the wider array of policy tools and enhanced operational cooperation to counter migrant-smuggling, which have been triggered by the crisis' (European Commission 2017d: 34) and concludes, therefore, that 'there is no sufficient evidence to draw firm conclusions about the need for a revision of the Facilitators package at this point in time' (European Commission 2017d: 35).

The Commission's decision not to revise EU criminal law on migrant-smuggling leaves much to be desired in terms of justification and coherence. Rather than examining critically the legality and effectiveness of the current EU substantive criminal law framework on migrant-smuggling, it justifies choices in criminalisation on the grounds of boosting investigatory and prosecutorial interests. In this manner, substantive criminal law becomes a mere tool for prosecutorial efficiency, rather than reflecting normative or societal choices for criminalisation (Mitsilegas 2018). By declining to adjust EU law, the Commission has missed three opportunities:

(i) aligning EU law with international law on the criminalisation of migrant-smuggling;
(ii) modernising (or 'Lisbonising') – as in the case of the 'parallel' offences of human trafficking (Mitsilegas and Vavoula 2015) – the EU legal framework on migrant-smuggling, by taking more fully into account the human rights obligations of the EU, which were enhanced after the entry into force of the Lisbon Treaty and the constitutionalisation of the EU Charter of Fundamental Rights (Mitsilegas 2016);
(iii) addressing decriminalisation in the field of EU criminal law (Mitsilegas 2018).

Since the emergence of the so-called 'European humanitarian refugee crisis' in 2015, not only has the EU's Facilitators Package been put in use, but so have various political and operational responses to tackling migrant-smuggling (see chapter three). Part II builds on the growing evidence of cases when 'helpers' have been prosecuted, intimidated and punished (PICUM 2017; Fekete, Weber and Edmond-Pettitt 2017; Gkliati 2016). It further elaborates on the increased involvement of EU-led operations in addressing migrant-smuggling, particularly in EU border countries such as Italy, Greece and Hungary.

## B. Awareness of EU Law among Civil Society Actors

Online survey respondents assigned very little weight to the EU's Facilitators Package alone in terms of the perceived origin of policies that 'criminalise' individuals and/or CSOs providing humanitarian assistance to migrants and asylum-seekers (see Figure 2.1). Nevertheless, the Facilitators Package was shown to have important cumulative effects in Italy, where EU and national policies slightly outweighed national policies alone as a perceived causal factor in criminalisation. However, in the remaining countries under investigation (Hungary, Greece and the UK), national policies were regarded by different CSAs as the main source or tool to punish both individuals and civil society actors assisting migrants.

**Figure 2.1** Perceived origin of the policies 'criminalising' individuals and/or CSOs providing humanitarian assistance by country

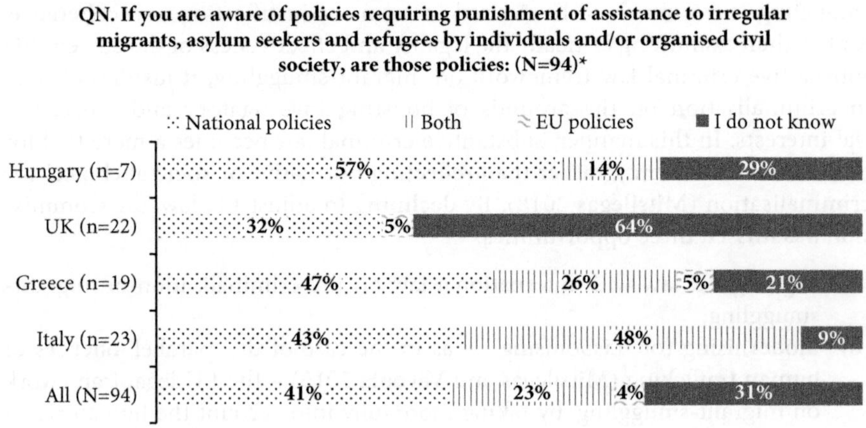


*Hungarian survey received only seven responses.

Source: Online Survey (2017).

As to who is at risk of being punished or prevented from assisting undocumented migrants or asylum-seekers, 14 per cent more respondents answered individuals and activists acting alone (see Figure 2.2) compared to respondents who answered members of a formally organised group (see Figure 2.3). This finding remained consistent across the national contexts covered by the research. The UK respondents were least aware of the source and impacts of such policies, although 26 (out of 27) respondents reported that they provide assistance themselves. Quite strikingly, two-thirds of respondents from the UK could not identify the source of 'criminalising' policies (see Figure 2.1). On the other hand, respondents in the most affected countries, Italy and Greece, were well aware of the possible negative consequences for individuals (more than two-thirds in both cases). Although perceived criminalisation of CSOs was reported by more than half of respondents in both countries, more respondents in Italy were unsure of this point (see Figure 2.3). This uncertainty is also evident in our chapter four analysis of the pre-existing laws and national implementation of the Facilitators' Package. It is also backed up by prior research (Carrera et al 2016a).

**Figure 2.2** Awareness of policies criminalising individuals by country

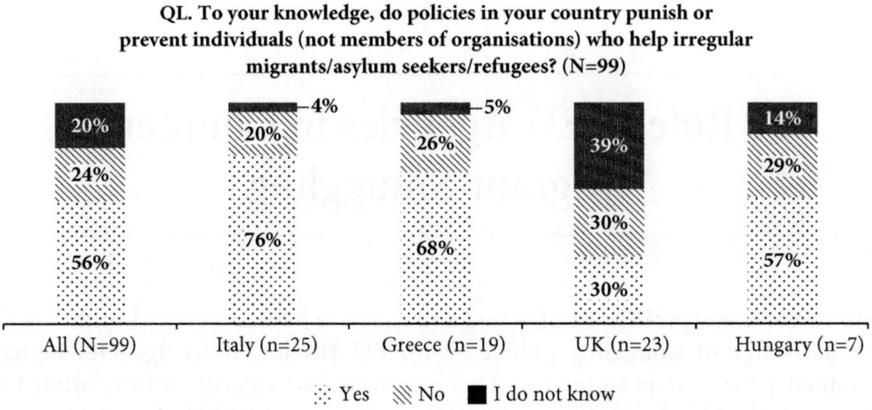


Source: Online Survey (2017).

**Figure 2.3** Awareness of policies criminalising members of CSOs by country

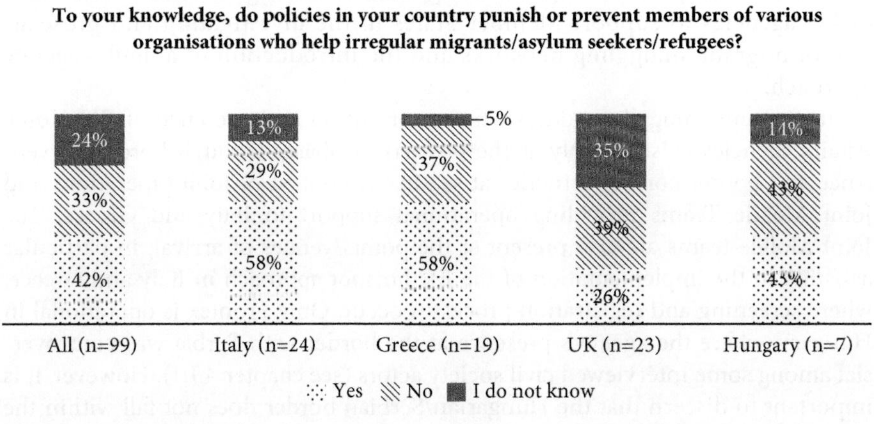


Source: Online Survey (2017).

While the EU, through the EU Facilitators Package, has played an increasingly active role in developing anti-migrant-smuggling policies and criminalising the facilitation of entry and residence of irregular immigrants, our research suggests that the ways in which it has been transposed and implemented at the domestic level in the four EU Member States under examination has left gaps and led to challenges and legal uncertainty.

# 3

# The Role of EU Agencies in Countering Migrant-Smuggling

An increasingly prolific set of actors and agencies have intervened in the field of anti-migrant-smuggling policies, with EU Home Affairs agencies being granted particular prominence. This has been particularly so in relation to Europol (the EU's law enforcement agency), Eurojust (the EU's Judicial Cooperation Unit), Frontex (the European Border and Coast Guard Agency), and EASO (the European Asylum Support Office). The Commission's EU Action Plan against Migrant Smuggling of May 2015 included concrete policy actions to counter and prevent migrant-smuggling, including increasing the tasks of EU agencies to support Member States in the investigation and prosecution of migrant-smuggling networks and the introduction of a 'multi-agency approach'.

In the anti-smuggling context, the contribution and presence of EU Home Affairs agencies exists mainly at the pre-arrival phases through border surveillance and border control activities at sea in the context of Joint Operations and Joint Mobile Teams providing operational support to Italy and Greece. The Joint Mobile teams are also present at the points/venues of arrival, in particular assisting in the implementation of the EU hotspot approach in Italy and Greece, where screening and registration processes occur. Only Frontex is operational in Hungary, where the agency's presence at the border with Serbia was controversial among some interviewed civil society actors (see chapter 4.III). However, it is important to discern that the Hungarian/Serbian border does not fall within the EU hotspot approach. Finally, at the external EU borders with the UK, there is no EU involvement at all.

In addition to a multi-agency approach, a multidisciplinary approach is mentioned. This does not mention explicitly but implies the involvement of CSAs which provide humanitarian assistance:

> This first EU Action Plan sets out concrete actions *to counter and prevent migrant-smuggling*, while ensuring the protection of the human rights of migrants. It is based on a multidisciplinary approach, involving actors and institutions at local, regional, national and international level.[1]

[1] European Commission (2015b) (original emphasis).

This chapter outlines how migrant-smuggling was set as a political priority across the EU and how this created pressure on both law enforcement and judicial authorities. This prioritisation has been translated into the establishment of separate formal structures, such as the European Migrant Smuggling Centre (EMSC), as well as various non-formal networks of practitioners created by the Commission and also initiated by Europol and Eurojust. The blurring of the law enforcement mandate increasingly includes not only Europol and Frontex, but also EUNAVFOR and EASO in various operational anti-smuggling activities. The field research trips revealed the concerning issue of a mixing and blending of mandates among the EU Justice and Home Affairs agencies. Indeed, 'who is doing what?' remains a topical question at both EU and national levels (see chapters four to seven for more elaboration).

## I. Europol

Europol is the EU's law enforcement agency. Europol focuses on 'the biggest security threats' in Europe among which migrant-smuggling is identified, along with terrorism, drug trafficking, money laundering, organised fraud and counterfeit euros (Europol 2015a). Europol hosts approximately 200 liaison officers from EU Member States. Crime investigations are supported by approximately 100 crime analysts. The interviewees in both Europol and Eurojust told us that they welcomed the support of analysts as they manage to identify the links between different ongoing investigations, and thus to investigate the larger networks.[2]

Europol's mandate has been strengthened and expanded by Regulation 2016/794 of 11 May 2016 (European Union 2016b). The regulation mentions 'immigrant smuggling' only in its Annex 1 as the explanation of the additional areas of organised crime covered by this EU agency. However, Recital 7 reminds us of Europol's raison d'être as a 'flanking measure' for the absence of internal borders in the Schengen area:

> Europol should also carry out risk analyses, including in respect of organised crime, insofar as the risks concerned may undermine the application of the Schengen acquis by the Member States.[3]

Europol's work methods are increasingly embedded in preventative policing logic. Use of large-scale databases, intelligence-gathering and information-sharing is intended to go beyond the traditional criminal justice approaches (Carrera et al 2016b). The closed-door discussion also confirmed this logic, as the migrant-smuggling business is 'a liquid phenomenon' and thus it was presumed by some practitioners that neither with traditional law enforcement measures, nor with

[2] Interview with EU agencies 24 August 2017, The Hague, the Netherlands; interview with national judicial authorities, 24 August 2017, The Hague, the Netherlands.

[3] European Union (2016b).

preventative approaches, can practitioners produce the desired effect of dismantling criminal networks.[4] One interviewee explained that there are 'too many different networks, routes and modus operandi. For example, in a bigger network there are "career criminals" who one day could sell arms, another [day] smuggle migrants.'[5]

In total Europol had nine priority crime areas under the 2013–17 EU Policy Cycle, where 'the facilitation of illegal immigration' was listed as a top priority with an aim to

> disrupt organized crime groups that facilitate illegal immigration through the main entry points to the EU, and in particular to fight their use of fraudulent documents to abuse legal channels for migration.[6]

The Council of the EU also has selected the fight against 'migrant-smuggling' as a top priority for its Serious and Organised Crime Assessment (SOCTA) for the upcoming EU Policy Cycle of 2018–21, leaving behind other types of crime, where criminal intent is more visible, such as child exploitation and pornography, tax fraud and even human trafficking (Council of the EU 2017a). Such political decisions have direct implications in allocated budgeting and human resources allocation:

> For each [priority], a multi-annual strategic plan, an EMPACT (European multidisciplinary platform against criminal threats) project and an operational action plan are implemented.[7]

In addition, this prioritisation raises the expectation among the public and policymakers that because of the allocated finances, law enforcement officers will solve the sensitive political and socio-economic phenomena of migration and refugee issues with criminal and law enforcement tools. Such political prioritisation is translated into the establishment of separate formal structures, such as the European Migrant Smuggling Centre (EMSC).

An earlier assessment (Carrera et al 2016b) of the added value of using such tools designed to fight organised crime found that prioritisation and institutionalisation of migrant-smuggling lack critical evaluation. Europol is using its own analyses, such as SOCTA reports, to support the further prioritisation of fighting certain areas of crime that are already under radar. This also needs to be seen in the context of inter-institutional competition among the EU's Justice and Home Affairs agencies, regarding who gets to suggest the solution to the issue of the political salience: stemming irregular migration. As a result, the prioritisation of 'migrant-smuggling' is reaffirmed, in a kind of vicious cycle owing to inadequate scrutiny. Europol's academic advisory board concluded on the SOCTA Report of

[4] Closed-door discussion with EU and national actors representing coastguards, law enforcement and judiciary, 21 September 2017, Brussels, Belgium.

[5] Interview with EU agencies, 24 August 2017, The Hague, the Netherlands.

[6] Europol (2015b).

[7] Europol (2015b).

2017 that in the area of migrant-smuggling, 'criminalisation and prosecution are not the only or necessarily the best strategy for dealing with the harms of organised crime groups and their activities' (Tailor et al 2017).

## A. Europol's European Migrant Smuggling Centre

The political priority of countering migrant-smuggling at the EU level led to the establishment of the European Migrant Smuggling Centre (EMSC) within Europol in February 2016 (Europol 2016a; 2016b). EMSC was established at the request of the EU Justice and Home Affairs Council, which invited Europol 'to strengthen its capacity to support Member States in better preventing and fighting against migrant-smuggling' (Council of the EU 2015f).

EMSC is a follow-up to the Joint Operation MARE, which began in 2014. The aim of EMSC is 'to combat people smuggling via the Mediterranean and … subsequent secondary movements to destination countries' (Europol 2016b). EMSC is seen more as a migration management than criminal justice tool, as confirmed in Europol's own report:

> Given the scale of migrant-smuggling, and its centrality to the migration challenge as a whole, leveraging *a greater law enforcement response through EMSC is critical to the EU's migration strategy*. Success depends, however, on the strong and consistent engagement of Member States and other partners through enhanced information sharing and operational cooperation.[8]

An interview with an EU Justice and Home Affairs agency confirmed that the reason for creating such a specialised centre within Europol was to create new intelligence and databases.[9] Such databases include vessels of interest. For example, between July 2016 and June 2017 there were '850 vessels of interest monitored' (Europol 2017a). Interestingly, the interviewees at the EU Justice and Home Affairs agencies in The Hague were unwilling to speak about the suspected NGO maritime vessels conducting search and rescue (SAR), but the researchers observed a map of the Mediterranean Sea that showed and described NGO SAR vessels. During the interviews at EU Justice and Home Affairs agencies in The Hague, the 'vessels of interest were mentioned' as a broad category of those suspected of drugs and weapons trafficking and migrant-smuggling.[10]

Another type of database covers a supply chain of satellite phones and rubber dinghies.[11] Intelligence gathered in the EMSC database can be shared with and among the Member States as well as with Frontex, Interpol, EUNAVFOR MED Sophia and other law enforcement actors. In the period between July 2016 and

[8] Europol (2016c: 14) (emphasis added).
[9] Interview with EU agencies, 24 August 2017, The Hague, the Netherlands.
[10] Interview with EU agencies, 24 August 2017, The Hague, the Netherlands.
[11] Interview with EU agencies, 24 August 2017, The Hague, the Netherlands.

June 2017 there were '20,000 data on suspects' reported to Europol and '11,700 SIENA [Europol's Secure Information Exchange Network Application] messages processed' (Europol 2017a).

Interviews revealed that Member States are free to 'label' who could see their posted 'intel' in the database and for what purpose. In addition, in this exercise Europol relies on the national definition of 'who is a smuggler', and does not see its role in promoting European standards and definitions laid out by the Facilitators Package.[12] This was also confirmed by subsequent interviews with national practitioners.[13] Thus, Europol does not play fully its role in harmonising the definition of smuggling across the EU.

Though the number of entries and cross-checks are impressive, interviews with judicial authorities confirmed that such a large amount of 'intel' does not help prosecutors. Quite the contrary, according to one respondent: the massive volume of personal exchanges in unknown languages may prolong the process of evidence-gathering.[14] National law enforcement practitioners, meanwhile, were divided about increased volumes of information. Whereas some interviewees regarded gathering more data entirely positively,[15] others were concerned with the usefulness of the additional data.[16] Nevertheless, both judicial actors and all national practitioners acknowledged the added value of 'better information analysis' – a job done by the EMSC analysts. At the EMSC, 45 experts and analysts provide operational and strategic support to national law enforcement agencies (Europol 2017a).

The EMSC produces specialised operational analyses either at the request of a Member State or on its own initiative. One interviewee confirmed that EMSC analyses can be aimed at 'finding targets in the databases that have not been further developed'.[17] EMSC also develops a strategic analysis which reveals migrant-smuggling business model trends. For example, Europol's report 'Migrant smuggling in the EU' (Europol 2016c) identifies the main nationalities, age and ways the suspect smugglers operate. For example:

> The most common nationalities or countries of birth for these suspects [of migrant-smuggling] are Bulgaria, Egypt, Hungary, Iraq, Kosovo, Pakistan, Poland, Romania, Serbia, Syria, Tunisia and Turkey.

Thus, EMSC create potential smuggler profiles using data entered on the basis of suspicion and not actual prosecution. Whereas such data may be useful in a

[12] Interview with EU agencies, 24 August 2017, The Hague, the Netherlands.

[13] Interview with national border/law enforcement authorities (a), (b), (c) and (d), 24 August 2017, The Hague, the Netherlands.

[14] Interview with national judicial authorities, 24 August 2017, The Hague, the Netherlands.

[15] Interview with national border/law enforcement authorities (a) and (b), 24 August 2017, The Hague, the Netherlands.

[16] Interview with national border/law enforcement authorities (c) and (d) 24 August 2017, The Hague, the Netherlands.

[17] Interview with EU agencies 24 August 2017, The Hague, the Netherlands.

concrete context, in their current form they raise questions of presumption of innocence (as it is only presumed that such persons are more likely than others to be smugglers). This goes against the EU's principle of 'non-discrimination', and may serve as a self-fulfilling prophecy of suspecting and more assiduously checking, for example, truck drivers with Bulgarian licence plates, than drivers with Dutch licence plates. One of the main concerns is that Europol, in this analytical exercise, is laying the groundwork for future interventions by relying on information in databases provided by national law enforcement agencies concerning suspect persons whose guilt is not yet proven in national courts.

The EMSC also develops data on migratory route trends, for example via the European Monitoring Team report (EPMT) (Europol 2017a) represented by Europol's graph in Figure 3.1.

**Figure 3.1** Europol's analysis of main trends in facilitation of illegal immigration

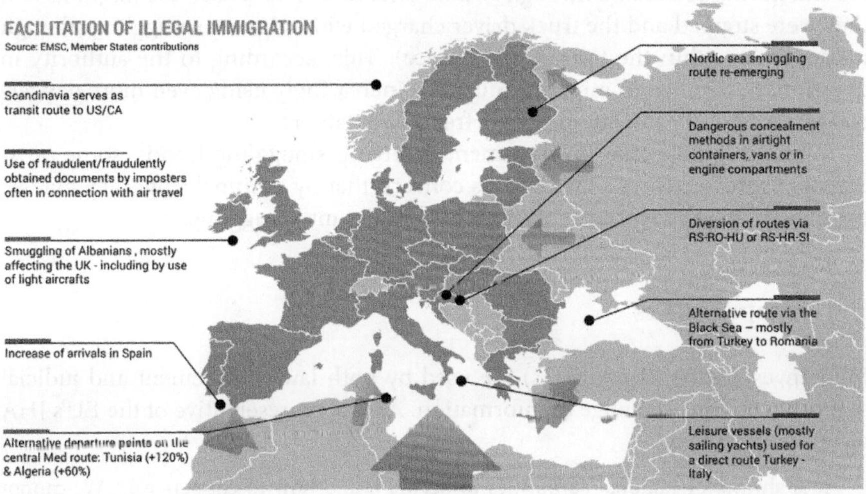


Source: Europol (2017a).

Figure 3.1 indicates new and emerging migrant-smuggling trends. It also sheds light on smugglers' new 'methods'. For example, Europol's recent publication highlights the concealment of migrants in small car boots as an outcome of increased police checks and the use of heat detection cameras on trucks (Europol 2017c). The closed-door discussion conducted for this research indicated that judicial practitioners were cautious about whether to prosecute such cases, since smugglers might then deploy even more life-endangering practices.[18] For example,

[18] Closed-door discussion with EU and national actors representing coastguards, law enforcement and judiciary, 21 September 2017, Brussels, Belgium.

in the UK, a code of conduct requires prosecutors to apply a two-stage test – 'Evidential' and 'Public Interest' – and cite potential adverse effects on the victim:

> Prosecutors also need to consider if a prosecution is likely to have *an adverse effect* on the victim's physical or mental health, always bearing in mind the seriousness of the offence. If there is evidence that prosecution is likely to have an adverse impact on the victim's health it may make a prosecution less likely, taking into account the victim's views.[19]

During the closed-door discussion, it was pointed out that at the EU level there is no similar oversight mechanism on assessing how law enforcement's focus on certain types of migrant-smuggling business will affect smugglers' strategies. An account was heard in Greece from a national border and law enforcement interviewee, who shared a story of how, with the help of deployed Frontex officers, heat detectors are being increasingly used to check trucks upon entry onto ferries.[20] The interviewee told a shocking account of migrants being concealed in salt containers and having to breathe through straws. Heat detectors sensed the migrants and they were stopped and the truck driver charged with migrant-smuggling (though it happened within the territory of Greece). This, according to the authority in question, in turn led to migrant smugglers increasingly using even more dangerous forms of concealment, including freezer containers.

While it is important to document emerging smuggling trends, some prosecutors expressed their simultaneous concern that by criminalising, they may be ushering in new, more dangerous models of migrant-smuggling.

## B. Europol's JITs

Joint Investigation Teams (JITs) are used by both law enforcement and judicial actors to ease the exchange of information. As one representative of the EU's JHA agencies explained,

> It is always for national authorities to decide if and how to cooperate … We cannot coordinate investigation – as their role is to support national law enforcement. For example, EMSC can be part of a JIT but not to set it up … we could advise to use it to a Member State and if Member State wants – Europol is included in co-operation.[21]

For example, in June, 2016 EMSC supported a Hungarian-Slovakian JIT by sending a Europol Mobile Investigation Team (EMIST) to Slovakia:

> The action led to the arrest of 7 suspects and the seizure of electronic and communication devices. Crucial data was extracted from the mobile phones seized and was cross-matched against Europol's databases which has allowed for further identification of new international links.[22]

[19] UK Crown Prosecution Service (2013: Art 4.12(c)) (emphasis added).
[20] Interview with national border/coastguard authorities, 9 June 2017, Lesvos, Greece.
[21] Interview with EU agencies 24 August 2017, The Hague, the Netherlands.
[22] Europol (2016d).

Europol's support led to three criminal investigations and identification of 15 suspects, who were brought to court. According to Europol (2016d), 'the mixed group of Slovakian, Hungarian and Afghan perpetrators facilitated the illegal journey of asylum-seekers to the EU for financial gain'. The Afghan nationals were suspected of recruiting migrants from asylum reception centres in Hungary, and the Slovakian and Hungarian nationals of smuggling migrants into Germany by car. In this case, Europol concluded,

> Foreign-based mobile criminal groups appear increasingly at the EU's external borders along the main migration channels and around refugee camps to offer their services to those who are stranded.[23]

Interestingly, 'migration channels' and 'refugee camps' are where civil society actors provide most of their services. Our civil society focus group discussion revealed that sometimes CSAs get attacked by smugglers, since they provide free and more impartial advice.[24] Nevertheless, without a clear exemption, CSAs are increasingly treated as potential smugglers. In addition, there is not always a willingness to make exemptions, as discussed in chapter two. As one of the participants in the closed-door discussion with coastguards, law enforcement and judicial actors pointed out, civil society actors themselves may not always be 'saints', that is, act with due respect for the law.[25]

## C. Operation Taurus in Greece

Europol can support authorities with or without a JIT. For example, the recent Operation Taurus was successfully conducted by the Hellenic Police, with the support of Europol. The operation was planned for five months and aimed at dismantling an 'organised crime group [that] smuggled illegal migrants by air from Greece to the United Kingdom, using falsified documents' (Europol 2017a). Europol assisted Greek authorities by

— organising an operational planning meeting at Europol headquarters upon the request of the Greek authorities, with the participation of Germany, Ireland, Italy, Portugal, Spain, Sweden and the UK;
— providing tailored analytical support;
— supporting expertise via Europol staff deployed to the European Regional Task Force (EURTF) in Piraeus, Greece (Europol 2017b).

Operations took place on 31 October and 1 November 2017: 90 Hellenic Police officers carried out 21 house searches in Athens, which led to the arrest

[23] Europol (2016d).
[24] Focus group with CSAs providing humanitarian assistance, 11 May 2017, Brussels, Belgium.
[25] Closed-door discussion with EU and national actors representing coastguards, law enforcement and judiciary, 21 September 2017, Brussels, Belgium.

of 20 suspects. The operation seized three 'document forgery labs' and related equipment, such as printers and scanners and €61,000 in cash (Europol 2017a). Interestingly, in addition to existing databases and cooperation in the EMSC, Europol as an institution has agreed on a separate national operational plan with Greek authorities:

> In 2016, Europol's Executive Director Rob Wainwright and the Chief of the Hellenic Police, Lt. Gen Konstaninos Tsouvalas signed the Greek National Operational Plan, whose main objective is to target organised migration crime in Greece. The Greek National Operation Plan reaffirmed Europol and the Hellenic Police's mutual commitment and provides a robust framework for the exchange of information between both parties.[26]

In this way, the EU's anti-smuggling priority is getting operationalised and translated into concrete actions. The focus on exchanging 'intel' rather than on gathering evidence is misleading, as intel often cannot be used in courts as an evidence for crime.

## D. Europol in Hotspots

Five Europol Mobile Investigation Team (EMSC) officers are deployed to European Regional Task Forces in Greece and Italy (Europol 2017a). Nevertheless, Europol liaison officers, who were deployed to hotspots in Greece, came mainly from Europol's European Counter Terrorism Centre (ECTC) and were tasked with cross-checking the names of migrants and refugees against the relevant terrorism-related databases. During interviews, it was explained that because of the deployment of Europol's officers to Regional Task Forces and liaison officers to hotspots, cooperation between relevant national law enforcement officers and Europol's staff is not as efficient as it could be.[27]

Europol supports over 40,000 international investigations each year (Europol 2015a). In 2017, regarding migrant-smuggling, Europol declared that there were '5,000 international organised crime groups currently under investigation in the EU' (Bianchini et al 2017). This means that 12.5 per cent of Europol's efforts are devoted to the investigation of migrant-smuggling. As the current research reveals, such investigations extend to asylum-seekers themselves, their family members and friends, individual activists, volunteers and civil society organisations, including Nobel Peace Prize nominees such as Eritrean priest Mussie Zerai (Ford 2017) and Team Humanity (Nobel Peace Prize Committee 2017). Europol gathers intelligence from a variety of actors including Frontex, Operation Sophia and national border and law enforcement officials along migration routes.

[26] Europol (2017a).
[27] Interview with EU agencies 24 August 2017, The Hague, the Netherlands.

## E. Challenges for Law Enforcement

The broad national interpretation of what constitutes the crime of 'migrant-smuggling', including criminalisation of acts without profit motivation (see national interpretations in chapter four) in the context of the high political priority for 'curbing migration' and involvement of competing EU JHA agencies with their operational capacities, makes it unfortunate and unavoidable that different modes of policing extend to all non-statutory actors that are involved in assisting migrants. The political quest to showcase the efficiency of EU interventions and boast a high number of cases has already led (and will increasingly do so) to the investigation of 'false positives'.

While chapter four shows heavy penalties in all four countries, the scale of implementation differs. For example, a number of interviewees in Hungary commented that at the national level, efforts to combat smuggling were 'half-hearted'. CSOs reported numerous examples of smugglers having been made known to the police or authorities, to no avail. Of acute concern was one report of smugglers infiltrating a camp and menacing unaccompanied minors.[28]

National law enforcement actors who were asked about the opportunity costs – lost chances to investigate much more evidently criminal phenomena, such as human trafficking – could only respond that they were following national and EU political priorities. According to law enforcement officials, evidence must come with intent – and there must be money to fund investigations. The interviews revealed that EU agencies approximate the proceeds of smugglers from the volume of people coming to Europe and the average fees they paid.[29] For other types of crime, such as human trafficking or labour exploitation, estimates are harder to make.

One of the closed-door event discussants shed light on the lack of political concern and the consequent lack of law enforcement which occurs once migrants and asylum-seekers are within the EU. Human traffickers and labour exploiters run very labour-intensive businesses in Europe, such as in the agriculture sector in both Italy and Greece. The discussant specified:

> Italian canned tomatoes costs less than one euro – consumers around the EU like it because it's cheap, State and local municipality in Italy likes [*sic*] it for the exports, the farmer likes it for additional income. Though, it is only possible to keep such [a] low price thanks to undeclared work of migrants and refugees.[30]

Another interviewee from a CSO in Rome was similarly concerned and predicted an explosion of human-trafficking cases, because the majority of the clients the CSO works with find precarious and undeclared jobs in fields such as prostitution and agriculture.[31]

[28] Interview with national welfare authority providing social and medical assistance, 31 August 2017, Subotica, Serbia.

[29] Interview with EU agencies 24 August 2017, The Hague, the Netherlands.

[30] Closed-door discussion with EU and national actors representing coastguards, law enforcement and judiciary, 21 September 2017, Brussels, Belgium.

[31] Interview with CSO, 8 November 2016, Rome, Italy.

The UNODC (2017) stated that the 'smuggling of migrants has become a very profitable business generating significant proceeds that can be disrupted by "following the money", as for other forms of organized crime'. Yet the 'follow the money' logic appears to have been replaced by a logic of following the migrants and those who assist them. In this way, humanitarian assistance is becoming not only increasingly 'politicised', but also policed and criminalised.

Member States' uploading of crime reports to Europol is voluntary. This was highlighted as a wasted opportunity by a Hungarian judicial actor:

> Whenever you give something to Europol whether you get a cross-check match or not it's random. It doesn't mean there aren't similar cases around you, but other countries might not share that information. In an ideal world, you'd have sharing of police intelligence all over the place.[32]

Blurring mandates is another acute concern. Interviews conducted with representatives of relevant EU agencies revealed that EASO supports Europol with anti-smuggling investigations by conducting social media monitoring using falsified Facebook profiles of 'potential migrants' and sharing this information weekly with other Home Affairs agencies.[33] Europol then requests Facebook to take down such pages or groups, where smugglers are advertising their services to potential migrants. The EMSC runs a similar exercise independently.

A further concern raised in the research relates to the lack of a holistic picture of migration and asylum issues, including within the EU's own legislation, and the narrow channels for legal migration. The latter includes the lack of speedy and realistic channels for asylum-seekers and refugees to arrive in Europe without resorting to smugglers. Also frequently raised as a concern by CSOs was the poor provision of – and access to – safe and legal pathways of secondary migration within the EU, per, for example, the right of unaccompanied minors eligible for family reunification under Dublin III (see chapter four on the case of France and the UK). Moreover, unilateral moves by Member States are not written into regionally focused law or practice. For example, nationally focused solutions such as the Hungarian one were widely perceived to be a sticking plaster or even, in the case of the border wall and transit zones, a means of redirecting smuggling operations to other routes into Europe.

During the closed-door discussion, it was similarly expressed that due to the closure of Balkan routes, agreements with Turkey and reliance on the Libyan Government of National Accord and even armed militias, smuggling networks were not dismantled but simply shifted to the Black Sea or reopened via the Mediterranean Sea arrival route in Spain (see Figure 3.1).[34] The closed-door discussion also highlighted the consensus among coastguards, law enforcement and judicial

[32] Interview with legal expert, 30 August 2017, Szeged, Hungary.

[33] Interview with EU agency, 6 June 2017, Athens, Greece; interview with EU agency on 24 August 2017, The Hague, the Netherlands.

[34] Closed-door discussion with EU and national actors representing coastguards, law enforcement and judiciary, 21 September 2017, Brussels, Belgium.

actors that essentially 'migrant-smuggling' is not a question of criminal justice but of migration management.

## II. Eurojust

Eurojust is the European Union's Judicial Cooperation Unit. It works with 29 national legal systems and the EU's own legal framework. An interviewee representing national judicial authorities commented that within Eurojust, 'co-operation is challenging, but necessary'.[35] In particular, due to delays in cooperation, refusals to cooperate and conflicts of jurisdiction, some criminals escape cross-border prosecutions. Article 85 of the Lisbon Treaty defines Eurojust's mandate as:

> to support and strengthen coordination and cooperation between national investigating and prosecuting authorities in relation to serious crime affecting two or more Member States or requiring a prosecution on common bases, on the basis of operations conducted and information supplied by the Member State's Authorities and by Europol.

Though a rigid reading would entail that crimes must be serious and cross-border, a previous study on organised crime ascertained that there is quite a broad reading of how the crime can 'affect' Member States and that practically any 'organised crime' conducted by two or more persons (depending on national legislation) can be regarded as serious (Carrera et al 2016). Eurojust has explicitly listed 'smuggling of *illegal* immigrants [*sic*]' among the open list of crimes for which the agency has competence.

Thus, in the area of migrant-smuggling, the multiplication of actors involved in gathering information on suspects extends far beyond Europol: to Frontex, EUNAVFOR Sophia, NATO and even EASO's social media monitoring. Eurojust has concluded cooperation agreements with two EU law-enforcement agencies: Europol and Frontex. Nevertheless, there are no such agreements with other actors. On 1 October 2015, Eurojust signed a Memorandum of Understanding with the EUNAFOR MED in which the parties, in light of the EU Action Plan against Migrant Smuggling, planned 'to exchange strategic information of a non-operational nature, best practice, expertise and experience in the field of *illegal* immigrant smuggling [*sic*]'.[36] It led to the 'increased cooperation with the EUNAVFOR MED' in investigating migrant-smuggling (Eurojust 2016a: 1).

On the same day (1 October 2015), the Italian National Anti-Mafia and Counterterrorism (DNAA) Prosecutor agreed to ensure the 'completeness and effectiveness of investigations at the national level and the involvement, through Eurojust, of the European partners in the fight against smugglers' networks' (DNAA 2015). Thus, EUNAVFOR MED, despite being a EU-led operation

[35] Interview with national judicial authorities, 24 August 2017, The Hague, the Netherlands.
[36] Eurojust (2015).

under the command of the Italian Navy, was included in the judicial aspects through Eurojust. Despite these insurances at a national level, regional Italian judicial authorities which were interviewed regarded such inclusion of non-law enforcement actors, particularly military personnel, in gathering information on criminals as difficult – moreover, the evidence gathered can rarely be used in national courts.[37]

The interviewee explained that evidentiary requirements set strict procedure on how information needs to be gathered in compliance with criminal law, for example, by following the decisions of the investigative judge or prosecutor to intercept the online communication between suspects.[38] Unless the information is gathered as 'intel' in accordance with this procedure, it cannot be presented before the independent judge. Therefore, efforts to exchange information between military and law enforcement may lead to counter-productive results – either gathering information that eventually cannot be used, or lowering the evidentiary requirements that are likely to 'unbalance' the criminal justice system.

## A. Eurojust's Thematic Group on Illegal Migrant-Smuggling

Increased politicisation and prioritisation of this crime type has led to the establishment of various institutions, such as Europol's EMSC and various informal networks of practitioners, including Eurojust's Thematic Group on Illegal Migrant-Smuggling (henceforth referred to as the Thematic Group). The Thematic Group was established on 29 September 2015. It was foreseen that the Thematic Group would

> work in cooperation with specialised prosecutors in the Member States to address the legal, judicial, operational and practical challenges faced in the investigation and prosecution of illegal immigrant-smuggling and to enhance judicial cooperation, including with third States.[39]

In reality, the Thematic Group's work seems more analytical, and has the potential to bring about more EU standards in relation to migrant-smuggling. It will focus on the following four areas:

- collecting and analysing selected national case law on illegal immigrant-smuggling to identify legal difficulties as well as gathering and sharing best practices;
- preparing a chart on the applicable legal framework at EU and international level on migrant-smuggling;

[37] Interview with national judicial authorities, 12 November 2016, Catania, Italy.
[38] Interview with national judicial authorities, 12 November 2016, Catania, Italy.
[39] Council of the EU (2015).

— mapping the definition of illegal immigrant-smuggling, and/or closely related crime types;
— organising the first Eurojust tactical meeting on illegal immigrant-smuggling.[40]

The European Commission itself has created the Network of National Contact Points on Migrant Smuggling. The network's first meeting took place in March 2017. It should be welcomed that the EU Fundamental Rights Agency (FRA) is involved. FRA representatives raised the point of importance 'not to criminalise humanitarian assistance given to irregular migrants' (Sandru 2017).

The spread of various informal networks for separate crime areas in order to enable swift exchanges of operational information and related criminal justice challenges was well documented in a previous study on organised crime (Carrera et al 2016b). While, in the current context, raising awareness, exchanging promising practices and discussing various challenges is welcomed, the risk is that such networks can become increasingly operational, particularly in third countries of transit, namely Turkey and Libya.

## B. Eurojust in Hotspots

Eurojust as a relevant EU Justice and Home Affairs agency 'supports the hotspot approach' (Eurojust 2016a). Nevertheless, the field research trips to Italy and Greece, particularly visits to EU Regional Task Forces (EURTF), confirmed that Eurojust's involvement is much less than that of Frontex, Europol or even EUNAVFOR Sophia (in the case of Italy), which are permanently present. For example, regarding the hotspot in Italy, the national Italian agency was entrusted to act on behalf of Eurojust to channel information through the national Italian desk:

> Eurojust supports the Operational Frontex Regional Team (OFRT) in Catania in facilitating mutual legal assistance requests and in coordinating between Member States' national authorities, also in cases involving third countries. Information related to illegal immigrant smuggling is collected by the *Direzione Nazionale Antimafia e Antiterrorismo* [National Anti-Mafia and Antiterrorism Directorate, DNAA]. The DNAA Coordinator is also appointed as Eurojust's Contact Point on illegal immigrant smuggling, and is regularly present in the hotspot and channels relevant information to the Italian Desk at Eurojust for judicial follow up and coordination at EU level.[41]

The identical arrangement was reached in Greece:

> Two Greek prosecutors from the Court of Appeals of Piraeus [Athens] have been appointed as Eurojust's Contact Points in the hotspot and they are in close cooperation

[40] Council of the EU (2015).
[41] Council of the EU (2015).

> with the Greek Desk at Eurojust. By having judicial contact points present in Piraeus, Eurojust is kept informed in real time of any information which might require the use of Eurojust's operational tools, i.e. coordination meetings or centres or the setting up of a joint investigation team.[42]

These 'light' arrangements of Eurojust's presence at the hotspots seem logical, given the low number of cases that reach prosecution. As mentioned above, despite the ample intel gathered and numerous information exchanges between the military and law enforcement actors, very little of the evidence that is gathered can be used before the courts. In addition, the majority of suspects are refugees or migrants themselves, of very 'low' rank, easily replacable, therefore their persecution would not bring desirable societal impact of stopping migrant-smuggling.

## C. Joint Investigation Teams on Migrant-Smuggling

In addition, Europol and Eurojust support and facilitate 'exchange of information' about smugglers and criminal smuggling networks, and the organisation of Joint Investigation Teams (JITs). Eurojust regards JITs as a judicial coordination and cooperation instrument, which can be established on the basis of a JIT agreement. An interviewee explained that each Member State has its own rules regarding how to establish a JIT, but those who delegate the power to establish a JIT to their national liaison officers at Eurojust can do it in a matter of minutes, which 'can be crucial for the ongoing crime'.[43] Whereas Mutual Legal Assistance (MLA) requests limited co-operation for specific purposes and provides rather passive engagement between partners, the JITs provide the opportunity for unlimited real-time exchange of information and participatory trust-building among partners.[44]

In Hungary, for example, lawyers and a judicial representative interviewed for this research commented that the most successful anti-smuggling efforts were those conducted across countries where states worked together.[45] All were keen to point out that this was because of the inherently transnational nature of the crime:

> Normally organisers are inside Western European countries on one end and on the other end in those countries where the migrants are coming from … we are the gatekeeper, we lack a lot of information which would be needed to see the big picture.[46]

Nevertheless, a number of shortcomings were noted in relation to transnational operations, including a lack of staff and resources. As one judicial representative commented,

> Those cases where we had some success were where international co-operation has been done primarily through Joint Investigation team cases. This is practically the only

[42] Council of the EU (2015).
[43] Interview with national judicial authorities, 24 August 2017, The Hague, the Netherlands.
[44] Interview with national judicial authorities, 24 August 2017, The Hague, the Netherlands.
[45] Interview with CSO providing legal assistance, 28 August 2017, Budapest, Hungary.
[46] Interview with legal expert, 30 August 2017, Szeged, Hungary.

> way. Traditional remedies are too slow to investigate cases due to lack of information. These criminal organisations are not firm, it's more like a cell, a fluid pool of perpetrators, not a solid structure of organised crime.[47]

Joint operations involve much skill and new technologies for telephone interception and surveillance – 'not the normal investigation methods of interrogating suspects and using witnesses', as one interviewee said.[48] Another difficult aspect in these operations concerns criminal jurisdiction, which is why coordination is key. There is often a need for parallel indictments across countries.

One judicial official explained a successful collaboration:

> In one case we had to indict two groups at the same time as there was no way to manage the issue of dual jurisdiction. We couldn't join the cases as had no jurisdiction over foreign citizens committing crimes abroad and they had no jurisdiction for the same even though the groups were the same so we did parallel indictments – two charges but pointing at each other.[49]

Three joint investigations were reported to have borne fruit in terms of prosecuting criminal smuggling – for example, the Parndorf case in Hungary (see example below) – but many others failed because of various challenges, detailed below.

## D. Parndorf Case in Hungary

On 27 August 2015 on an Austrian motorway, a lorry was found containing the decomposing bodies of 71 individuals, including a baby, who had been smuggled through Hungary (Smalemay 2017). There was no JIT formed and this started a new investigation.

Both Eurojust and Europol provided speedy operational support:

> A coordination meeting [at Eurojust] preceded by an operational meeting at the Europol were organized within 48 hours of the request. At the Eurojust's coordination meeting, the existence of more than 10 ongoing investigations in Germany concerning migrant transports planned, organized and carried out by the same OCG [organised crime group] became clear; underlining the need for cooperation and exchange of information.[50]

In this case, the JIT was considered, but due to differences at this stage of the investigation, and because some MLA requests had already been sent by other partners, it was decided that a traditional MLA request was more suitable. As a result,

> Four suspects of Bulgarian nationality and one Afghan suspect, all belonging to an OCG involved in IIS [illegal migrant-smuggling], were identified and arrested in Hungary

[47] Interview with legal expert, 30 August 2017, Szeged, Hungary.
[48] Interview with legal expert, 30 August 2017, Szeged, Hungary.
[49] Interview with legal expert, 30 August 2017, Szeged, Hungary.
[50] Eurojust (2016b: 32).

> days later. Alleged facilitators of the crimes were later arrested in Germany and cases were also brought against suspects in Bulgaria and Serbia.[51]

Fieldwork for this research, backed up by other research in the public domain, revealed that the smuggling network involved in this case was being tracked by several national authorities, none of whom were able to interpret the intercepted distress call – and act – in time:

> All of those conversations were recorded but no one was there. Not the Austrians, not the Slovakians, not the Hungarians. No one was there to understand what they were talking about. In retrospect, it took place under the authorities' noses but no one was there to listen to it … there's poor co-operation. Why were we intercepting the same phone three times into three different systems anyway?[52]

This leads back to another challenge of translation and interpretation, mentioned during the closed-door discussion: when criminals use obscure or non-European languages. This incident was claimed at the time to have been one of a series of sparks for more intense measures pursued by the Orbán government to combat smuggling and irregular migration (see chapter 4.II).[53] Some have nevertheless criticised the government for using the incident as an excuse to pursue an anti-migrant agenda without being fully committed to stopping migrant-smuggling.[54] Others have pointed out that the Orbán government's anti-migrant agenda was well underway before the incident:

> I would like to cast some doubt on the argument that the changes were proposed in relation to the death[s] of 71 people in a lorry on 27 August 2015. The [amendments to the Hungarian Criminal Code] Bill was introduced to the Parliament on 28 August 2015, making it very unlikely that the detailed changes were drafted within a day. Moreover, neither the reasoning section of the bill mentions the incident, nor the request for an accelerated procedure, filed the same day, has any reference to it.[55]

## E. Challenges for Judicial Actors

When speaking about the EU's Justice and Home Affairs agencies, at best the secondary role is assigned to Eurojust – the EU's unit for judicial cooperation and a criminal justice approach as such. The closed-door discussion revealed that the fight against smuggling has been heavily funded and supported on the side of law enforcement (including justifying the involvement of military actors), but that this was not 'followed all the way through to prosecution'.[56]

[51] Eurojust (2016b: 32).

[52] Interview with legal expert, 30 August 2017, Szeged, Hungary.

[53] Interview with think tank advising the government on anti-smuggling and immigration, 30 August 2017, Budapest, Hungary.

[54] Focus group with CSAs providing humanitarian assistance, 11 May 2017, Brussels, Belgium.

[55] Email correspondence with Hungarian CSO providing legal assistance, 6 November 2017.

[56] Closed-door discussion with EU and national actors representing coastguards, law enforcement and judiciary, 21 September 2017, Brussels, Belgium.

The challenges related to gathering evidence were mentioned in the EU stakeholder meeting, including the 'different legal requirements' and 'different data retention regimes' (Eurojust 2016a: 6). Another challenge, as interviews in The Hague indicated, is that national prosecutors see the increased volumes of gathered 'intel' as a challenge for efficient and speedy investigations.[57] An even more important challenge for the judicial authorities is admissibility of the evidence before the independent judge:

> Admissibility of evidence gathered abroad through the execution of the MLA requests is hampered when the legal requirements of the forum State are not entirely met. For example limitations may be present both in activating and also using telephone interceptions or special investigative techniques (e.g. undercover agents).[58]

Cooperation with key third countries on the migration route was regarded as 'crucial, but is influenced by different social systems and cultures' (Eurojust 2016a: 6). The interviews revealed how challenging it is for prosecutors to be tasked and asked to work in contexts where international judicial cooperation is hardly possible, such as in the context of conflict-torn Libya or even Turkey.[59] This was confirmed during the practitioners' discussion at the UNODC (2017: iii), where it was strongly emphasised that bringing top-level smugglers to justice 'requires political will, prioritization of resources, concerted efforts as well as a common understanding and *very solid judicial cooperation* along smuggling routes' [emphasis added]. In addition, Eurojust 'appointed contact points in the key third countries':

> The College of Eurojust is discussing the posting of liaison magistrates to third states, in particular the role of such liaison magistrate and the criteria for selecting countries, and other ways to step up cooperation with third states. In relation to the MENA (Middle East and Northern Africa) region, Eurojust contact points have recently been nominated in Algeria, Jordan, Lebanon, Palestinian Authority, Saudi Arabia and Iraq, in addition to those already appointed in Egypt, Israel and Tunisia.[60]

Nevertheless, the interviews revealed high costs owing to the security risks facing prosecutors deployed to these countries, as well as plans to send prosecutors to Libya.[61] Investigations of migrant-smuggling and trafficking cases remain inefficient due to deficiencies of the rule of law standards in Libya. A Statewatch-leaked Strategic Review of the EUBAM mission in Libya and Operation Sophia mentions serious rule of law challenges, including a 'rudimentary level of central coordination' and 'tribal courts' (Council of the EU 2017b: paras 46–56). National law enforcement and judicial practitioners as well as relevant EU JHA agencies have confirmed that, at the moment, they can do nothing with the evidence gathered

[57] Closed-door discussion with EU and national actors representing coastguards, law enforcement and judiciary, 21 September 2017, Brussels, Belgium.
[58] Eurojust (2016a: 6).
[59] Interview with national judicial authorities, 12 November 2016, Catania, Italy; interview with national judicial authorities, 24 August 2017, The Hague, the Netherlands.
[60] Council of the EU (2015).
[61] Interview with national judicial authorities, 24 August 2017, The Hague, the Netherlands.

from migrants who are rescued, since the Libyan situation does not allow effective prosecution.[62] Moreover, another rule of law and competencies-related challenge emerges in Turkey, since after the 2016 'coup attempt' many prosecutors, who were cooperating with the EU agencies, were accused of being Gülenists, and their replacements hardly speak English.[63]

The closed-door discussion also highlighted the difference in legal regimes and definitions of 'what is smuggling' and 'what is an organised criminal group'. One of the discussants highlighted that what is considered a felony in some European countries can be regarded in countries of origin and transit as not even a crime.[64] This issue also featured in the discussion among practitioners in the Tactical Meeting, who elaborated on the challenges for national authorities of cooperating with North African countries as including 'extradition proceedings [which] often fail to meet the double criminality requirement … [and] execution letters of request on identification of suspects and tracing and seizure of assets' (Eurojust, 2016a).

Civil society actors in Hungary stressed that both Eurojust and Europol also provide support to Member States not only at the external EU sea borders but also along the Balkan corridor and within the EU, where there is a need to stop smuggling.[65] A contrasting 'lack of the EU' was witnessed in the Calais region. Whereas Austria, Hungary, Slovakia and other countries on the Balkan route and the UK work together in JITs and participate in Thematic Groups against migrant-smuggling, there does not seem to be such a coordinated approach in Italy and Greece, where Regional Task Forces are established.

To conclude, the EU's great ambition to fight smuggling and its significant allocation of funds to diverse actors results, in practice, in quite a low number of successful prosecutions. Both EU law enforcement and judicial actors agreed during the closed-door discussion that when it comes to both prosecutions and successful prosecutions, the numbers are extremely modest: Eurojust had 60 cases in 2015, 65 in 2016 and 34 as of mid-2017.[66] EU and national judicial actors during the closed door discussion agreed that many such cases, once started, are dropped due to the challenges identified above and because they lack quality evidence and criminal intent. Moreover, where prosecutions do take place, they often end up criminalising very minor actors, including smuggled migrants themselves, as elaborated in chapter four.[67]

[62] Interview with national judicial authorities, 24 August 2017, The Hague, the Netherlands.

[63] Interview with national judicial authorities, 24 August 2017, The Hague, the Netherlands.

[64] Closed-door discussion with EU and national actors representing coastguards, law enforcement and judiciary, 21 September 2017, Brussels, Belgium.

[65] Interview with CSO providing legal assistance, 28 August 2017, Budapest, Hungary.

[66] Closed-door discussion with EU and national actors representing coastguards, law enforcement and judiciary, 21 September 2017, Brussels, Belgium.

[67] Closed-door discussion with EU and national actors representing coastguards, law enforcement and judiciary, 21 September 2017, Brussels, Belgium.

# III. Frontex

The new mandate of Frontex, following the adoption of the European Border and Coast Guard Regulation (EU/2016/1624), gives the agency new powers in countering (preventing and detecting) the smuggling of migrants as part of 'cross-border crimes' (European Union 2016). Article 15.5 provides for the possibility of joint operations or rapid intervention teams to cover 'multipurpose' objectives, such as 'coast guard functions and the prevention of cross-border crime, including the fight against migrant-smuggling'. Article 52 meanwhile foresees the possibility for the agency to cooperate with EU Home Affairs agencies and other EU institutions in 'preventing and detecting cross-border crime such as migrant-smuggling'. Interestingly, paragraph 19 of the new Frontex Regulation states:

> Cross-border crimes necessarily entail a cross-border dimension … characterized by crimes directly linked to unauthorized crossings of the external borders, including trafficking in human beings or smuggling of migrants. That said, Article 1(2) of Council Directive 2002/90/EC allows Member States not to impose sanctions where the aim of the behaviour is to provide humanitarian assistance to migrant[s].[68]

Thus, new Frontex regulation stresses on the humanitarian exemption clause in the Facilitators' Package. The excerpt above once again highlights the optional nature of this provision, as it is left up for the responsibility of Member States. Nevertheless, there is no clear prohibition for Frontex not to assist in criminalising humanitarian acts, though the EU-added value of such action would be highly questionable from EU's own legal standards, such as Fundamental Rights and Rule of Law.

## A. Frontex Joint Operations at Sea and in Hotspots

Frontex is one of the most visible actors in the implementation of EU anti-smuggling policies in border controls and surveillance. This has mainly taken place in relation to two Frontex-coordinated maritime joint operations (JOs), where other EU Member States deploy experts, officers and equipment: Joint Operation Triton in Italy, and Joint Operation Poseidon Sea in Greece. The operations' main objective has been to support the two Member States in conducting border controls and surveillance, yet both became 'multipurpose' operations so as to cover other aspects, such as migrant-smuggling (European Commission 2016d; Frontex 2016b and 2016c). The description of Joint Operation Poseidon Sea, for instance, states:

> Debriefing officers deployed by the agency collect intelligence about people smuggling networks operating in Turkey and migrants' countries of origin. The agency shares this information with the Greek authorities and Europol.[69]

[68] European Union (2016).
[69] Frontex (2016b).

The cases of Italy and Greece present different issues and challenges when it comes to Frontex sea operations, the involvement of other supranational actors such as the military, and the presence and contributions of CSAs in SAR activities. In October 2013, Italy launched a unilateral and ad hoc operation in the central Mediterranean called Operation Mare Nostrum (OMN). OMN took responsibility for people in need of rescue and protection in the Mediterranean. It focused mainly on SAR and disembarkation of those rescued to Italian territory and presented a predominantly humanitarian approach, rescuing some 150,000 people at sea during its existence (Italian Navy 2014). After the Italian authorities announced that OMN would end in 2014, several civil society actors expressed concerns regarding the gap of SAR in the Mediterranean (eg, Amnesty International 2014).

These concerns were not addressed after the closing of OMN in December 2014 and the launch of Frontex JO Triton. The European Commission and Frontex made clear that Triton would not replace OMN (European Commission 2014a, 2014b). Compared with OMN, Triton covered a different geographical area and was conducted by national authorities responsible for Schengen cooperation; it had distinct purposes and practical aims. Its main goal and mandate were 'border control and surveillance'. Triton did formally engage in SAR as a general obligation under international law, but *only* in the context of border controls and surveillance activities and not as part of its official mandate (see Frontex 2016a).[70] The launch of the EUNAVFOR-MED Operation (Operation Sophia) in May 2015 did not address the SAR gap either (see below).

Frontex officers conduct voluntary debriefing of migrants, whereas Europol's European Migrant Smuggling Centre in the headquarters in The Hague analyses the gathered information. Europol's operational officer in Italy only checks the validity of documents. According to interviewees from European agencies, Europol's operational officers ('mobile units') deployed in Greece are more involved in the investigation of terrorism-related threats.[71]

In both Italy and Greece, deployed EU officials and liaison officers have stressed that their role is 'only' to support national authorities, who hold ultimate responsibility for their activities.[72] While the competences of these EU Agencies have been said to be mainly 'soft' in nature, focused on supporting and coordinating EU Member States' actions, their actions have been proven to have profound effects on the ground (see Carrera et al 2013). In Greece, EU support is much more apparent than in Italy: as of 18 September 2017, Greece was host to 1,183 deployed EASO and Frontex officers (European Commission 2017b).

[70] According to Frontex (2016a), 'International law obliges all captains of vessels to provide assistance to any persons found in distress at sea. SAR is also a specific objective of the operational plan of every Frontex joint maritime operation. For this reason, vessels deployed by Frontex to an operational area are always ready to provide support to the national authorities in SAR operations'.

[71] Interview with EU agencies/official, 24 August 2017, The Hague, the Netherlands; interview with EU agencies/officials, 8 June 2017, Lesvos island, Greece.

[72] Interview with EU agency, 6 June 2017, Athens, Greece; interview with EU agency, 7 June 2017, Athens, Greece; interview with EU agencies/officials, 8 June 2017, Lesvos island, Greece; interview with EU agencies/officials, 9 June 2017, Lesvos island, Greece; interview with EU agencies, 9 November 2016, Rome, Italy; interview with EU agencies/officials, 13 November 2016, Catania, Italy.

## B. Frontex Operations on Land – The Hungarian Border: Complicity or Compliance?

This section considers how the EU has both criticised and sought to practically support Hungary's management of the external Schengen border with Serbia, including through the controversial deployment of Frontex officers. The debate between the EU and Hungarian government in relation to the management of the external Schengen borders during the 'European humanitarian refugee crisis' has had important implications for the EU's involvement at the border, including in relation to the presence of Frontex, among other EU Home Affairs actors. Neither Frontex nor other EU law enforcement is present in the transit zones.

The Hungarian National Immigration and Asylum Office performs asylum interviews in the transit zones; meanwhile, the security of the zones is assured by private contractors and police. Healthcare is provided by military doctors. UNHCR is there to represent the international community, as are various state-funded civil society organisations which provide assistance. UNHCR has been critical of the existence of and conditions in the transit zones as well as issues concerning the process by which decisions as to who is allowed to enter are conducted.[73]

UNHCR refers to its monitoring role as one of 'protection by presence' and has played a role in successfully intervening to resolve various transit zone abuses, including police violence and handcuffing of pregnant women.[74] Meanwhile, for fear of losing funds and/or access, others have remained quiet after witnessing abuses (see chapters 5.II.A and 7.III). Some interviewees suggested that it was anticipated that Frontex would work in Serbia in the near future. Currently, Serbian border guards are present in Hungary as legal observers – in an advisory role with no administrative powers.

Despite condemning the stance of Hungarian Prime Minister Victor Orbán, and rejecting his demand that the EU pay for the costs of the external Schengen border wall, in a recent letter sent from the European Commission to Prime Minister Orbán, EU Commission President Jean-Claude Juncker acknowledged that the EU was offering some support to Hungary, including posting 19 Frontex border agents from EU Member States at the Hungary-Serbia border (Juncker 2017). Frontex has been operational in Hungary for many years, but since January 2017 it has had a more prominent role and is now a permanent presence.

Interviews conducted as part of fieldwork revealed an element of mystery surrounding the deployment of these officers, including where they are and what their function is. This confusion was also found among international and UN organisations.[75] Interviews with EU agencies revealed that Frontex has

[73] Interview with UN actor, 31 August 2017, Szeged, Budapest.
[74] Interview with UN actor, 31 August 2017, Szeged, Budapest.
[75] Interview with UN actor, 31 August 2017, Szeged, Hungary.

two permanent functions in Hungary: (i) support with border surveillance activities; and ii) support with border checks at crossing points. Frontex posts experienced officers from Member States at the border crossing points to assist local authorities with border control and anti-smuggling checks, for example, checking vehicles.[76] All of their activities are in keeping with national legislation, but the Schengen Handbook is the main legal document on which the operations are based.[77]

In terms of border patrols, interviewees from EU Home Affairs agencies were keen to stress that the deployed Frontex officers had no direct practical control themselves but rather were integrated into the local police force. They also had a role in supporting 'border surveillance activity'. At the request of the Hungarian authorities,[78] these surveillance operations take place within an eight-kilometre zone of the border fence, not directly along the fence itself. EU interviewees confirmed that only Hungarian authorities were present at the fence itself. Other interviewees nevertheless claimed to have witnessed directly or heard evidence indirectly of Frontex officers involved in conducting border patrols and interacting with migrants and activists.[79]

When Frontex officers detect irregular migrants they hand them over to the Hungarian authorities to take care of the case. They are also under an obligation to raise any concerns of trafficking before handing them over, although this is also the operational competence of the Hungarian authorities and no specific training has been conducted in this domain. The lack of adequate trafficking screening was raised by numerous civil society interviewees and representatives of UN organisations.[80] One interviewee from an EU Home Affairs agency commented that the role of the deployed Frontex officers was ultimately not to judge but to help people: 'It's criminal as a police officer not to help people in need.'[81]

EU officials indicated both in interviews and at the closed-door stakeholder event that the heightened border patrols could have the effect of redirecting migrants through other routes, such as the Serbian-Bulgarian border or Ukrainian border. This concern was raised by multiple interviewees from EU and international institutions as well as CSOs. Indeed, most interviewees saw the Hungarian solution as unhelpful to the regional anti-smuggling response as a whole. Frontex has no presence at the internal EU Romania-Hungarian border. Other migrants remain undeterred and seek to cross multiple times, staying in the woodland areas by the border fence.[82]

[76] Interview with EU agencies/officials, 30 August 2017, via Skype.

[77] Interview with EU agencies/officials, 30 August 2017, via Skype.

[78] Interview with EU agencies/officials, 30 August 2017, via Skype.

[79] Interview with non-formal group (activists) providing social assistance, 31 August 2017, Subotica, Serbia.

[80] Interview with lawyer, 31 August 2017, Szeged, Hungary; interview with UN actor, 31 August 2017, Szeged, Hungary.

[81] Interview with EU agencies/officials, 30 August 2017, via Skype.

[82] Interview with non-formal group (activists) providing social assistance, 31 August 2017, Subotica, Serbia.

## C. Controversy Related to Frontex Deployment on Serbian-Hungarian Borders

Some interviewees from international organisations[83] and international CSOs[84] expressed concern that the presence of Frontex officers at the Hungary-Serbia border served the function of legitimising the border fence. In light of reports of extreme violence and even torture (*Médecins Sans Frontières* 2017) committed against migrants at the border as part of anti-smuggling and anti-border crossing patrols (see chapters 5.II.A and 7.III), some felt that by being present, the EU was condoning such violence.[85] Representatives from EU agencies were nevertheless keen to stress that while the primary function of the deployed Frontex officers was operational support, they also provided a monitoring function. This is reminiscent of the stated function of UNHCR in the transit camps of 'protection by presence' (see above).

## D. Accountability of Frontex Activities

Frontex has an accountability structure centred on the Fundamental Rights Officer, which gives it some protective function. Through the Frontex Fundamental Rights Officer complaints mechanism, members of the Frontex consultative forum can highlight cases of concern which will be investigated. Deployed officers also have the possibility to report incidents of concern. Meanwhile, anybody is free to submit a complaint against a Frontex officer through a new complaints mechanism.[86]

Some CSOs reported that the complaint mechanism was more of a public relations exercise than an act of genuine transparency in Hungary.[87] For example, a group of NGOs addressed a letter directly to the Frontex executive director regarding possible violent practices by police officers at the Serbia-Hungary border. Interviewees from an EU organisation confirmed that concerns had been investigated and no evidence for rights abuses was found. The same interviewees confirmed that the reports of violence had been investigated by Hungarian authorities who reported back, since Frontex has 'no mandate to do its own investigations'.[88] A representative from an EU agency commented:

> In our operations there haven't been such observations. We have a separate reporting mechanism and no such incidents have been reported. We have heard of no cases of mistreatment by Hungarian police via our team members deployed there, however we are not present in the transit zones so we don't know what happens there.[89]

[83] Interview with UN actor, 31 August 2017, Szeged, Hungary.
[84] Interview with CSO providing social assistance, 30 August 2017, Budapest, Hungary.
[85] Interview with CSO providing social assistance, 30 August 2017, Budapest, Hungary; focus group with CSAs providing humanitarian assistance, 11 May 2017, Brussels, Belgium.
[86] Interview with EU agencies/officials, 30 August 2017, via Skype.
[87] Focus group with CSAs providing humanitarian assistance, 11 May 2017, Brussels, Belgium.
[88] Interview with EU agencies/officials, 30 August 2017, via Skype.
[89] Interview with EU agencies/officials, 30 August, via Skype.

The European Commission has conducted visits to the transit zones, as it is their responsibility to monitor the implementation of the Schengen border code. Frontex has no direct links to IOM and UNHCR or CSOs on the ground in Hungary, only via the consultative forum. One CSO which provides legal support commented on the role of Frontex and accountability at the border:

> We've been in touch with them [about] abuse and push backs. Their human rights monitor came on a monitoring mission this year [after the publication of our report on violence and pushbacks]. We also wrote to the director complaining about the abuse, he responding saying thanks, they are considering what their role is … we are aware of the new Frontex complaint mechanism but it started a bit later and … took a while to operationalise.[90]

CSAs commented that in reality it was very difficult to identify agents of violence against migrants are at the border, because uniforms are hard to differentiate. Similar issues have been confirmed in Italy and Greece. In Italy, an Amnesty International (2016) investigation into forced fingerprinting practices outlined that physical fingerprinting was left to national officials, but Frontex liaison officers should have known of the methods used. Nevertheless, as chapter 6.I further details, interviewed governmental officials as well as international organisations and EU JHA agencies either denied or refused to comment on the findings of the Amnesty International report.

Two CSAs providing legal assistance to migrants in Hungary nevertheless reported that there had been cases where migrants who had reported violence explained that the beatings had stopped when 'uniformed, foreign-speaking officers' were present. This may suggest that the presence of Frontex officers serves a protective function in upholding migrant rights at the border, although any evidence in this regard is speculative at best. One CSO which provides legal assistance commented,

> We were thinking if Frontex increased its observing capacity it could help stop the violence. When we travelled to Subotica last time there were people lying on the floor with open wounds – they didn't just fall into something.[91]

The same CSO has also reported incidents of violence to the Serbian police, who have acknowledged the issue. A common perspective among CSOs in Hungary, Greece and Italy was that the deployment of more and better trained border guards from across Member States through a Frontex operation would have been a preferable option to the establishment of more ad hoc national programmes. For example, at the Hungarian-Serbian border approximately 2,500 'border hunters' (a civilian border patrol) out of a total 3,000 foreseen had been deployed at the time of fieldwork in summer 2017. Border-hunters are Hungarian citizens who undergo a short training programme and receive a small salary to perform border guarding functions. They are less accountable than the police (see further discussion in chapters 5.II.A and 7.III).

[90] Interview with CSO providing legal assistance, 28 August 2017, Budapest, Hungary.
[91] Interview with CSO providing legal assistance, 16 August 2017, via Skype.

## IV. Role of EASO in Hotspots

Unlike in Italy, where EASO acts in a supportive role to enable relocations, in Greece EASO liaison officers de facto assess asylum claims by issuing opinions on both admissibility and merits. Such opinions are later referred to and approved by the Greek Asylum Service. CSA interviewees expressed that they were happy for the EU to step in to deal with the backlog of cases, but they were critical regarding the lack of subsequent responsibility for EASO 'opinions', since all appeals are happening against the Greek Asylum Service itself.[92] In Greece, in addition to Frontex and Europol representatives, EASO and Commission (DG Home) representatives in each of the five islands are also taking an active role in tackling migrant-smuggling. The situation seems to be different in Italy, where EASO is supporting the Ministry of the Interior to implement the relocation mechanism.

Finally, there was evidence that while EU cooperation in asylum determinations and relocations was working well in some instances along the Balkan route, in other cases countries were cooperating without EASO being physically present. For example, in Hungary there were some successful cases of unaccompanied minors being reunited with family members in other parts of Europe under Dublin III procedures. Other cases reported during fieldwork nevertheless concerned unaccompanied minors who, tired of long delays in transit zones, or having been pushed back to Serbia multiple times, turned to smugglers instead of legal pathways to reunite with relatives in other EU Member States.[93]

## V. Role of EU-led Military Operations – EUNAVFOR MED Sophia in Central Mediterranean

Operation Sophia is a Common Security and Defence Policy (CSDP) to tackle migrant-smuggling with a prominent military nature, and yet with the main official goal of dismantling the criminal smuggling networks' business model. It was granted a legal mandate by UN Resolution 2240(2015) to intercept, inspect, seize and destroy vessels on the high seas off the coast of Libya for a period of one year in cases where there are 'reasonable grounds to believe' that these vessels are being used for smuggling and human trafficking. Search and Rescue (SAR) was therefore not at the core of its objectives.

In June 2016, Operation Sophia's mandate was extended for another year and two new tasks were added: training the Libyan Coast Guard and contributing to the implementation of the UN arms embargo on the high seas (UN Resolution 2291(2016)). The effectiveness and proportionality of Operation Sophia has been

[92] Interview with CSO providing legal assistance, 6 June 2017, Athens, Greece; interview with CSO providing social assistance to refugees, 7 June 2017, Athens, Greece; interview CSO providing legal assistance, 8 June 2017, Lesvos island, Greece.

[93] Interview with CSO providing legal assistance, 28 August 2017, Budapest, Hungary.

questioned, not least by the UK's House of Lords, which concluded that it 'has not in any meaningful way deterred the flow of migrants, disrupted the smugglers' networks or impeded the business of people smuggling on the central Mediterranean route' (UK House of Lords 2017: 14).

EUNAVFOR MED is a military crisis management operation that was initially established by Council Decision (CFSP) 2015/778 (Council of the EU 2015b). Article 1 of this Council Decision describes that its mission is to contribute to the disruption of the business model of migrant-smuggling and trafficking networks in the Southern Central Mediterranean by undertaking systematic efforts to identify, capture and dispose of vessels and assets used or suspected of being used by smugglers or traffickers.

Article 2 of Council Decision (CFSP) 2015/778 (2015b) envisages the operation being conducted in sequential phases, corresponding to a gradation of measures and strategies. In the first phase, the operation would take place in the form of supporting the detection and monitoring of migration networks through information-gathering and patrolling on the high seas. The second phase would involve boarding, search, seizure and diversion on the high seas of vessels suspected of being used for migrant-smuggling or trafficking, under the conditions provided for by applicable international law, including UNCLOS and the Protocol against the Smuggling of Migrants; and, in accordance with any applicable UN Security Council Resolution or consent by the coastal state concerned, boarding, search, seizure and diversion on the high seas or in the territorial and internal waters of that state of vessels suspected of being used for migrant-smuggling or trafficking, under the conditions set out in that resolution or consent. In the final phase, all necessary measures can be taken against vessel and related assets if they are suspected of being used for migrant-smuggling or trafficking in the territory of that state. Such an operation can take place in accordance with any applicable UN Security Council Resolution or consent by the coastal state concerned.

In June 2015, EUNAVFOR MED officially launched its first phase with the Council Decision (CFSP) 2015/972 (Council of the EU 2015c). The Council would assess whether the conditions for transition beyond the first phase of the operation had been met, taking into account any applicable UN Security Council Resolution and consent by the coastal states concerned. Consequently, Article 2 of (CFSP) 2015/972 (2015c) on the basis of that assessment and in accordance with Article 6(1) of Decision (CFSP) 2015/778, the Political and Security Committee would have the power to decide when to make the transition between the phases of the operation. The Political and Security Committee adopted a Decision to that effect on 28 September 2015(CFSP) 2015/1772 (Council of the EU 2015d), which authorised moving to the second stage on 7 October 2015 (in accordance with Article 1), two days before the eventual adoption of a UN Security Council Resolution (Papastavridis 2016). A follow-up Council Decision (CFSP) 1926/2015 (Council of the EU 2015e) of 26 October 2015 added to the designation of Operation EUNAVFOR MED the name Operation Sophia. It was named after a baby born aboard one of the mission's ships off the coast of Libya.

The evolution of the EU legislative framework has been inextricably linked with action by the UN Security Council. On 9 October 2015, the UN Security Council adopted Resolution 2240 (2015), which reinforced the authority to take measures against the smuggling of migrants and human trafficking from the territory of Libya and off its coast. Its underlying aim was the disruption of organised criminal networks engaged in migrant-smuggling and trafficking, whilst preventing the exploitation of smuggled migrants or trafficked persons and the loss of lives (UN Security Council Recital 19).

To that end, the UN Security Council Resolution 2240 (2015: Arts 5–6) called upon Member States acting at the domestic level, but also through regional organisations, to inspect on the high seas off the coast of Libya both unflagged and flagged vessels that they reasonably believed to be used by organised criminal enterprises for smuggling or trafficking purposes. In the case of the flagged vessels, such inspection must take place after securing the consent of the flag state. The reference to the role of regional organisations in that respect is noteworthy, as it is through this reference that the EU is authorised to act. In this manner, the UN Security Council Resolution provides a legal basis for the further development of EU Operation Sophia (Butler and Ratcovic 2016: 255). Having in mind the objective of saving the lives of migrants under threat, the Resolution further decided to authorise, for one year, the inspection of vessels on the high seas off the coast of Libya when there are reasonable grounds to believe that they are suspicious, even without the consent of the flag state, provided that good faith efforts have been made in that respect (UN Security Council 2015: Art 7). In case it is confirmed that the suspicious vessels have been indeed used for smuggling or trafficking purposes, the resolution authorises their seizure (UN Security Council 2015: Art 8). Resolution 2240/2015 was implemented in the framework of Operation Sofia, as agreed by the Council on 18 January 2016. As a result, the operation was authorised to conduct boarding, search, seizure and diversion on the high seas of any suspicious vessels according to Council Decision (CFSP) 2016/118 (Council of the EU 2016c).

This approach continued in the next year with parallel developments at the UN and the EU level. In June 2016, Resolution 2292 (2016d) was adopted by the UN Security Council (2016) concerning the arms embargo on Libya. The Council of the EU (2016d) extended until 27 July 2017 the mandate of EUNAVFOR MED Operation Sophia, adding two supporting tasks: capacity building and training the Libyan coastguard and navy, particularly in law enforcement tasks at sea (UN Security Council 2016: Art 3) and contributing to the implementation of the UN arms embargo and to information-sharing.

Assistance in training commenced on 30 August 2016 following the adoption of Council Decision 2016/1635 of the Political and Security Committee (Council of the EU 2016e). In addition, on 19 December 2016, the Council adopted Decision (CFSP) 2016/2314, increasing the authorisations granted to EUNAVFOR MED Operation Sophia to exchange information with relevant actors (Council of the EU 2016f). Then, in June 2017, the UN Security Council (2017a) renewed the authorisations prescribed in Resolution 2292(2016) and the European Council stressed the key role of training and equipping the Libyan coastguard as a means of dismantling the business model of smugglers and traffickers (European Council 2017).

With the deadline of the operation's mandate approaching, on 25 July 2017 the Council extended the mandate of Operation Sophia until 31 December 2018 and further increased the information exchange possibilities, by enabling the transmission not only of data on vessels and their equipment, but also of the relevant information acquired during the performance of core operation tasks (Council of the EU 2017c: Art 1). Another key change has been the establishment of a monitoring mechanism and the authorisation of the conduct of surveillance activities and information gathering on illegal trafficking, both of which contribute to situational awareness and to maritime security. Importantly, this information may be released not only to national law enforcement authorities but also to the 'legitimate Libyan authorities'. The UN Security Council has in turn renewed the mandate of its earlier resolutions via a new Resolution 2380 adopted in October 2017 (UN Security Council 2017b).

## VI. A Multi-Agency Approach to Countering Migrant-Smuggling

In examining the different channels of policing migrant-smuggling at the EU level, it is important to point out that these channels have not developed in isolation. Rather, they are increasingly designed to operate in a synergetic manner (see Mitsilegas 2018, on which this section is based) – constituting a model described by Bigo (2014: 220) as 'global preventive surveillance'. From an operational perspective, the activities of Operation Sophia demonstrate the focus on synergies with other actors within and outside the EU. Operation Sophia has developed synergies with Frontex and the Italian authorities regarding search and rescue, as well as with NATO, which has launched Operation Sea Guardian working in close co-operation with Operation Sophia, with the view of establishing joint patrols with the Libyan authorities in the future (Council of the EU 2017c).

In addition to operational co-operation, including search and rescue, the interagency model of cooperation has emerged prominently in the fight against migrant-smuggling in the context of intelligence gathering and sharing, including with third states (UN Security Council 2017b). In October 2017 the UN Security Council reiterated:

> the call on Member States acting nationally or through regional organisations, including the EU, to cooperate with the Government of National Accord and with each other, including by sharing information to assist Libya, upon request, in building needed capacity including to secure its borders and to prevent, investigate and prosecute acts of smuggling of migrants and human trafficking through its territory and in its territorial sea; and in order to prevent the further proliferation of, and endangerment of lives by,

the smuggling of migrants and human trafficking into, through and from the territory of Libya and off its coast.[94]

Two new models of intelligence cooperation have emerged in efforts to tackle migrant-smuggling. One model involves – as in the field of criminalisation and prosecution – the privatisation of immigration control via intelligence-gathering and sharing. NGOs are now required by the code of conduct adopted by Italy to commit to 'loyal cooperation' with the public security authority of the migrants' intended place of disembarkation, including by transmitting relevant information of interest for investigation purposes to the Italian police authorities. Another model involves extending the activities of existing law enforcement agencies – in this case Europol – to focus specifically on migrant-smuggling. This has been achieved by the establishment of a specific Europol smuggling unit, the European Migrant Smuggling Centre (EMSC), which was launched in February 2016 (as discussed in section I.A above).

The EMSC's stated goal is to proactively support EU Member States in dismantling criminal networks involved in organised migrant-smuggling. It focuses on geographical criminal hotspots, and builds a better capability across the EU to fight migrant-smuggling networks (Europol 2016b). Interagency co-operation is key to the remit of the EMSC, including co-operation with Frontex and Eurojust (Council of the EU 2015f), and co-operation with EUNAVFOR MED Operation Sophia. The latter has seconded a police advisor to the EMSC 'to consolidate cooperation and facilitate timely information exchange' (Europol 2017c).

In addition to the newly established mechanisms analysed above and justified on the grounds of tackling migrant-smuggling, existing border surveillance structures are also relevant in this context. This is particularly the case regarding the European Border Surveillance System (EUROSUR) (European Union 2013). A key component of EUROSUR is the development of situational pictures at the national and EU levels (European Union 2013: Arts 8–10) and of a common pre-frontier intelligence picture which will be maintained by Frontex in order to provide the national coordination centres with effective, accurate and timely information and analysis on the pre-frontier area (ibid: Art 11(1)). Key to the operation of EUROSUR is the common application of surveillance tools which will be coordinated by Frontex (ibid: Art 12(1)). According the EUROSUR Regulation Frontex will provide a national coordination centre, at its request, with information on the external borders of the requesting Member State and on the pre-frontier area which may be derived from, inter alia:

— selective monitoring of designated third-country ports and coasts which have been identified through risk analysis and information as being embarkation or transit points for vessels or other craft used for illegal immigration or cross-border crime;

[94] UN Security Council (2017b: Art 2).

— tracking vessels or other craft over high seas which are suspected of, or have been identified as, being used for illegal immigration or cross-border crime;
— monitoring designated areas in the maritime domain in order to detect, identify and track vessels and other craft being used for, or suspected of being used for, illegal immigration or cross-border crime; and
— selective monitoring of designated pre-frontier areas at the external borders which have been identified through risk analysis and information as being potential departure or transit areas for illegal immigration or cross-border crime (European Union 2013: Art 12(2)).

It was declared that the purpose of EUROSUR is not only fighting irregular migration, but also saving lives at sea. The preamble of the EUROSUR Regulation lays out that:

> EUROSUR should considerably improve the operational and technical ability of the Agency and the Member States to detect such small vessels and to improve the reaction capability of the Member States, thereby contributing to reducing the loss of lives of migrants.[95]

Nevertheless, in practice, EUROSUR is a system of supranational extraterritorial surveillance, involving information gathering outside the border and in third states, based on technology, with the aim of, in essence, providing intelligence which aims to prevent or deflect migration flows to the EU external border (Mitsilegas 2015). The practical application of EUROSUR has raised a number of ethical questions that have been discussed in academic and policy debates in the context of the European integrated border management (Jeandesboz 2011).

[95] European Union (2013: Art 12(2)).

# PART II

# The Impacts of Anti-Migrant-Smuggling Policies on Civil Society

# 4

# Anti-Smuggling in National Law and Perceptions among Civil Society Actors

The following sections focus on the main issues emerging from the national implementation of the EU Facilitators Package in the four countries under investigation: Italy, Greece, Hungary and the UK. The analysis does not seek to carry out an exhaustive examination of the domestic transposition of the Facilitators Package (see discussion in chapter two). It instead pays particular attention to the main issues and dilemmas related to the elements of 'financial and material benefit' as well as to the so-called 'humanitarian exception' in each of the four countries. Such analysis provides an overview of the breadth of definitions of anti-smuggling laws and humanitarian exemptions. Whether these translate into practical experiences of policing by CSAs is discussed in chapters five to seven.

## I. Italy

This section outlines the legislation in force regarding the facilitation of entry (section I.A) which was made applicable to civil society actors engaging in SAR activities (section I.B).

### A. Facilitation of Entry

The Italian Migration Law of 1998 (Legislative Decree of 18/08/1998) which governs immigration and the status of foreigners criminalises the facilitation of irregular entry. Article 12 contains provisions against clandestine immigration, stating [unofficial translation; emphasis added]:

> 1. Unless the offence is the most serious offence, anyone who, in violation of the provisions of this single text, promotes, directs, organises, finances or carries out the transportation of foreigners in the territory of the state, or acts in other ways to illegally entrust them to the territory of the state or another state of which the person is not a citizen or has no permanent residence, is *punished by imprisonment from one to five years and* a fine of €15,000 per person.

2. Notwithstanding Article 54 of the Criminal Code, no rescue and humanitarian assistance services provided in Italy to foreigners in a state of necessity, present in the territory of the state, shall constitute a criminal offense.
3. Unless the offense is the most serious offense, anyone who, in violation of the provisions of this single text, promotes, directs, organises, finances or carries out the movement of foreigners in the territory of the state, or acts in other ways to illegally let them into the territory of the state or into another state of which the person is not a citizen or has no permanent residence, is punished by imprisonment from *five to fifteen years and* with a fine of *€15,000 for each person in case:*
   - *(a)* the fact is that the entry or stay in the territory of the state of five or more persons is illegal;
   - *(b)* the person transported has been at risk of his/her life or his/her safety in order to obtain entry or residence;
   - *(c)* the person transported has been subjected to inhuman or degrading treatment in order to obtain their illegal entry or stay;
   - *(d)* the act is committed by three or more persons co-operating with one another or using international transport services, or counterfeit or altered or otherwise illegally obtained documents;
   - *(e)* the perpetrators have weapons or explosive materials.

3-bis. If the facts referred to in paragraph 3 are committed using two or more of the hypotheses referred to in points *(a)*, *(b)*, *(c)*, *(d)* and *(e)* of the same paragraph, the penalty provided there is increased;

3-ter. The imprisonment sentence is increased *by one third to half and the fine of €25,000* applies to each person if the acts referred to in paragraphs 1 and 3:

- *(a)* are committed in order to recruit persons for prostitution or for sexual exploitation or labour, or for the admission of minors to be used in illicit activities in order to facilitate their exploitation;
- *(b)* are committed in order to make a profit, even indirectly.[1]

The article referred to above has been amended on at least four occasions.[2] Interestingly, in the original version, paragraph 1 contained the shorter penalty of 'imprisonment of up to three years'.[3] The original article also contained a humanitarian exemption clause within the territory of the country. Aggravated sentences were also lower: from four to 12 years.

Article 416 of the Italian Criminal Code can be applied to smuggling cases of the nature of 'organised crime'. This provision is applicable when 'three or more

[1] Unofficial English translation found at OSCE Legislation Online database, Legislationline (www.legislationline.org), a free-of-charge online legislative database, created in 2002 to assist OSCE participating States in bringing their legislation into line with relevant international human-rights standards. The Italian Migration Law may be downloaded from www.legislationline.org/download/action/download/id/4982/file/Ialy_Decree_immigration_foreigners_1998_en.pdf.

[2] Legislative Decree 13 April 1999, no 113, Legislative Decree 4 April 2002, no 51, Law 30 July 2002, no 189 and Legislative Decree 14 September 2004, no 241, Law No 94 15 July 2009.

[3] Legislative Decree 25 July 1998, no 286 'Consolidated text of the provisions concerning the immigration rules and rules on the status of a foreigner' published in the Official Journal no 191 18 August 1998 Ordinary Supplement no 139.

persons associate in order to commit multiple criminal offences (organising, participating in, directing such association, etc)'.

Italian migration law remains the main law to prosecute this 'migration crime'. Article 12, paragraph 2 explicitly excludes humanitarian actors from criminalisation, but only when acting in 'the state of necessity', and the wording of this article relates to situations *within* the state. However, this exception is applied also outside of the territory, to organisations conducting SAR operations on the high seas. On the other hand, a refusal to rescue people in distress would also impose the criminal liability of failing to comply with international obligations at sea.

A UNODC (2017) report reveals how the humanitarian facilitation of entry has, until now, only been exempted by a broad interpretation of Italian law, which provides exemption for the 'facilitation of stay' but not for humanitarian 'facilitation of entry'. A participant from the Italian border and coastguard authorities confirmed, at the closed-door discussion conducted for this research, that political pressure to reduce numbers of entries and to stop rescuers led to an inquiry in the Senate and, recently, to criminal investigations of CSAs conducting SAR operations.[4] As section I.A further elaborates, the interpretation of situations of 'distress' or 'necessity' to rescue is currently being challenged by the Trapani prosecutor.

At the time of writing, under Italian migration law, family members can be and are prosecuted for the facilitation of entry. In addition, under Article 12, paragraph 3, direct or indirect profit is not a requirement to establish the crime but can serve as an aggravating circumstance for the offence (UNODC 2017: 38 and 41).

One such indirect profit concerns a reduced fee for the family, or travel without fee, for the migrant who steers the boat or holds the compass. In such cases of indirect benefit, accused smugglers 'can be treated more leniently' (UNODC 2017: 41). In addition, Italian practitioners consulted for this research were divided on whether the mere intention to obtain profit is adequate to establish aggravated circumstances, or whether the profit has to be obtained (UNODC 2017: 41). Interviews in Italy with national judicial authorities and CSO representatives confirmed that the majority of people charged with the crime of smuggling have actually themselves been migrants who were steering and holding the compass in the boat carrying irregular migrants to Europe.[5] In order to identify such 'low key smugglers' in Italy, the prosecutors have developed potential 'smuggler profiles' as 'some migrants (especially from Mali, Gambia and Senegal) [are] deemed to be good fishermen, able and willing to sail, who accept the smugglers' proposal to steer the ship in exchange of travelling without paying any cost' (Ragazzi 2016: 6). An Italian investigative judge elaborating on this issue comments that while in theory a strategy of 'smugglers profiles' might be useful, in practice it helps

[4] Closed-door discussion with EU and national actors representing coastguards, law enforcement and judiciary, 21 September 2017, Brussels, Belgium.

[5] Interview with national judicial authorities 12 November 2016, Catania, Italy; interview with CSO providing legal and social assistance, 11 November 2016, Catania, Italy.

smugglers to avoid prosecution: 'to prosecute such occasional skippers has got no sense, as they are not participants in the criminal networks responsible for the smuggling' (Ragazzi 2016: 6).

One of the CSOs interviewed in Catania commented that very vulnerable migrants, minors or poor individuals continue to be prosecuted for smuggling and that they are sometimes pushed to steer just before the boat is rescued but then still face arrest by the police.[6] The same interviewee mentioned that one commercial lawyer was known among CSAs in Sicily for the deceptive practice of taking advantage of desperate detained migrants in this position by promising to quickly free the clients from prison. The trick was to convince clients to plead guilty: 'but the clients were not told that the moment you have a criminal record, you will not get the subsidiary protection or asylum.'[7] In such cases, persons are sentenced to two years of suspended penalty and indeed are released from prison, but within seven days they receive an expulsion paper. Some CSOs are trying to appeal in such cases, as accused migrants are not smugglers but persons in clear need of international protection. In order to demonstrate that these migrants or refugees are innocent, CSOs have to open a new case to reverse the prior judgment. However, some clients do not want to go through this process, particularly as judges can detain them in prison again for the duration of the case. Such cases not only lack the impact of dismantling the smuggling modus operandi, but also have related opportunity costs in relation to the investigation of more serious crimes. These costs are in addition to those accrued by the individual migrant: of detention and detrimental effects to the individual's well-being and rights, including inability to access the international protection.

During the closed-door discussion, EU and national judicial authorities confirmed that punishing such 'low key actors' (migrants themselves, their family members or 'humanitarian actors') for the facilitation of entry has no visible impact on dismantling or disrupting the smuggling business model, but can only lead to more risks for victims of smuggling.[8] It is, some hypothesised, a dangerous smokescreen.

Participants at the closed-door meeting had no common view regarding the salience of the profit aspect for the criminalisation of smuggling in Italy. Practitioners were unwilling to accept direct or indirect profits as constitutive elements of the crime, but only as an aggravating factor, as 'it would be hard to find evidence of it in each and every case, as it is mostly cash involved'. On the other hand, among the participants, smuggling was still perceived as 'a very profitable business'.[9] Participants agreed that the 'follow the money model' could indeed lead to tracking and revealing major smugglers and to the confiscation of their assets.

[6] Interview with CSO providing legal and social assistance, 11 November 2016, Catania, Italy.

[7] Interview with CSO providing legal and social assistance, 11 November 2016, Catania, Italy.

[8] Closed-door discussion with EU and national actors representing coastguards, law enforcement and judiciary, 21 September 2017, Brussels.

[9] Closed-door discussion with EU and national actors representing coastguards, law enforcement and judiciary, 21 September 2017, Brussels, Belgium.

Our discussion confirmed UNODC findings that '[Italian legal practitioners] noted the need to build political will and capacity around international legal cooperation in relation to financial investigations' (UNODC 2017). Nevertheless, minor cases, without a profit element, continue to be willingly investigated and prosecuted, as one of the discussants representing national border and coastguard authorities pointed out, 'because of political pressures'.[10] During the UNODC discussions, '[Italian] practitioners emphasized the importance of establishing the profit element – not just in terms of securing more severe penalties under both the Criminal Code and Legislative Decree 92/2008, but also in securing the information necessary to identify and disrupt high-profit organized smuggling networks' (UNODC 2017: 39).

Continuous political pressure to 'curb migration' by fighting 'smuggling' leads to a dangerous 'feedback loop' of prosecutors in Italy being expected to find and prosecute 'smugglers' and thus to solve the 'migration problem'. Prosecutors may search for the easier ways to prosecute smuggling without following the money and disrupting the networks at the core. This leads to the creation of new 'potential' smugglers profiles, one of them being humanitarian civil society actors.

## B. Facilitation of Stay

As mentioned above, 'within the country' facilitation of stay by humanitarian actors is not officially a crime in Italy. Nevertheless, there is growing evidence of policing of such actors (see further discussion in chapters 6.I and 7.I).

Profit, in the Italian legal framework, is broadly framed as 'unfair advantage'. It is applied as a requirement to criminalise the facilitation of residence and stay. As the UNODC study shows (2017: 39), concepts such as 'unfair advantage', though quite broad, are 'considered to be well understood and not difficult to establish' by Italian practitioners. The study mentions an Italian Supreme Court case where it was established 'that in order to be criminally liable, the persons offering accommodation or renting property must consciously impose particularly onerous and exorbitant conditions on migrants'.[11]

Nevertheless, further elaboration by practitioners on what can actually constitute such 'unfair' conditions are vague: for example, in the event that the conditions of a rental contract are more beneficial to the landlord and yet not necessarily in clear detriment of the tenant's/migrant's rights, could such a situation be deemed as an 'unfair advantage' (UNODC 2017: 40)? The Italian Supreme Court established

[10] Closed-door discussion with EU and national actors representing coastguards, law enforcement and judiciary, 21 September 2017, Brussels, Belgium.

[11] Italian Criminal Court of Cassation (Cassazione Penale, Sez. I) (2013) No 26457, 18 June 2013 (24 April 2013).

that 'such a purpose can be drawn from contract terms much more beneficial to the owner, even if such terms are not excessively detrimental to the migrant'.[12]

The online survey conducted for this study shows that half of the respondents in Italy were not aware of reporting obligations of social service actors in relation to irregular migrants or asylum-seekers (see Figure 4.1). There was nevertheless some perception among respondents that labour inspectorates and employers, as well as landlords, might be implicated in cases of reporting. Nevertheless, two-thirds of survey representatives claimed that any reporting obligations of other actors had no impact on their activities (see Figure 4.2). The perceived risks of 'criminalisation' and actual experiences of policing do, however, illustrate how broadly construed notions of 'what is smuggling' are, raising legal uncertainty and

**Figure 4.1** Awareness of duties to report irregular migrants and/or asylum-seekers in Italy

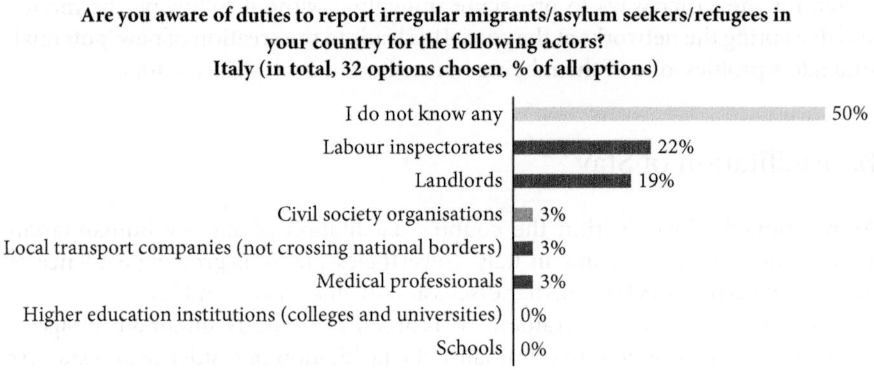


Source: CSA Online Survey (2017).

**Figure 4.2** Impact of reporting duties on humanitarian actors in Italy

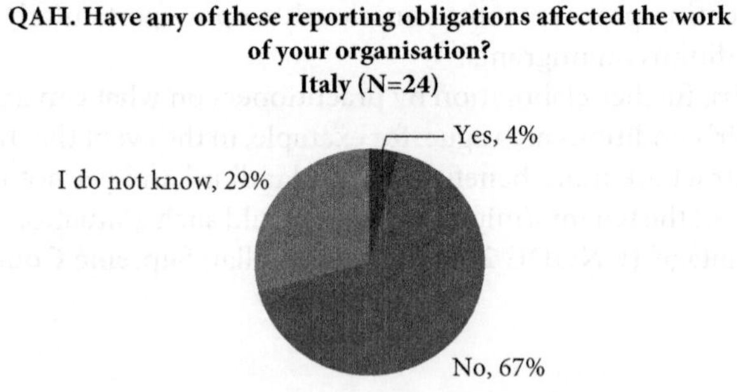


Source: CSA Online Survey (2017).

[12] Italian Supreme Court, Judgment no 17117, 20 January 2015, the meaning and effect of 'intent to gain'; Court of Catania, Proc. n. 93/2016 RIMC, 21 January 2016.

decreasing the trust between civil society, law enforcement and other actors tasked with reporting obligations. During the focus group discussion, CSOs mainly agreed that they would cooperate with law enforcement and other actors if they were authorised by their clients to do so, or if their clients or staff were in immediate danger or victims of crime – sexual or domestic violence was given as an example.[13]

## C. Perceptions of Anti-Smuggling Laws in Italy among Civil Society Actors

The respondents were split in their opinions of the origins of broad anti-smuggling laws in Italy – whether they stemmed from national migration law or national law combined with the EU's Facilitators Package provisions (see Figure 4.3 below). The Italian CSAs surveyed primarily attributed the causality of these laws to the cumulative effects of interactions between the EU's Facilitators Package and the Dublin Regulation on the one hand, and national immigration law, criminal law and the recent Minnitti law (189/02) on the other. During the closed-door discussion, a national border and coastguard authority representative also stressed that the targeting of CSOs by law enforcement, especially those CSOs conducting SAR, was influenced by the lack of solidarity within the EU concerning the Common European Asylum System (CEAS) as well as by the lack of development cooperation with the countries of origin and transit.[14]

**Figure 4.3** Perceived origin of the policies 'criminalising' individuals and/or CSOs providing humanitarian assistance in Italy

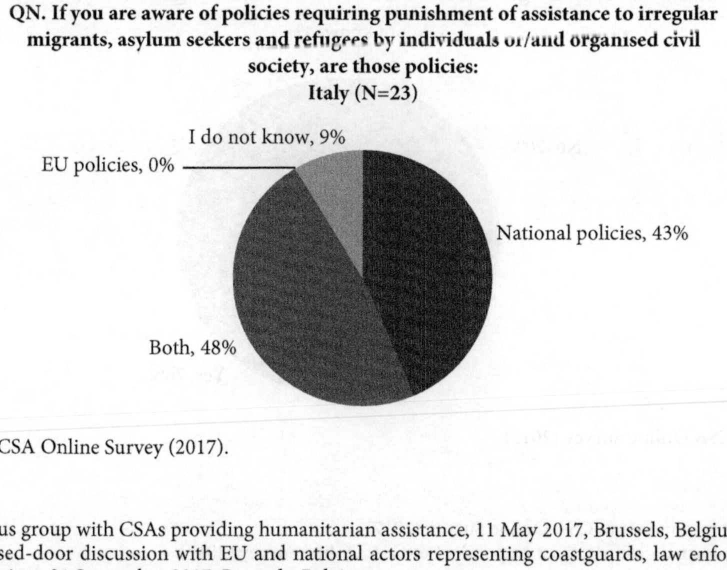


Source: CSA Online Survey (2017).

[13] Focus group with CSAs providing humanitarian assistance, 11 May 2017, Brussels, Belgium.
[14] Closed-door discussion with EU and national actors representing coastguards, law enforcement and judiciary, 21 September 2017, Brussels, Belgium.

Some of the comments received through the survey indicated unclear limits of application regarding Italian anti-smuggling laws. Survey respondents representing CSAs varied from those believing that only clear criminal cases are prosecuted, to those who saw the emergence of a creeping policing logic for any act that helps undocumented migrants. For example, a respondent from a formalised CSO working in the reception centre believed that 'the punishment is only for who helps irregular migrants (asylum-seekers and refugees are not included): normally smugglers or criminal organisations like the mafia … under the law 189/02'.[15] In contrast, a respondent belonging to an activist group claimed, 'In Italy, whoever helps undocumented migrants with housing or work is punished by law. We have news that also members of NGOs are being criminally charged with facilitating undocumented migrants'.[16] These divergent responses echo previous research that suggests the experience of policing may be highly subjective, depending on a range of factors including type of organisation, type of assistance provided, context in which assistance is provided, geographical location, and personal disposition and perceptions of fear and intimidation (Carrera et al 2016a).

Survey respondents reported that the humanitarian assistance scene in Italy is largely uncertain and insecure for both individuals and volunteers as well as formalised CSOs (see Figures 4.4 and 4.5 below). Whereas more than two-thirds of respondents mentioned that individuals are likely to be punished or prevented (18 per cent more than those who answered civil society), the uncertainty is 9 per cent higher on the question related to organised civil society. It is important to stress that 86 per cent of online survey respondents from Italy had direct

**Figure 4.4** Do policies in Italy punish or prevent individuals (not members of organisations) who help irregular migrants/asylum-seekers/refugees? (Italy, n=25)

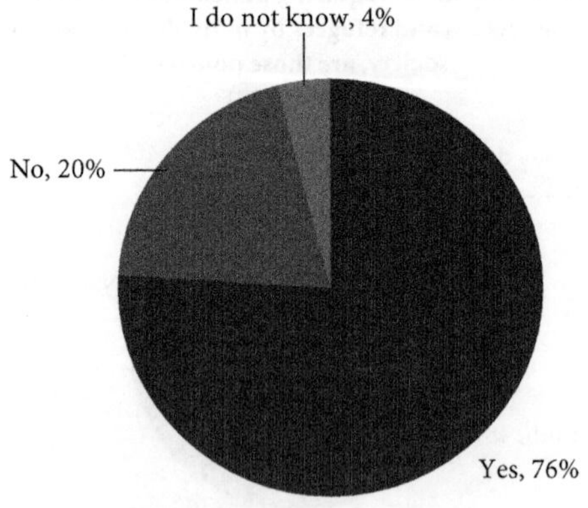


Source: CSA Online Survey (2017).

[15] CSO respondent to CSA Online Survey (2017).
[16] Non-formal group/activist respondent to CSA Online Survey (2017).

**Figure 4.5** Do policies in Italy punish or prevent members of various organisations which help irregular migrants/asylum-seekers/refugees? (Italy, n=24)

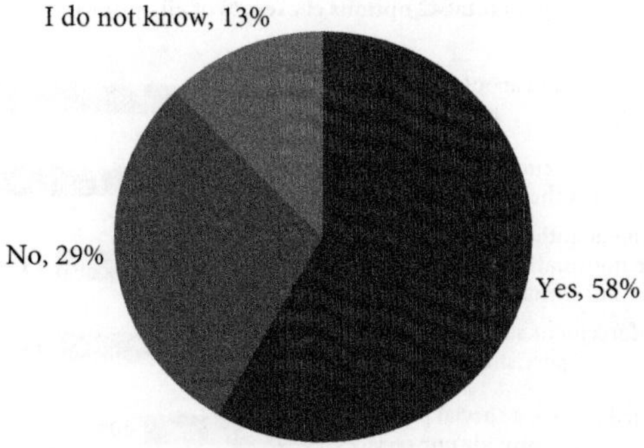


Source: CSA Online Survey (2017).

**Figure 4.6** Perceived change in policing humanitarian assistance in Italy

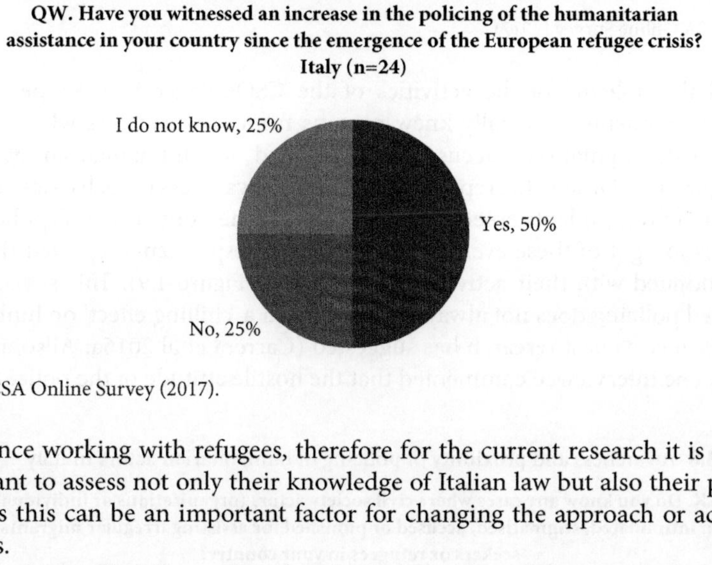


Source: CSA Online Survey (2017).

experience working with refugees, therefore for the current research it is equally important to assess not only their knowledge of Italian law but also their perceptions, as this can be an important factor for changing the approach or activities of CSAs.

More than half of all actors surveyed in Italy confirmed that they had witnessed increased policing of their activities in Italy after 2015, when the period referred to as the 'European humanitarian refugee crisis' began (see Figure 4.6). However, in the Italian context, the number of persons arriving in Italy remained relatively stable in comparison with those arriving in Greece.

When asked how they experience policing, survey respondents drew most attention to extensive policing forms by local authorities and occasional supervision by the police and law enforcement (see Figure 4.7). More intense forms of policing by law enforcement constituted less than one-third of practices. Only 10 per cent of respondents reported no kind of policing.

**Figure 4.7** CSAs' experiences of policing in Italy

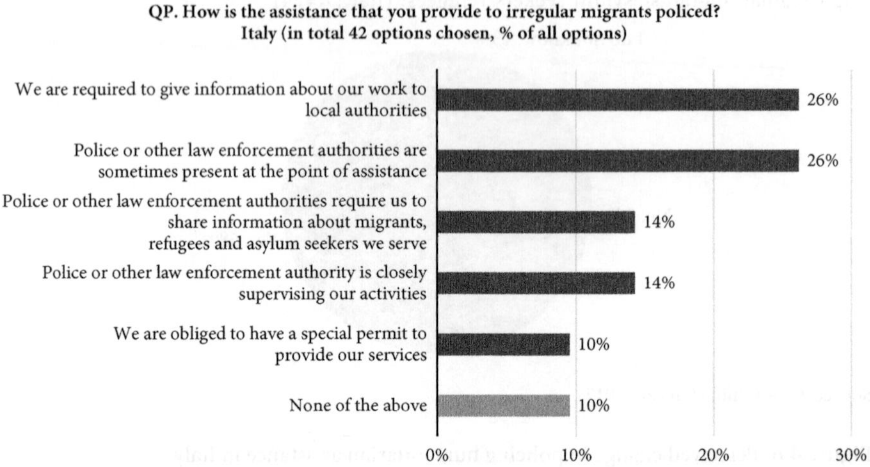


Source: CSA Online Survey (2017).

Beyond the policing of the activities of the CSOs concerned, 81 per cent of Italian respondents personally knew persons from various CSAs who had been intimidated, stigmatised, accused or punished for humanitarian assistance (see Figure 4.8). Despite the reported high level of awareness of such cases, less than one-third of respondents opted to adapt or change their organisation's policies and practices in light of these events: the majority of respondents reported that they had continued with their activities as before (see Figure 4.9). This suggests that enhanced policing does not always correlate with a 'chilling effect' on humanitarian assistance as past research has suggested (Carrera et al 2016a; Allsopp 2016). Indeed, one interviewee commented that the hostile attitude of the police to their

**Figure 4.8** Awareness and proximity of policing of humanitarian actors in Italy

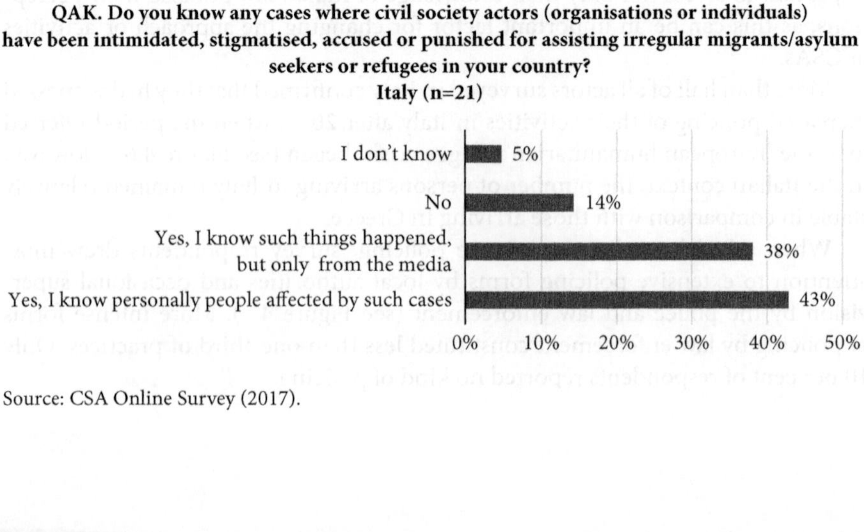


Source: CSA Online Survey (2017).

**Figure 4.9** Impact of policing of humanitarian actors in Italy on respondent's organisation

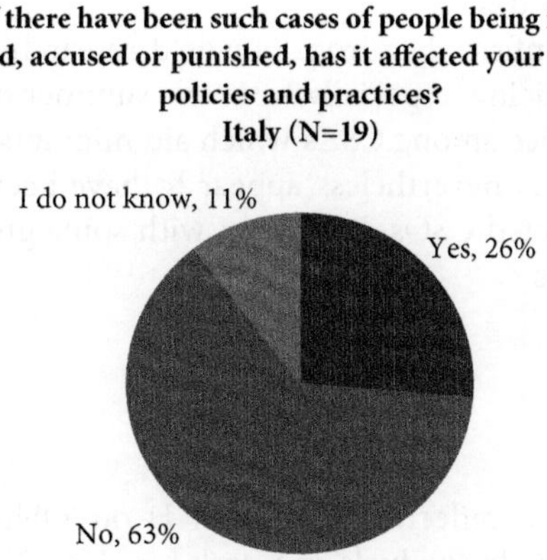


Source: CSA Online Survey (2017).

work in Ventimiglia at the height of 2015 served to unify activist groups and make them 'more determined' to uphold migrants' rights.[17]

Interestingly, asked to rank what is most at stake for CSAs in Italy, most respondents answered negative public opinion (see Figure 4.10). The trust of clients and funding were also high on the priority list for CSOs, whereas internal organisational

**Figure 4.10** Ranking of the key costs of policing for CSAs in Italy

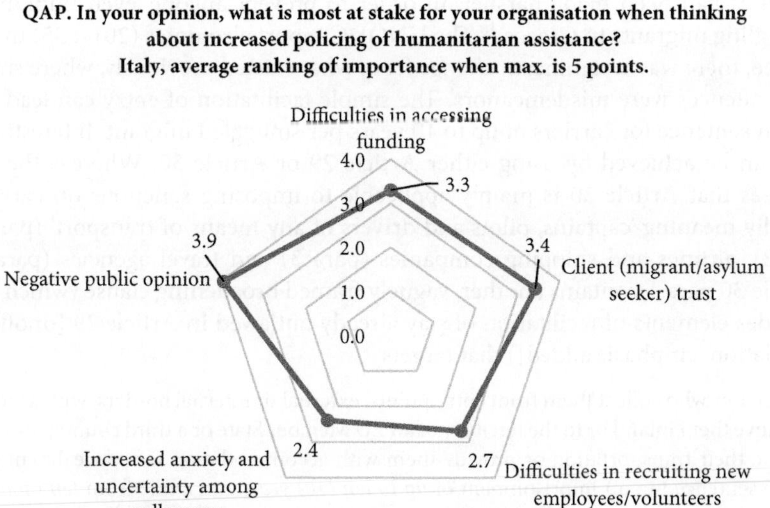


Source: CSA Online Survey (2017).

[17] Interview with non-formal group (activists) in Ventimiglia, 20 February 2017, via Skype.

issues – such as anxiety among colleagues and difficulties in recruiting volunteers – were seen as secondary issues.

The survey results confirm data from our field research (see chapters five to seven) that increased policing, especially from the summer of 2015 onwards, has been a common experience among CSAs which aid migrants and asylum-seekers in Italy. The consequences nevertheless appear to have been somewhat diffuse. Moreover, they have affected CSOs differently, with some groups and operations more targeted than others.

## II. Greece

The Facilitators Package is reflected in Chapter H on 'Obligations of Agencies, Public Officers and Private Individuals' in Greek Law No 4251/2014 Immigration and Social Integration Code (2014). Whereas Articles 26–28 outline penalties for the facilitation of residence and undeclared work of undocumented migrants, Articles 29 and 30 established a felony for facilitation of entry.

### A. Facilitation of Entry and Exit

Interviewed national border and coastguard authorities all commented that in Greece, smuggling is a very serious crime; moreover, they were of the view that penalties had been made harsher, in order to prevent anyone 'even thinking of smuggling migrants to Greece'.[18] The UNODC report also notes (2017: 35) that in Greece, there was 'a significant change from what existed previously, where smuggling offences were misdemeanors'. The simple facilitation of entry can lead to a prison sentence for carriers of up to 10 years per smuggled migrant. Interestingly, this can be achieved by using either Article 29 or Article 30. Whereas the title foresees that Article 30 is mainly applicable to imposing sanctions on carriers, broadly meaning 'captains, pilots and drivers of any means of transport' (paras 1 and 2), airlines and shipping companies (para 3) and travel agencies (para 4), Article 30 para 1 contains another, vaguely framed broadening clause (which also includes elements of facilitation of stay already outlawed in Article 29 [unofficial translation; emphasis added]) that targets

> persons who collect them from entry points, external or internal borders, with a view to move them inland or to the territory of an EU Member State or a third country, or facilitate their transportation or provide them with accommodation for concealment shall be sentenced to a.) imprisonment of *up to ten (10) years* and a fine from *ten thousand (10,000) to thirty thousand (30,000)* euros *for each transported person.*[19]

[18] Interview with expert on border/coast guard authorities, 12 June 2017, Athens, Greece.

[19] Unofficial translation available at UNHCR's Refworld online database (emphasis added), www.refworld.org/docid/54eb40114.html.

Article 29 para 5 [emphasis added] on the other hand, applies to any persons 'who facilitate the *entry or exit* from the Greek territory of third-country nationals without performance of the checks stipulated in Article 5 [visa requirements; such persons] shall be sentenced *up to ten (10) years of imprisonment* and a *minimum fine of twenty thousand (20,000) euros*'. This basic sentence is increased to 'at least 10 years of imprisonment and a minimum fine of fifty thousand (50,000) euros, if the act was carried out with a view to making a profit or by profession or habit' or if 'two or more persons acted jointly', ie, if it was organised crime (Greek Law No 4251/2014 Art 29 para 5 [Emphasis added]. In the closed-door discussion, participants found it unusual for an EU Member State to prosecute not only the entry but also the exit from Greece/the EU. The representative of Greek law enforcement actors posited that in this way Greece sought to step up solidarity with its neighbours, but could not explain the rationale behind the law.[20]

Article 30 para 1(b) indicates that 'intent to get a profit' is not necessary to establish the felony but is used rather as an aggravating circumstance and makes the penalty at least 10 years of prison for each smuggled migrant. The 'profit' is interpreted as a 'financial gain', but the transfer of money does not need to actually happen. Practitioners agreed that the evidence can be quite simply established by a migrant witnessing that s/he paid for the suspect smuggler or that the 'smuggler' was found to have the amount in cash (UNODC 2017: 37). This also means that various transport companies are at risk of being punished by default, as they are carrying passengers for profit 'by profession'. Other, aggravating circumstances also are considered to increase the penalty to at least 15 years – if a migrant smuggler is endangering human life – and to life imprisonment when there is a loss of life.[21]

The UNODC report highlighted anecdotal examples of ethical dilemmas faced by judicial practitioners who are required by law to apply such harsh penalties for acts lacking clear criminal intent, such as

> a taxi driver transporting several irregular migrants within Greece being captured by the aggravated provisions of the base offence [for profit, thus at least 10 years per person], and thereby subject to lengthy sentences of imprisonment … or … a minor smuggler [steering the boat] associated with negligent death is liable to a much harsher sanction than a person charged with murder.[22]

[20] Closed-door discussion with EU and national actors representing coastguards, law enforcement and judiciary, 21 September 2017, Brussels.

[21] Art 30 para 1 of the Greek Law No 4251/2014, foresees the following aggravating circumstances [unofficial translation]: '… b. at least ten (10) years of imprisonment and a fine from thirty thousand (30 000) to sixty thousand (60 000) euros for each transported person, if the offender acted with a view to making a profit or by profession or habit, or is a relapsing offender, or acts in the capacity of civil servant or tour or shipping or travel agent, or if two or more persons acted jointly; c. at least fifteen (15) years of imprisonment and a fine of two hundred thousand (200 000) euros as a minimum for each transported person, if the act could endanger human life; d. life imprisonment and a fine of seven hundred thousand (700 000) euros as a minimum for each transported person, if the act referred to in c) above resulted in the loss of life.'

[22] UNODC (2017: 37).

The intended deterrent effect of such harsh penalties remains questionable. The closed-door discussants representing experts on national border and coastguard authorities as well as judicial authorities were well aware that due to the harsh penalties, smugglers themselves were no longer piloting boats to the Greek islands.[23] This had contributed to a change of 'modus operandi' of smugglers, which was even more 'endangering to life'. This was documented in the increased death rates in the Aegean (see chapter 5.I.B). According to the discussants, detrimental impacts of the application of anti-smuggling laws on migrant lives should be carefully assessed as part of judicial practice.[24] Nevertheless, discussants agreed that it becomes increasingly harder as the context becomes more and more politically sensitive.[25]

Article 30 para 6 of Greek Law No 4251/2014 contains a humanitarian exemption clause, which reads: 'The above penalties shall not be imposed in case of *rescue of people at sea* or *transport of people in need of international protection* as required by international law' (unofficial translation; emphasis added). This humanitarian exemption clause was positively evaluated by the EU's Fundamental Rights Agency (FRA) (2014: 10). CSOs interviewed in Greece were well aware of the transposition of the humanitarian exemption clause from the EU's Facilitators Package into Greek law.[26] Nevertheless, they also mentioned some humanitarian actors, particularly those involved in SAR cases, who had still been prosecuted for facilitation of entry (see chapter 5.I.B).

The UNODC (2017) report elaborated on the lack of clarity in the application of this exemption, as it only excludes assistance to 'people in need of international protection', but not assistance to undocumented and irregular migrants. Whereas it is recognised that in SAR cases rescuers are not in a position to identify the legal status of rescued persons, this seems to be a central question regarding assistance in other contexts. Thus

> the situation of humanitarian actors who facilitate the entry of migrants … is considered to be *a significant grey area from a policy perspective*. While the law clearly captures such acts [as migrant-smuggling], it is not yet determined in policy whether it should be applied to prosecute them.[27]

During the closed-door meeting, a discussant representing Greek judicial authorities expressed doubt regarding the 'humanitarian' motivations of CSAs, as

[23] Closed-door discussion with EU and national actors representing coastguards, law enforcement and judiciary, 21 September 2017, Brussels.
[24] Closed-door discussion with EU and national actors representing coastguards, law enforcement and judiciary, 21 September 2017, Brussels.
[25] Closed-door discussion with EU and national actors representing coastguards, law enforcement and judiciary, 21 September 2017, Brussels.
[26] Interview with civil society organisation providing legal assistance, 6 June 2017, Athens, Greece; interview with civil society organisation providing legal assistance, 8 June 2017, Lesvos island, Greece.
[27] UNODC (2017: 36) (emphasis added).

'they are not all saints'.[28] Such suspicion interestingly leads to a reversal of the presumption of innocence of humanitarian actors, who are regarded as not sincere in their intentions to save lives. This confirms explanations by Greek CSAs regarding experiences of statutory suspicion of their activities; this was particularly true of 'foreign' organisations established in other EU countries.[29] This line of thinking was already identified in the UNODC (2017: 36) discussions, where Greek practitioners feared that a clearer application of the humanitarian exemption clause could translate into abuse, since 'facilitators could take on the role of rescuers.'

Similar to Italian legislation, the Greek law does not exempt acts of 'migrant-smuggling' by family members when there is no intent of financial gain. The practitioners in this case have two possibilities: 'criminal justice agencies may choose to not proceed to prosecution where this is considered to be against the interests of the State' or 'courts can mitigate the punishment' (UNODC 2017: 36). Nevertheless, interviews with national and coastguard agencies showed that desperate efforts to bring loved ones into Greece or out of Greece are indeed considered to be 'migrant-smuggling'.[30]

## B. Facilitation of Stay

Greek Law No 4251/2014 foresees various penalties for the facilitation of stay of irregular migrants including via the help of public agencies and their employees (Article 26), notaries capable of producing documents (Article 27), employers and human traffickers (Article 28) and landlords, hotel managers and other individuals facilitating residence or entry/exit or hiding migrants from police (Article 29).

The law also establishes an offence for facilitation of stay in Greece of an irregular citizen of a third country, even when there is no intention to reap financial gain. The penalties are increased when there is an intent to gain profit or exploit and abuse irregular migrants, as for example in Article 28.

Interestingly, the law outlines not only the reporting obligations but a prohibition from providing services to undocumented migrants by a wide spectrum of public actors:

> Public services, legal entities of public law, local authorities, public utilities and social security organisations *shall not provide their services* to third country nationals who do not have a passport or any other travel document recognised by international conventions, an entry visa or a residence permit and, generally, who cannot prove that they have entered and reside legally in Greece.[31]

[28] Closed-door discussion with EU and national actors representing coastguards, law enforcement and judiciary, 21 September 2017, Brussels, Belgium.

[29] Interview with civil society organisation providing legal assistance, 8 June 2017, Lesvos island, Greece.

[30] Interview with national border/coastguard authorities, 9 June 2017, Lesvos island, Greece; interview with expert on border/coastguard authorities, 12 June 2017, Athens, Greece.

[31] Art 26 para 1 Greek Law No 4251/2014 (emphasis added).

The exemptions are outlined in Article 26 para 2 and apply only to a narrow set of circumstances: the health and social security sector can assist only undocumented minors and adults in medical emergencies or individuals in instances of childbirth (cl a); attorneys and other judicial actors can provide support to undocumented migrants in the context of court proceedings (cll b–c and h); and services can be provided in the context of 'voluntary departures' from Greece (cll d–f) or while competent authorities are issuing residence permits (cll e–g).

Article 29 criminalises not only landlords and real estate agents by prohibiting them to conclude rental contracts with undocumented migrants (para 1); it also imposes reporting obligations on hotel managers (para 2) and any other persons who 'facilitate the illegal residence of a third-country national or obstructs the investigations of police authorities to locate, apprehend and deport such national' (para 6). The facilitation of stay is regarded as a misdemeanour and can invoke the penalty of 'at least one (1) year of imprisonment and a minimum fine of five thousand (5,000) euros' (Art 29 para 6). If there is intent to reap financial gain, the minimum fine and imprisonment is doubled.

There is no mitigation for family members in any of the relevant Articles (27–29) on facilitation of entry or residence in Greek law. Rather, Article 28 para 5 regards the exploitation of minor undocumented migrants for prostitution by family members or related persons as an aggravating circumstance.

Interestingly, though the provisions in Greek law are broad and all-encompassing and overlap with particularly harsh penalties, CSAs which responded to the online questionnaire seemed not to be entirely aware of – or witness to – this phenomenon. More than half of the respondents did not know of any such obligations (see Figure 4.11).

**Figure 4.11** Awareness of duties to report irregular migrants and/or asylum-seekers in Greece

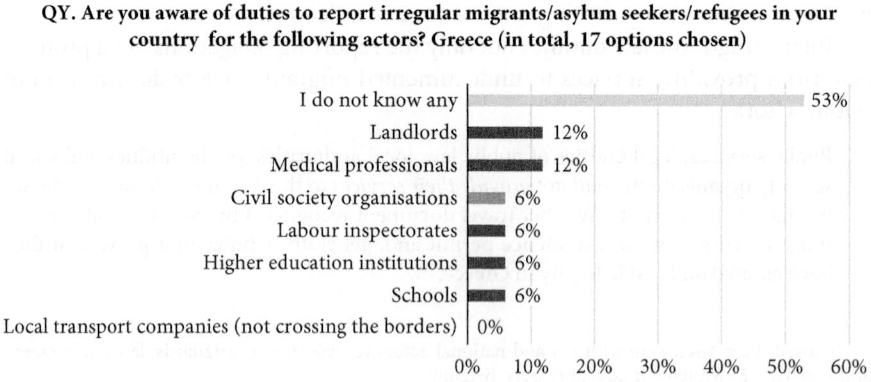


Source: CSA Online Survey (2017).

The most commonly known obligations to report were those of landlords and medical professionals. Whereas landlords were also identified as having reporting duties by CSAs in Italy (Figure 4.11) and in the UK (Figure 4.28), the reporting duties of medical professionals were more visible in Greece and in the UK. In comparison with doctors and landlords, the reporting obligations of CSOs were much lesser known. Interestingly, CSA online respondents were not aware of the sweeping prohibitions of Greek Law No 4251/2014, as discussed above, on local transport companies, schools and universities from providing services to undocumented migrants. This can perhaps be explained by the fact that some of the respondents came from other EU Member States to work and volunteer in Greece. In addition, the interviews in Lesvos with CSO and UN actors revealed that many CSAs have very little contact with private service providers, since, for example, the majority of services in the Greek islands are covered by the 'hot-spot approach': shelter, transportation and even schooling are provided by certain CSOs, which are funded and coordinated by UNHCR, and not the local authorities.[32] See chapter 6.II for further discussion.

Other actors' reporting obligations were perceived by almost two-thirds of survey respondents as having no effect on the activities of CSAs in Greece (see Figure 4.12). Although the percentage of respondents concerned with reporting obligations was overall quite low in Greece (13 per cent), it was comparably higher than in Italy (only 4 per cent) (see Figure 4.2).

**Figure 4.12** Impact of reporting duties on humanitarian actors in Greece

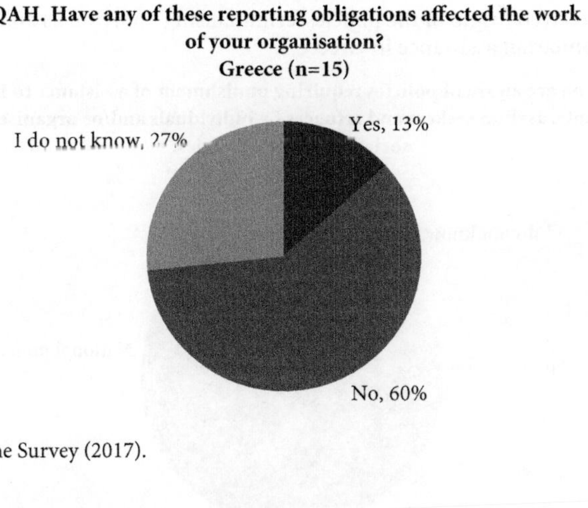


Source: CSA Online Survey (2017).

[32] Interview with civil society organisation providing legal assistance, 8 June 2017, Lesvos island, Greece; interview with the UN actor (a), 9 June 2017, Lesvos island, Greece; interview with the UN actor (b), 9 June 2017, Lesvos island, Greece.

## C. Perceptions of Greek Anti-Smuggling Laws among Civil Society Actors

Almost half of the CSA respondents in Greece traced the origins of the laws criminalising or preventing humanitarian assistance back to Greek national policies (see Figure 4.13). The combination of EU and national policies was considered to be the cause by less than one-third of respondents. One-fifth of all respondents were not aware of such policies, which is double the percentage of respondents who were not aware of such policies in Italy. Again, the explanation may be that respondents are not Greeks but citizens of another EU Member State or third country, or that these were individuals and activists driven by the intention to help the asylum-seekers they meet rather than professionals with knowledge of the laws. Some interesting testimonies were gathered on how CSAs in Greece were prevented from assisting migrants, but opinions differed on whether this stemmed from anti-smuggling laws or other kinds of laws applied to impede CSOs.

For example, one of the volunteers who provided assistance in detention centres and the community in Thessaloniki said, 'There is no clear policy on that topic but policies on other subjects are used as an excuse to prevent aid workers and volunteers from assisting migrants'.[33] Whereas another CSO employee of a CSO working at various sites in Thessaloniki claimed that the policies were indeed '[t]endentiously [applied], policies that aid and abet smuggling, trafficking and

**Figure 4.13** Perceived origin of the policies 'criminalising' individuals and/or CSOs providing humanitarian assistance in Greece

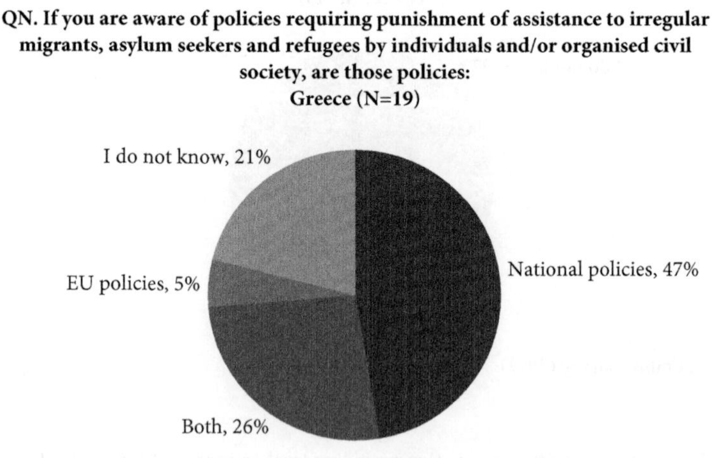


Source: CSA Online Survey (2017).

[33] Respondent volunteering for CSO in Greece, CSA Online Survey (2017).

irregular movement'.[34] Another respondent gave an example of how easily CSAs can be arrested in northern Greece 'for having a refugee in your car (regardless if he is an asylum-seeker or not and regardless if you are driving away from the border or not) and being charged for smuggling'.[35] Another survey respondent working for a CSO said 'preventative' policies relate to all sites where humanitarian assistance is provided (as covered further in chapters five to seven), including 'criminalization of driving refugees … entrance to detention facilities … search and rescue'.[36]

The CSA Online Survey indicates that formal humanitarian exemption in Greek Law No 4251/2014 does not provide sufficient protection for various humanitarian actors in practice. In Greece, the policies were regarded by more than half of respondents as 'punitive' towards both individuals and CSOs providing humanitarian assistance (see Figures 4.14 and 4.15). Nevertheless, individuals were seen to be slightly more targeted (by 10 per cent more respondents) than formally organised CSOs (see Figure 4.14). This also corresponds to interview findings: activists and individual volunteers, in particular those who are not Greek nationals, were said to be targeted by various measures of policing (see chapters 5.I.B, 6.II and 7.II).

**Figure 4.14** Do policies in Greece punish or prevent *individuals* (not members of organisations) who help irregular migrants/asylum-seekers/refugees? (Greece, n=19)

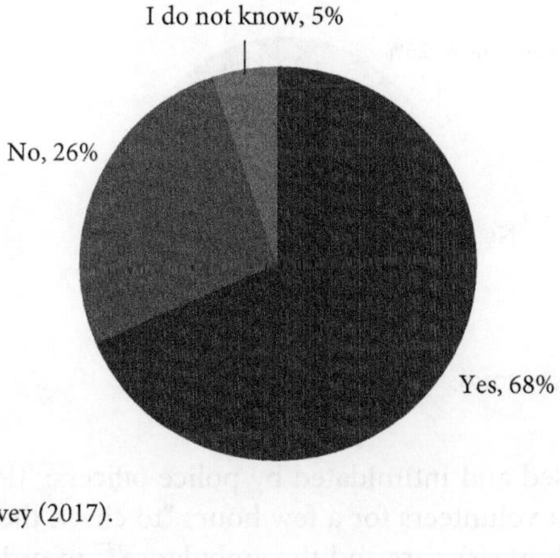


Source: CSA Online Survey (2017).

Two-thirds of all respondents in Greece confirmed that with the emergence of the so-called European humanitarian refugee crisis in 2015, CSAs became more policed (Figure 4.16). Worrying examples were provided. For example, a volunteer for a CSO in Thessaloniki explained how a CSO assisting failed asylum-seekers

[34] Respondent working for CSO in Greece, CSA Online Survey (2017).
[35] Respondent volunteering for CSO in Greece, CSA Online Survey (2017).
[36] Respondent working for CSO in Greece, CSA Online Survey (2017).

**Figure 4.15** Do policies in Greece punish or prevent members of various *organisations* who help irregular migrants/asylum-seekers/refugees? (Greece, n=19)

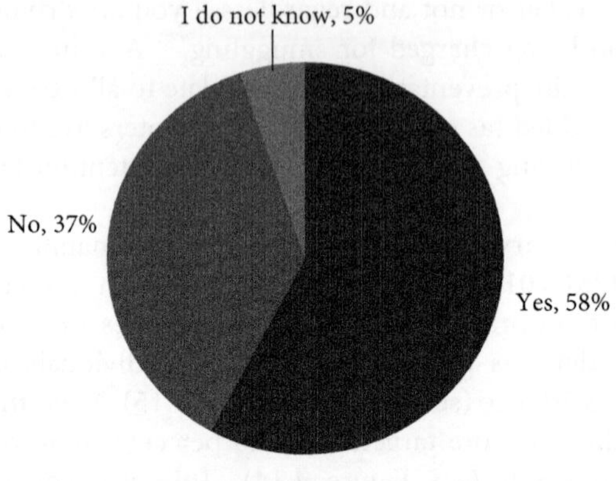


Source: CSA Online Survey (2017).

**Figure 4.16** Perceived change in policing humanitarian assistance in Greece

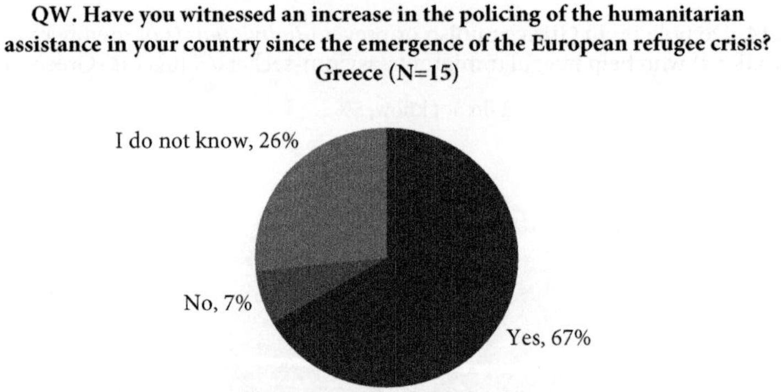


Source: CSA Online Survey (2017).

in squats was harassed and intimidated by police officers: '[P]olice come almost every day and detain volunteers for a few hours "to check their documents", take the plates off the volunteer's cars and the ambulance'[37] in order to make humanitarian assistance more difficult (see also chapters 6.II and 7.II) Such practices, according to some interviewees, do not follow from any anti-smuggling law but rather from a widespread belief among national authorities that more humane conditions, access to rights and CSO assistance can be perceived as a 'pull factor' for irregular migration.[38] Another survey respondent indicated on the basis of

[37] A respondent volunteering for CSO in Greece, Online Survey (2017).
[38] Interview with civil society organisation providing legal assistance, 6 June 2017, Athens, Greece.

personal experience in Greece that there is '[i]ncreased [police] presence at sites of services, increased harassment of legal teams, increased harassment of foreigners, increased harassment of local solidarity groups'.[39] The practice of repetitive police checks on CSAs and volunteers in Greece reveals the systemic nature of the disciplining and intimidating measures. Interviews with CSAs revealed that volunteers are checked, not because it is unclear who they are, but precisely because police and border guards know who they are and what they are doing.[40]

CSOs working in Greece have expressed that they experience various ways of policing, including the most intense form of 'close supervision' by police or other law enforcement authorities. Although special permits amount to 22 per cent of all choices, it was illustrated during interviews and in survey responses as one of the prevalent ways in which CSAs activities are policed in Greece (see Figure 4.17). This was reported to be especially so in relation to CSAs from other EU Member States or third countries and to those who wish to assist migrants and asylum-seekers in detention centres (see chapter 6.II).

**Figure 4.17** CSAs' experiences of policing in Greece

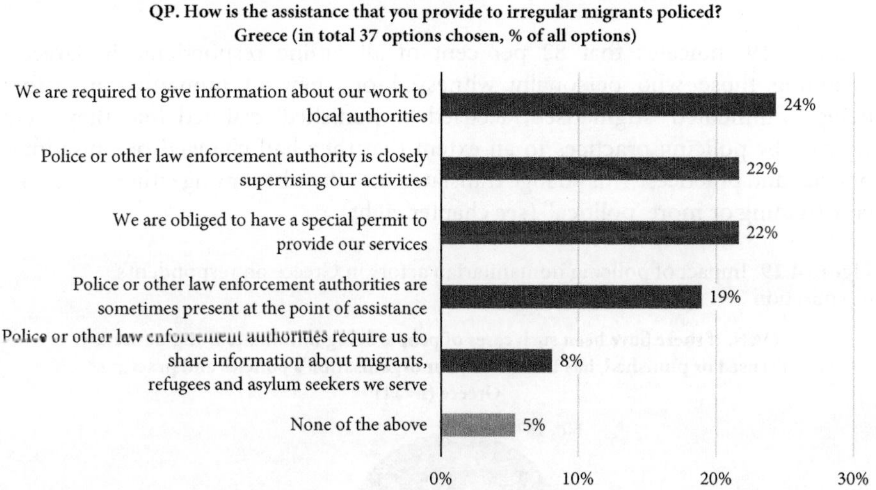


Source: CSA Online Survey (2017).

The online survey indicated that there is no 'in between' situation in Greece. More than three-quarters of all respondents knew someone personally who was 'intimidated, stigmatised, accused or punished' for providing humanitarian assistance, and one-quarter of respondents were not aware of it at all, even from media

[39] Respondent volunteering for CSO in Greece, Online Survey (2017).

[40] Interview with civil society organisation providing legal assistance, 6 June 2017, Athens, Greece; Interview with civil society organisation providing legal assistance, 8 June 2017, Lesvos island, Greece.

(see Figure 4.18). The examples of policing are further elaborated in the following sections: chapters 5.I.B, 6.II and 7.II.

**Figure 4.18** Awareness and proximity of policing humanitarian actors in Greece

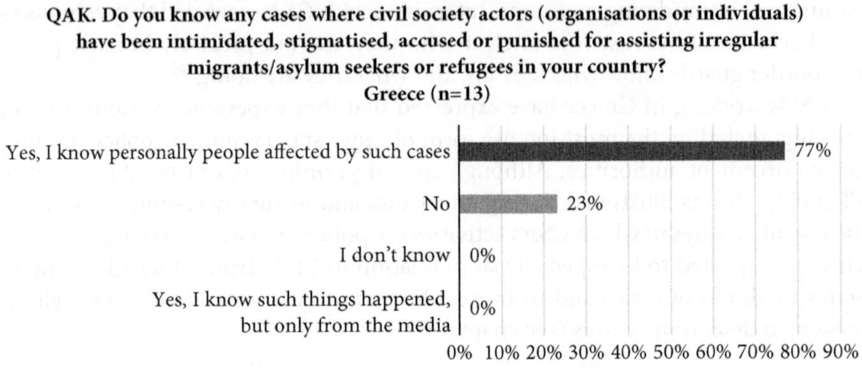


Source: CSA Online Survey (2017).

Figure 4.19 indicates that 82 per cent of all online respondents in Greece, including those who personally witnessed or knew of humanitarian actors being 'intimidated, stigmatised, accused or punished', claimed that they were affected by policing practices to an extent that they had changed organisations' policies and practices. This change translated into their becoming either more self-constraining or more 'political' (see chapter eight).

**Figure 4.19** Impact of policing humanitarian actors in Greece on respondent's organisation

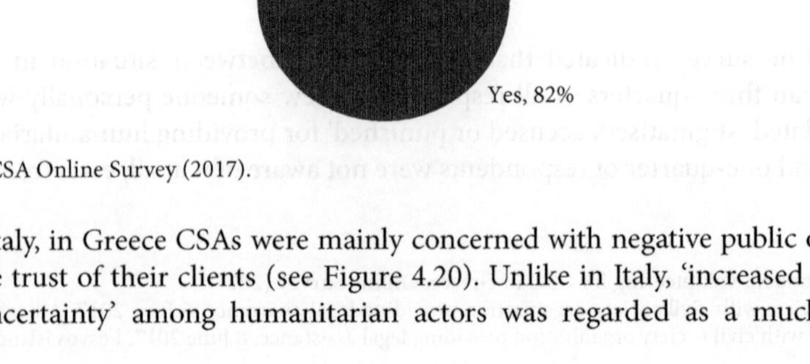


Source: CSA Online Survey (2017).

As in Italy, in Greece CSAs were mainly concerned with negative public opinion and the trust of their clients (see Figure 4.20). Unlike in Italy, 'increased anxiety and uncertainty' among humanitarian actors was regarded as a much more

**Figure 4.20** Ranking of the key costs of policing for CSAs in Greece

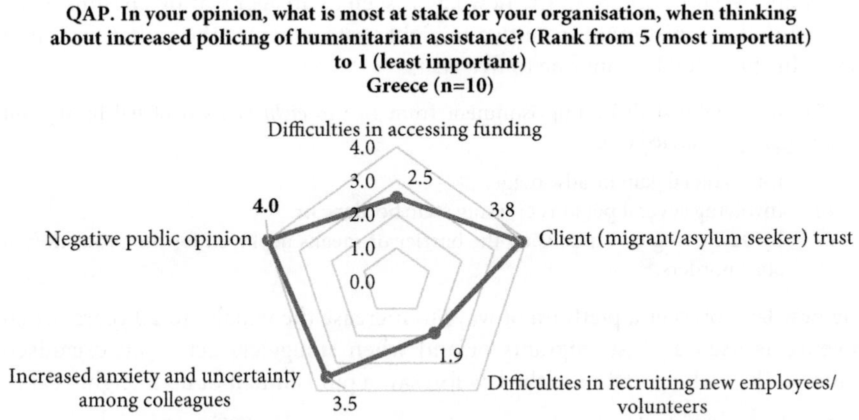


Source: CSA Online Survey (2017).

important concern, even more than accessing funding. 'Anxiety and uncertainty' are indicators of the hostile environment that has been created in Greece over the last few years. This is further illustrated in chapter 5.I.B in the context of SAR operations, chapter 6.II in the context of 'hot-spots', and chapter 7.II in the zones of 'transit through Greece and/or destination'.

# III. Hungary

## A. Facilitation of Entry

A number of new laws have been introduced following the Hungarian government's hardening stance on migration, which have affected the provision on facilitation of entry in Hungarian law. A raft of new measures has been introduced since 2015 in response to the 'European humanitarian refugee crisis'. Under the new section 353 of the Hungarian Criminal Code on 'Illegal Immigrant Smuggling', which entered into force on 15 September 2015, the following base offence is foreseen [unofficial translation; emphasis added]

> (1) Any person who provides aid to another person for crossing state borders in violation of statutory provisions is guilty of a felony punishable by imprisonment from *one to five years.*[41]

[41] Section 353 para 1, unofficial translation; emphasis added.

The earlier law foresaw the same base offence but with a penalty of up to three years. The financial gain element in the new law is seen as an aggravating circumstance, increasing the punishment from two to eight years, whereas the earlier provision made this punishable from one to five years:

> (2) The penalty shall be imprisonment from *two to eight* years if illegal immigrant smuggling is carried out:
>
> *a)* for financial gain or advantage;
> *b)* involving several persons crossing state borders; or
> *c)* by destroying or vandalising the barrier or means deployed for the protection of state borders.[42]

The new law foresees a plethora of ways to increase the penalty to 20 years, when violence is used against migrants or/and when smugglers act in an organised manner. The earlier version of the law foresaw a punishment of up to eight years:

> (3) The penalty shall be imprisonment from *five to ten* years if illegal immigrant smuggling is carried out:
>
> *a)* by tormenting the smuggled person;
> *b)* by displaying a deadly weapon;
> *c)* by carrying a deadly weapon;
> *d)* on a commercial scale; or
> *e)* in criminal association with accomplices.
>
> (4) The penalty shall be imprisonment from *five to fifteen* years if:
>
> *a)* illegal immigrant smuggling as referred to in Paragraph *a)* of Subsection (3) is committed in the manner defined in Paragraphs *b)–e)* thereof;
> *b)* illegal immigrant smuggling as referred to in Paragraph *b)* of Subsection (3) is committed in the manner defined in Paragraphs *a), c)–e)* thereof.
>
> (5) Any person who is engaged in organising or supervising the criminal offense defined in Subsection (3) or (4) is punishable by imprisonment of *ten to twenty years.*
>
> (6) Any person who engages in preparations for illegal immigrant smuggling is punishable by imprisonment *not exceeding three years.*[43]

As commented on in an interview with a representative from a Hungarian CSO which provides legal assistance, '[T]he fight against smuggling [in Hungary] is strongly linked to stopping refugees entering the country'.[44] A number of specific new felonies criminalising migrants and those mobilising for their rights were included in the revised Hungarian Criminal Code, specifically in relation to protecting the 'border barrier'. Section 352/A criminalises 'any person who enters the territory of Hungary by unlawfully crossing the barrier' with imprisonment of up to three years. Whereas Section 352/B criminalises anyone who 'destroys and

[42] Section 353 para 2 (unofficial translation; emphasis added).
[43] Section 353 paras 3–6 (unofficial translation; emphasis added).
[44] Interview with formal CSO providing legal assistance, 28 August 2017, Budapest, Hungary.

vandalises the barrier' with one to five years' imprisonment. Penalties for both of these offences can be increased:

a) by displaying a deadly weapon;
b) by carrying a deadly weapon;
c) by participating in civil disturbance.

It is not entirely clear what can be defined as a 'civil disturbance', but it would appear that any mobilisation of migrants, asylum-seekers and refugees and those who support them would invoke much heavier penalties. This provision makes explicit the link inherent in the EU's approach to what we call policing the mobility society – between the treatment of those who move and those who mobilise with or on behalf of migrants and asylum-seekers (including, of course, migrants mobilising for their own rights – see chapter 5.II.A for the case of Ahmed H).

Finally, section 352/C foresees the misdemeanour as punishable with one year of imprisonment for those who 'obstruct the construction or maintenance of the barrier'. The latter offence would appear to be designed to prevent any kind of demonstrations of civil society or individuals who disagree with the erection of fences at the EU's external border. The aforementioned provisions also leave ample opportunities to increase the penalties if persons are armed or endanger the life of migrants. Thus, in comparison with earlier laws, punishments for the act of smuggling an irregular migrant across the external Schengen border and of interfering in other ways with the border were increased in Hungary.

The act of facilitating the transit of irregular migrants – such as offering rides in a car, even without a profit motive, is also criminalised in Hungary (Frayer 2015). Under section 23(1) of the previous Hungarian Criminal Code of 2012, individuals were not punished under certain conditions if the act was committed to prevent harm to a person, property or public interest (EU Fundamental Rights Agency 2014). The code refers to this humanitarian exemption as 'Means of Last Result' and is worded as follows (authors' unofficial translation):

> (1) Any person who engages in conduct to save his own person or property or the person or property of others from an imminent danger that cannot otherwise be prevented, or acts so in the defense of the public interest, shall not be prosecuted, provided that the harm caused by the act does not exceed the peril with which he was threatened.

In addition to sanctions which include a possible fine and imprisonment, coercive measures can be taken to remove the person from the territory.

Some CSAs consulted for this research were dismissive of the new Hungarian anti-smuggling powers, seeing them as part of broader political move linked to the creation of an increasingly 'hostile environment' towards migrants and refugees which did not come with the requisite resources and human rights capacity to mount a genuine commitment to tackle smuggling and the associated crime of human trafficking[45] (see chapter 5.II.A). Other CSO interviewees interpreted

[45] Interview with legal expert, 30 August 2017, Budapest, Hungary; focus group with CSAs providing humanitarian assistance, 11 May 2017, Brussels, Belgium.

these specific anti-smuggling measures as a legitimate response to the risks associated with migrant-smuggling.[46] International civil society organisations were nevertheless keen to disassociate these 'legitimate anti-migrant-smuggling laws' from what they saw to be the unjustified new measures which criminalise asylum-seekers themselves and target the work of NGOs (see chapter 5.II.A).[47]

## B. Facilitation of Stay

Section 354 of the revised Hungarian Criminal Code on the Facilitation of Unauthorised Residence states (unofficial translation):

> (2) Any person who provides aid for financial gain to a foreign national to reside unlawfully … is guilty of a misdemeanor punishable by imprisonment not exceeding two years, insofar as the act did not result in a more serious criminal offence.

Penalties may include imprisonment for up to two years. Facilitating the residence of an irregular migrant then is punishable in Hungary under the 2012 Criminal Code only if undertaken for profit. Under these rules, under Hungarian law, as under UK law, landlords renting accommodation to irregular migrants may be at risk of a fine and/or imprisonment (European Fundamental Rights Agency 2014). In the cases of facilitation of either entry and stay, in addition to sanctions which include a possible fine and imprisonment, coercive measures can be taken to remove the person from the territory.

Meanwhile, Section 208 of the Hungarian Petty Offences Act states,

> (1) Anyone violating the rules on reporting foreigners, on registration of foreigners, or on stay of foreigners within the territory of the state, commits a petty offence.
>
> (2) The procedure concerning the above paragraph (1) falls under the competence of the police.

Penalties range from a fine of HUF 5,000 to HUF 150,000 (€16 to €510). In this case, no profit motive is required to constitute a crime.

With significant reductions in support available to migrants and refugees in Hungary and more time-limited legal statuses being granted to those recognised as being in need of protection (see section 7.III), some CSOs have expressed concern that any ambiguity over the ability of civil society to provide assistance to irregular migrants could have a 'chilling effect' and dissuade service providers such as landlords or community centres from granting vital services to asylum-seekers and refugees.[48]

[46] Focus group with CSAs providing humanitarian assistance, 11 May, 2017, Brussels, Belgium.
[47] Interview with UN actor, 31 August 2017, Szeged, Hungary.
[48] Interview with CSO providing social assistance, 29 August 2017, Budapest, Hungary.

## C. Perceptions of Civil Society

Both the survey data and field trip data showed that the new laws to criminalise irregular entry, transit and residence have come with an increase in the policing of humanitarian assistance which has affected the work of CSOs (see Figure 4.21). As one interviewee from an international organisation commented,

> Hungary is a very good example of how [anti-smuggling laws impact civil society] as government actions here that are designed at least on the surface to address security and control including anti-smuggling measures have very direct implications on access to asylum, reception conditions, safety of individuals and it has a very big impact also on the perception that the population has of people who in need of protection.[49]

**Figure 4.21** Perceived change in policing humanitarian assistance in Hungary

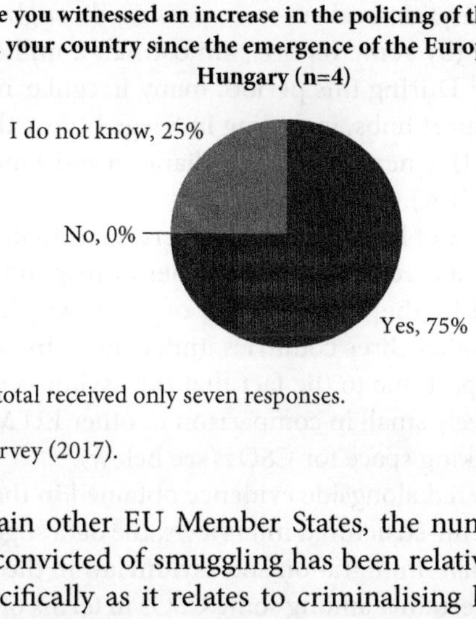


* Hungarian survey in total received only seven responses.

Source: CSA Online Survey (2017).

Compared to certain other EU Member States, the number of CSOs and individual volunteers convicted of smuggling has been relatively insignificant. Nor is the legislation specifically as it relates to criminalising humanitarian assistance especially harsh. As one lawyer working for a CSO interviewed for this research commented,

> In Hungary, I've only been aware of one single case where someone assisting asylum-seekers had to go through a criminal procedure but in the end they were acquitted I think. So this is not a major issue here. The corresponding legislation is sort of in line with average strictness in Europe in this regard, not excessively punished or harassed. The problem here is rather different … there are lots of other obstacles.[50]

[49] Interview with UN actor, 29 August 2017, Budapest, Hungary.
[50] Interview with CSO providing legal assistance, 16 August 2017, via Skype.

These main obstacles (discussed in more detail in chapters 5.II.A and 7.III) include issues of:

(i) access to migrant populations in need of assistance, in the light of new 'closed centre' asylum processes;
(ii) reputational harms to migrant support NGOs; and
(iii) a range of new bureaucratic restrictions placed on the work of NGOs.

Meanwhile, it is important to note that issues directly concerning the legal risks to CSOs and volunteers of providing of humanitarian assistance to irregular migrants entering, transiting and residing in Hungary were also reported to be of direct concern to some CSOs during the crisis of 2015.

Police powers to pursue individuals for petty offences for not complying with rules of 'reporting, registering and stay' of foreigners within the Hungarian territory was reported to be a source of confusion among CSOs from 2015 onwards, when large numbers of asylum-seekers were passing through Hungary en route to other parts of Europe (by some reports, almost half a million passed through Hungary during 2015).[51] During this period, many irregular migrants were resident for periods in transport hubs, including in Szeged (near the Serbian border) and Budapest (the capital), where they were reliant on assistance from volunteers and CSOs (see chapter 5.II.A).

Results from our survey of Hungarian CSOs were fewer than for other countries and they are not representative. The small number of respondents can nevertheless in part be explained by the small number of CSOs which assist migrants in Hungary, relative to the other three countries under study. Interviewees suggested that this context was in part due to the fact that the asylum-seeker population in Hungary has been relatively small in comparison to other EU Member States, and also because of the shrinking space for CSOs (see below).[52]

Nevertheless, considered alongside evidence obtained in the focus groups and through field trips and semi-structured interviews, the data suggest that the significant changes in Hungarian immigration and asylum law in the last two years have led to confusion and uncertainty among some CSOs in terms of what services they can provide to irregular migrants and under what conditions. A majority of CSOs which took part in the research said that they felt actors seeking to assist irregular migrants or asylum-seekers were punished or prevented from assisting them (see Figures 4.22 and 4.23). Several survey respondents and interviewees claimed the issue was primarily one of policing access, because since the creation of the new transit zones in which asylum-seekers are held during their applications, getting access to asylum-seekers in order to deliver services in the first place was

[51] Interview with non-formal group (activists) providing social assistance, 30 August 2017, Budapest, Hungary; interview with non-formal group (activists) providing social assistance, 31 August 2017, Szeged, Hungary.

[52] Interview with CSO providing social assistance, 29 August 2017, Budapest, Hungary.

becoming more and more difficult. As one respondent to our survey who provides services (such as providing medical aid, legal aid, shelter, etc) in the zones of transit in Hungary commented,

> Assisting irregular migrants in border crossings or even in approaching the border is forbidden. Providing assistance at the Serbian-Hungarian and Croatian-Hungarian border areas and also transit zones [has] been severely restricted.

A CSO interviewee who provides social assistance and whose organisation at the time of research had recently been prevented from providing services in the transit zones said, 'The real issue is that in practice the new laws have meant that as

**Figure 4.22** Do policies in Hungary punish or prevent *individuals* (not members of organisations) who help irregular migrants/asylum-seekers/refugees?*

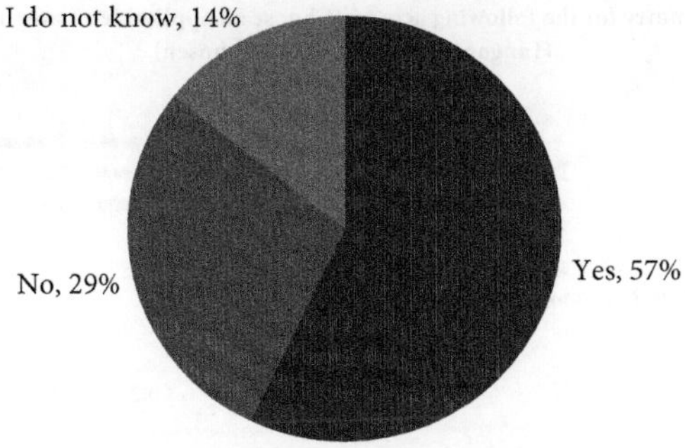


* Hungarian survey received in total only seven responses.

Source: CSA Online Survey (2017).

**Figure 4.23** Do policies in Hungary punish or prevent members of various *organisations* which help irregular migrants/asylum-seekers/refugees?*

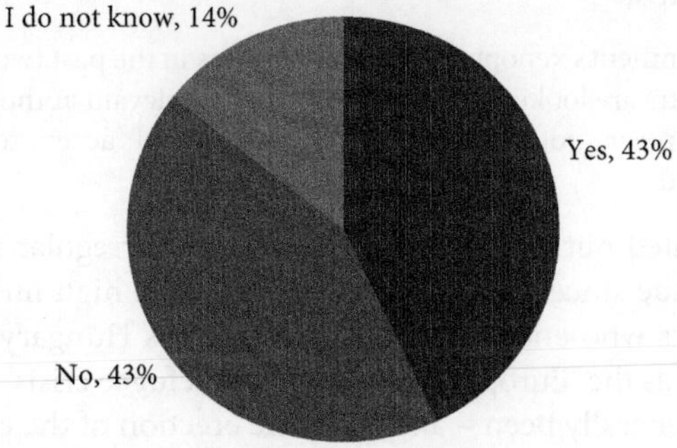


* Hungarian survey received in total only seven responses.

Source: CSA Online Survey (2017).

humanitarian actors we cannot even access asylum-seekers to help them. We can't be criminalised for helping them if we can't even to talk to them anymore!'[53]

Another CSO respondent to our survey commented in relation to access to the transit zones that 'entry permits are given for a shorter period of time, and issuance takes more time due to clearance'. This was one of a number of highlighted new bureaucratic obstacles.

Respondents to the survey were unsure whether they had duties to report irregular migrants in-country (see Figure 4.24), although one respondent commented, '[S]chools must report all non-Hungarian attendants' and 'this report must contain title of residences'.

**Figure 4.24** Awareness of duties to report irregular migrants and/or asylum-seekers in Hungary

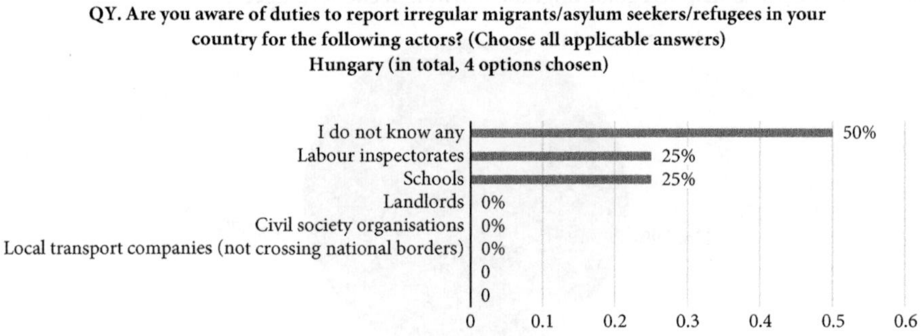


* Hungarian survey received in total only seven responses.

Source: CSA Online Survey (2017).

Respondents to the survey felt that the origin of policies criminalising assistance to migrants in Hungary were part of a nationalist agenda and not linked to EU anti-smuggling laws (see Figure 4.25). As one respondent working for a CSO in Hungary commented,

> Due to the government's xenophobic hate campaigns in the past two years, those assisting asylum-seekers are looked upon with suspicion. Relevant authorities usually refuse offers from volunteer groups to provide services or aid, access to asylum-seekers is severely restricted.

Several CSAs pointed out that the issue of reporting irregular migrants had not been a pressing issue since. This is because despite the high number of migrants and asylum-seekers who entered and transited across Hungary during what has come to be known as the 'European humanitarian refugee crisis' of 2015, Hungary nevertheless has generally been – and since the erection of the external Schengen

[53] Interview with CSO providing social and medical assistance, 30 August 2017, via Skype.

**Figure 4.25** Impact of reporting duties on humanitarian actors in Hungary

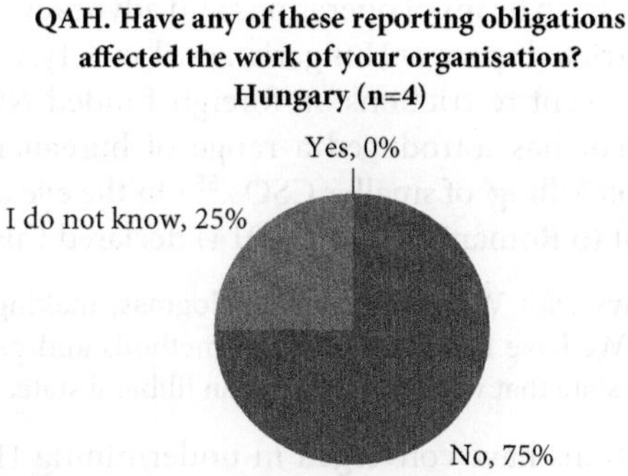


* Hungarian survey received in total only seven responses.

Source: CSA Online Survey (2017).

border is still – home to a relatively small population of undocumented or asylum-seeking migrants and refugees relative to its neighbouring European countries.

Under new emergency powers in place since spring 2017, irregular migrants detected in Hungary can nevertheless be sent back to the border from any part of the country. This means that in theory, an undocumented migrant seeking access to public services could be removed. At the time of writing, most CSAs we spoke to did not experience a proactive obligation to report irregular migrants to police or other authorities, although more than one was seeking legal counsel on this issue. Two CSOs and one international organisation spoke of being in talks with authorities in Budapest to set up advice services for migrants – potentially including irregular migrants – in the city.[54]

## D. Other Laws Impacting Humanitarian Assistance

CSAs consulted for this research were also keen to point out a range of other laws which are peripheral to the anti-smuggling framework but which have also been shown to impact the work of CSAs assisting irregular migrant and refugees in Hungary. In the words of one survey respondent working for a CSO:

> I am not sure whether it is relevant but [the] Hungarian government restricts NGOs in the field by different tools (mostly by communication). Those can and cannot be considered as punishment.

Most interviewees saw these new measures as part not so much of anti-smuggling policies per se but as of a general turn away from liberal democratic values on the part of the Orbán government. But most also agreed that they had a substantial

[54] Interview with CSO providing social assistance, 29 August 2017, Budapest, Hungary; interview with UN actor, 29 August 2017, Budapest, Hungary.

impact on their ability to provide services to asylum-seekers and irregular migrants and to continue existing, in terms of operations and advocacy, as an active presence in an increasingly restricted space of Hungarian civil society. One CSA commented that alongside more recent restrictions on foreign-funded NGOs, since 2012 the Hungarian government has introduced a range of bureaucratic logistical challenges as a form of 'soft killing' of smaller CSOs.[55] On the eve of the 2014 elections, during an official visit to Romania, Orbán (2014) declared this intent:

> We are parting ways with Western European dogmas, making ourselves independent from them … We have to abandon liberal methods and principles of organising society … The new state that we are building is an illiberal state, a non-liberal state.

The government's actions have converged in undermining Hungarian civil society (and thus affected migrant support actors) and were reported to have pursued two main objectives: centralisation of power and promotion of nationalism. Belonging to the former category are numerous amendments to the constitution (Krugman 2012), which in the words of a UN special rapporteur have resulted in 'the centralization and tightening of government's control over the judiciary, the media and, religious organisations and other spheres of public life' (UN Special rapporteur on human rights defenders 2016). Part of this move has included a reshaping and restructuring of civil society. The latter includes media laws[56] which restrict freedom of expression (ALB 2012) and the 2017 National Higher Education Act, which places new restrictions on foreign-funded higher education institutions.[57]

A controversial new law of June 2017 (Law on the Transparency of Organisations Receiving Support from Abroad) requires 'foreign-funded' NGOs to declare sources of international funding and state this in all public outputs. Civil society in Hungary is now composed of religious, 'charitable' organisations and what are now known as 'internationally funded organisations'. The adoption of these legislative acts did not unfold in complete compliance with the rules of democratic scrutiny, due to the lack of consultation with entitled concerned actors before submission to the Parliament in both instances (see Council of Europe 2017). The new laws are an attempt to tackle what according to the government is the challenge represented by foreign interest groups which are influencing Hungarian political life through various means.

Entities financed by George Soros seem to be one of the direct targets of the law on the transparency of organisations receiving support from abroad. During

[55] Interview with CSO providing social assistance, 29 August 2017, Budapest, Hungary.

[56] The Hungarian Media Package is composed of two laws adopted in 2010: the Media Act restructuring the media regulatory system, and the Press Act concerning media content and press regulation. The package was supplemented in 2014 with the Advertisement Tax Act, which introduced new taxes for companies with a high advertising revenue. These were subject to scrutiny by the Council of Europe's Venice Commission.

[57] The main target of the changes to the National Higher Education Act appears to be George Soros's Central European University (CEU) in Budapest, which is at risk of closing. The policies of the Hungarian government have been denounced by various observers, eg, Council of Europe.

the process of elaboration and discussion of the draft law, public officials directly referred to NGOs funded by Open Society Foundations. Here, two statements are cases in point: (i) in January 2017, the Fidesz vice-president (who is also an MP) stated, 'The Soros empire's fake civilian organisations … have to be rolled back by every means … and have to be swept out of here'; (ii) in February 2017, during the annual speech on the state of the nation, Orbán said,

> In 2017 we will also need to take up the struggle against international organisations' increasingly strong activists … it is a problem that foreign funding is being used to influence Hungarian politics … the organisations of George Soros are working tirelessly to bring thousands of migrants into Europe.[58]

The latter quotation highlights the semantic link on the part of the government between the justification for placing restrictions on the work of foreign-funded NGOs and an effort to combat migrant-smuggling. This link was also stressed in an interview with a senior official in a think tank close to the government, who highlighted NGOs as one of the three main causes of 'smuggling to Hungary' which needed to be addressed in order to tackle the problem.[59]

Soon after the adoption of the draft law, the Council of Europe raised a number of concerns, including:

- the lack of public consultation prior to its submission to the Hungarian Parliament;
- the obligation of NGOs receiving foreign funding to indicate this on all published and distributed materials;
- the obligation for NGOs to submit the detailed personal data of foreign donors, including private individuals;
- the gravity of the sanctions provided in the draft, including ultimately the dissolution of the association for non compliance with administrative obligations;
- the scope of application of the draft law, which applies to certain associations and excludes others, such as sports and religious organisations.

The Venice Commission was then called to issue a more detailed opinion on the draft law in order to help the Hungarian government address the shortcomings. The Commission released its preliminary report on 2 June 2017 (Council of Europe Venice Commission 2017a). In 13 June 2017, Hungary adopted some amendments to the draft law on foreign-funded NGOs. Nevertheless, in its final opinion of 20 June, the Venice Commission stated that even though it

> recognizes that some of the amendments represent an important improvement … some of the concerns were not addressed and the amendments do not suffice to alleviate the

[58] These statements are cited by the Parliamentary Assembly of the Council of Europe as to delineate the context in which the law was adopted, or rather as '[raising] doubts about the real aims of the … legislation'.

[59] Interview with government-affiliated think tank, 30 August 2017, Budapest, Hungary.

> Venice Commission's concerns that the Law will cause a disproportionate and unnecessary interference with the freedoms of association and expression, the right to privacy, and the prohibition of discrimination, including due to the absence of comparable transparency obligations which apply to domestic financing of NGOs.[60]

Given the government's failure to address the shortcomings that the law raised from a human rights perspective, on 13 July 2017, the EU Commission launched an infringement procedure, sending to the government a letter of formal notice (European Commission 2017e).

These new legal changes have been experienced by some NGOs as intentional stigmatisation or a 'smear campaign against NGOs and organizations working with migrants'.[61] One interviewee commented, 'Foreign-funded NGOs are seen as working against the national interest'.[62] The Amnesty International section in Hungary has decided not to comply with the law and will try to challenge it in the courts, and the same course of action is being pursued by the Helsinki Committee, a major provider of legal support for irregular migrants and asylum-seekers in Hungary.

As well as being challenged by the European Parliament for being anti-democratic in nature and intent (European Commission 2017e), the law has also been challenged by the United Nations (Dearden 2017a). After his visit to the country in early 2016, the UN special rapporteur on human rights defenders portrayed a gloomy picture of the climate in which Hungarian civil society is operating. He defined such an environment as polarised and politicised, and denounced the government's attempts 'to de-legitimize defenders and undermine their peaceful and legitimate activities through criminal defamation and excessive administrative and financial pressure', adding that 'defenders are exposed to serious challenges which, in some instances, appear to amount to violations of their fundamental rights and freedoms, as well as of their legitimate right to promote and defend human rights' (UN High Commissioner for Human Rights 2016).

As grantees of the Open Society Foundations, the following Hungarian CSOs working on migration are affected by the law:[63]

— Rosa Parks Foundation;
— Migráns Segítség Magyarország Association;
— Menedék: Hungarian Association for Migrants;
— Hungarian Civil Liberties Union;
— Hungarian Helsinki Committee.

[60] Council of Europe Venice Commission (2017b: 18).

[61] Interview with CSO providing legal assistance, 16 August 2017, via Skype.

[62] Interview with non-formal group (activist) providing social assistance, 31 August 2017, Budapest, Hungary.

[63] For the complete list of the OSF grantees in Hungary see Open Society Foundations 'List of Our Hungarian Grantees 2016', www.opensocietyfoundations.org/publications/open-society-hungarian-grantees-2016.

CSA interviewees were nevertheless all keen to point out that the law also impacted NGOs which were not in receipt of foreign funding, since 'just the fact of working with migrants casts you under suspicion'.[64]

Moreover, field research revealed that beyond the legislative level, freedom of expression has been violated through more direct attacks against journalists, notably within the context of the refugee crisis. In 2015, as reported by Freedom House (2016), a leaked report revealed that a public agency had instructed TV journalists to refrain from showing women and children when covering the refugee crisis. The same year, between September and October, seven journalists reporting on the crisis were victims of physical attacks by the police. In its 2017 World Report, Human Rights Watch asserted that during 2016 'journalists continued to work in a hostile environment' and reported on the case of Budapest Business Journal Editor-in-Chief Tom Popper, who resigned after he was told by his publisher to stop mentioning refugee issues in the editorial column (Human Rights Watch 2017). This is highly relevant since, as chapters five to seven show, over the course of the 'European refugee crisis' the media have played an important role in monitoring and holding to account humanitarian violations against vulnerable migrants and refugees.

## IV. UK

Alongside sweeping new measures to criminalise acts of irregular migration in itself, which have been introduced in successive Immigration Acts and Bills (2014, 2015–16 and 2017), a range of established and new laws affect the work of CSAs providing assistance to migrants and refugees in the UK or who are seeking to enter the UK via sea and land borders by stowing away, via spontaneous sea arrival and falsification of documents.

### A. Facilitation of Entry and Residence

Section 25 of the 1971 Immigration Act outlines the crime of facilitating irregular entry, transit and stay. It states in subsection (1) that a person commits an offence if he or she:

- (a) does an act which facilitates the commission of a breach of immigration law by an individual who is not a citizen of the European Union,
- (b) knows or has reasonable cause for believing that the act facilitates the commission of a breach of immigration law by the individual, and
- (c) knows or has reasonable cause for believing that the individual is not a citizen of the European Union.[65]

[64] Interview with CSO providing social assistance, 29 August 2017, Budapest, Hungary.
[65] www.legislation.gov.uk/ukpga/1971/77.

Subsection (2) clarifies that 'in subsection (1) "immigration law" means a law which has effect in a Member State and which controls, in respect of some or all persons who are not nationals of the State, entitlement to – (a) enter the State, (b) transit across the State, or (c) be in the State'. The facilitation of entry, transit and residence in another Member States is therefore also punishable in the UK.

Subsection (3) states

> a person commits an offence if – (a) he knowingly and for gain facilitates the arrival in, or the entry into, the United Kingdom of an individual, and (b) he knows or has reasonable cause to believe that the individual is an asylum-seeker.

The offence is punished on summary conviction by imprisonment of up to six months, or a fine not exceeding the statutory maximum; or both. It is punished on conviction to indictment with imprisonment of up to 14 years, and/or a fine (EU Fundamental Rights Agency 2014).

In the 1971 UK Immigration Act, the safeguard not to impose sanctions where irregular entry and transit are facilitated for humanitarian purposes only applies in cases where entry is facilitated by a person acting without a profit-making motive on behalf of an organisation that seeks to assist asylum-seekers. It relates to 'arrival' rather than to residence, and only applies to a person acting on behalf of an organisation that aims to assist asylum-seekers and does not charge for its services. The exemption does not cover the general offence of assisting unlawful immigration.

Guidance from the UK Crown Prosecution Service draws attention to the case of *Kapoor & Ors* [2012] EWCA Crim 435, in which there were difficulties in obtaining evidence of direct (financial) gain to support a charge under section 25A and cautions:

> Prosecutors should consider whether there might be sufficient evidence to infer gain in return for assistance in facilitating a breach of immigration law by those who then may go on to (falsely) claim asylum. The offence is an either-way offence and the maximum sentence on indictment is up to 14 years' imprisonment, a fine or both. It is also a 'lifestyle offence' under schedule 2 of the Proceeds of Crime Act 2002. Bearing in mind the nature of the offences and the likely sentence to be imposed, the majority of cases will not be suitable for summary trial unless there are significant and exceptional circumstances to justify this course of action.[66]

A 2016 study (Carrera et al) revealed shortcomings in the availability of data to show instances of criminalisation for humanitarian facilitation. UK crime statistics do not offer a detailed breakdown on types of offences. No specific data related to crimes in the scope of facilitation are available.

Publicly available statistics nevertheless do give a picture of the number of individuals prosecuted and found guilty at Crown Courts for generally assisting undocumented migrants. Domestic case law indicates evidence that family members and those assisting refugees to enter have been criminalised.

[66] www.cps.gov.uk/legal/h_to_k/immigration/.

Aliverti's 2013 study of UK case law related to facilitation revealed that 25 per cent of charged defendants were alleged to be family members of the person involved (Aliverti 2013). From 2005 to 2014, 2,420 individuals were prosecuted in a magistrates' court for assisting unlawful immigration in the UK; 220 were found guilty. In addition, 1,963 were tried in the Crown Court, of whom 1,521 individuals were found guilty (Carrera et al 2016: 42–43).

## B. New Controls in the 'Hostile Environment'

In recent years, in addition to the crime of facilitating irregular entry, a raft of measures has been introduced or enhanced in the UK which shift the burden of anti-smuggling and immigration law enforcement onto the general public (Yeo 2017). The majority of these proposals became law via the 2014 Immigration Act and have since been tightened or expanded under the 2016 Immigration Act. In an interview in 2012, Theresa May, then Home Secretary, was quoted as saying,

> The aim is to create here in Britain a really hostile environment for illegal migration … What we don't want is a situation where people think that they can come here and overstay because they're able to access everything they need.[67]

In 2012, at a policy level, the 2010–15 coalition government created a 'Hostile Environment Working Group' to devise new forms of hostility (Aitkenhead and Wintour 2013). This was renamed the more anodyne 'Inter-Ministerial Group on Migrants' Access to Benefits and Public Services'.

This phenomenon of shifting immigration control to members of the general public and service sectors has been a key feature of this 'hostile environment' (see chapter 7.IV for more detail on the impacts of these new measures). These measures impose new monitoring obligations on certain sectors and service providers with the possibility of civil or criminal sanction for negligence or failure to perform such duties in the case of, for example, renting property to an irregular migrant. Other measures, such as data sharing agreements between the National Health Service (NHS) and the Home Office are not written in law but create ambiguity surrounding what service providers can provide and when they are obliged to report irregular migrants seeking access to services (see chapter 7.IV).

In recent years, with the intensification of the fight against smuggling across land/sea borders, haulage companies and individual drivers have also faced greater penalties for the crime of facilitating irregular entry of migrants who may have stowed away in their vehicles. Lorry drivers are fined £2,000 for each 'stowaway' if they are caught in the UK. Drivers are fined €20,000 (£16,000) if illegal immigrants are found in their vehicles in France. Between 2012 and 2015, penalties for lorries carrying stowaways into the UK have more than tripled (Kent Online 2015).

[67] Yeo (2017).

Other legislation of note is section 32(6)(a) of the 2014 Immigration Act, which holds landlords responsible for checking tenants' immigration status. This legislation came into force gradually across certain regions and is outlined in the UK Home Office Code of Practice on Illegal Immigrants and Private Rented Accommodation (2016), which came into force for tenancies on 1 February 2016.[68]

Under section 22 of the 2014 Immigration Act, a landlord is required not to rent to someone unless the adult is a British citizen, or a European Economic Area (EEA) or Swiss national, or has a 'right to rent' in the UK. Someone will have the 'right to rent' in the UK provided they are present lawfully in accordance with immigration laws. Section 23 of the Act allows the Secretary of State to serve a landlord with a notice requiring the payment of a penalty of a specified amount where they have let property to an unqualified person in a tenancy subject to the scheme.

Landlords can establish a statutory excuse against liability for a civil penalty by conducting document checks before allowing adults to occupy rented accommodation (right to rent check). Where a landlord has previously let accommodation to a person with a time-limited right to rent, they are required to maintain their excuse against a penalty by conducting follow-up checks as detailed in the aforementioned code. The Home Office guidance is clear:

> If follow-up checks indicate that the person no longer has the right to rent, to maintain their excuse the landlord should make a report to the Home Office as soon as reasonably practicable. Landlords will need to keep records of the checks they have undertaken for those people who will occupy their accommodation.[69]

Landlords have the option to appoint an agent to act on their behalf. Where an agent has accepted responsibility for compliance with the scheme, the agent will be the liable party in place of the landlord. The UK Home Office Code of Practice stresses the logic of this approach:

> Housing illegal immigrants in the private rented sector allows such people to establish a settled life in the UK and frustrate the necessary process of returning them to their home country. This creates a significant cost to the public purse and also reduces the amount of housing stock available to British citizens and others residing here legally. As a landlord, you have a responsibility to restrict illegal immigrants accessing the private rented sector.[70]

A 2010 report by the EU Fundamental Rights Agency cautions against this approach, stressing that it is 'resulting in further reluctance to rent housing to migrants. This, in turn, increases migrants' vulnerability to exploitation and the risk that they must accept substandard housing' (FRA 2010: 13).

[68] www.gov.uk/government/publications/right-to-rent-landlords-code-of-practice/code-of-practice-on-illegal-immigrants-and-private-rented-accommodation-for-tenancies-starting-on-or-after-1-february-2016.

[69] UK Home Office (2016).

[70] UK Home Office (2016).

Employers have faced increasingly harsh civil and criminal sanctions for employing irregular migrant workers as part of the British government's self-professed 'Fight against Modern Day Slavery' (UK Home Office 2017). The government has appointed an independent anti-slavery commissioner to fight the phenomenon of modern slavery (UK Anti-Slavery Commissioner 2018). In a briefing paper published in September 2015, the UK government states that its aims are to 'make it harder' for undocumented migrants to live and work in the UK, by imposing 'tougher penalties and sanctions on rogue employers' (Bloch and McKay 2015). In UK law, employers can be jailed for five years and pay an unlimited fine if found guilty of employing someone whom they knew or had 'reasonable cause to believe' didn't have the right to work in the UK (UK Government 2017).

Employers can also be penalised with a civil fine of up to £20,000 for each illegal worker if they employ someone who doesn't have the right to work and they didn't do the correct checks, or if they did not do the checks properly. In the past, Home Office guidance has implied that undocumented migrants should not be allowed to volunteer, although this has not been pursued in law (Refugee Action 2013). The government has rapidly increased the number of raids on businesses in recent years (Yeo 2016). Prime Minister David Cameron was filmed by media attending such a raid in 2014 in what some dismissed as a 'PR stunt' (Mason 2014).

Banks are prohibited from opening current accounts for those identified as being in the UK unlawfully. Under controversial new laws, access to public services such as the National Health Service (NHS) is also restricted for irregular migrants; however it is still unclear the extent to which professionals can use their discretion and avoid sanction in relation to these rules. Moreover, asylum-seekers are, theoretically, excluded from current rules. Universities are also required to conduct checks on migrant students and to monitor their attendance, or face sanctions for failing to comply. In 2012, London Metropolitan University took the UK government to court after it had its visa-issuing licence revoked for failing to carry out adequate checks on students (The Telegraph 2012). Legal expert Colin Yeo is among those who have pointed out the wide-ranging impacts of these new rules:

> [I]t is not only unlawful migrants who are affected by the hostile environment. The privatisation of immigration control requires non-governmental actors and public services to check the immigration status of all users and customers. An increasingly wide range of service providers and service users are therefore affected: employers, landlords, banks and doctors and everyone who has contact with them are all affected. The effects are not equal; migrants, ethnic minorities, young people and women are disproportionately affected.[71]

Another law cited by several CSO interviewees which was reported to have an impact on the advocacy work of migrant support organisations in the UK concerns the 2014 Lobbying Act. The Act introduced new rules for charities, NGOs and

[71] Yeo (2017).

campaigning groups undertaking public-facing campaigns in the run-up to national elections, including the 2015 general election.

Well-established international NGOs Friends of the Earth and Greenpeace were fined under the Lobbying Act for breaking campaigning rules during the 2015 general election.

Prior to the 2017 general election, 50 different charities wrote a letter outlining their 'deep concerns' about the effect of the Lobbying Act. The letter stated that a number of charities have 'altered or reduced campaigning activities before the election as a result of the act', and calling on the next government to repeal it. 'Voices are being lost at this crucial time, and our democracy is the poorer for it' (Sharman 2017). Interviewees indicated that the criteria for becoming a 'charity' in the UK were also becoming stricter. One migrant support CSO interviewed for this research explained that they had deliberately refrained from registering as a charity, for fear that it might limit their advocacy and monitoring work.[72]

## C. Perceptions of the UK Law among Civil Society Actors

As with past studies (Carrera et al 2015), our survey and interview data revealed a high level of confusion on the part of UK CSOs regarding what services they could provide to irregular migrants (and other categories of migrants) and what the potential sanctions for failing to comply with rules might be. Respondents were undecided over whether UK policies punish individuals or organisations who help irregular migrants/asylum-seekers/refugees (see Figures 4.26 and 4.27).

**Figure 4.26** Do policies in the UK punish or prevent *individuals* (not members of organisations) who help irregular migrants/asylum-seekers/refugees? (UK, n=23)

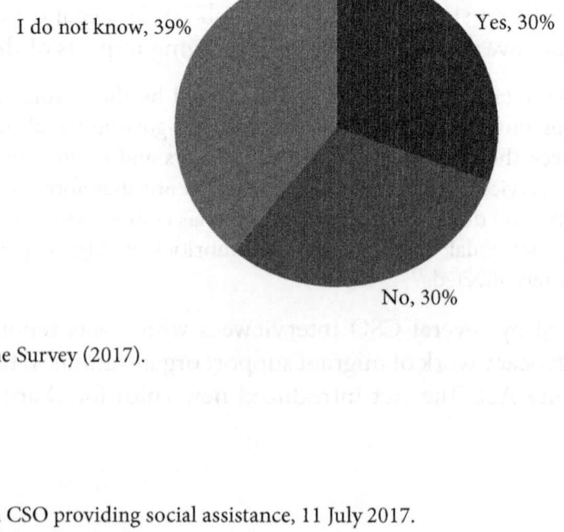


Source: CSA Online Survey (2017).

[72] Interview with CSO providing social assistance, 11 July 2017.

**Figure 4.27** Do policies in the UK punish or prevent members of various *organisations* which help irregular migrants/asylum-seekers/refugees? (UK, n=23)

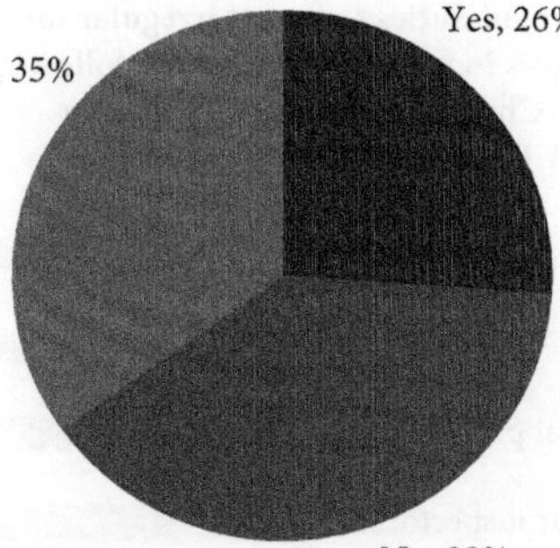


Source: CSA Online Survey (2017).

Several interviewees explained that the confusion was exacerbated by the proliferation of different legal statuses with different access to particular social rights which had been a trend over the last decade, as documented by the concept of 'stratification of social rights' advanced by Morris (2009). 'It's hard to keep up with who is entitled to what and then the rules keep changing so you feel like as a social worker you have to be an immigration lawyer', explained one CSO interviewee who works for a government service providing social advice at an office based in a London hospital.[73] The online survey respondents showed that due to the national debate, some of them were aware of the reporting duties for landlords, schools and also medical professionals (Figure 4.28).

There is sometimes a tendency to 'err on the side of caution'. One respondent belonging to an activist group in the UK said,

> There are restrictions on supporting non-registered asylum-seekers. I have looked into it but it's still a bit confusing. There are some here who cannot claim because they under threat to work illegal to repay debt to smugglers. We are not sure how to help these people without incurring liability for aiding illegal immigration.

Respondents also expressed confusion regarding what information they are legally obliged to share with authorities and what is discretionary, as demonstrated in Figure 4.29.

As one survey respondent working for a CSO in the UK explained, '[E]mployers, marriage Registry Offices, and schools don't have a duty but are being pressured to share information about nationality and country of birth of students through the school census'. Controversy emerged this year over school census data, which can now be shared with the Home Office under a new

[73] Interview with national welfare authority providing social and medical assistance, 12 July, London, UK.

**Figure 4.28** Awareness of duties to report irregular migrants and/or asylum-seekers in the UK

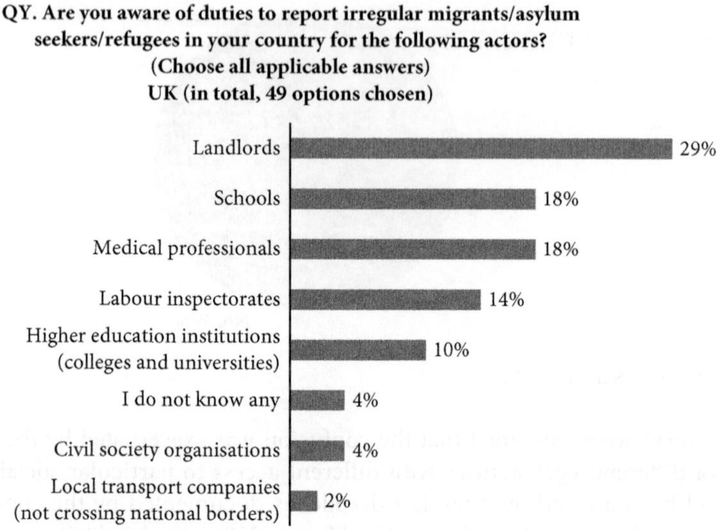


Source: CSA Online Survey (2017).

**Figure 4.29** CSAs' experiences of policing in the UK

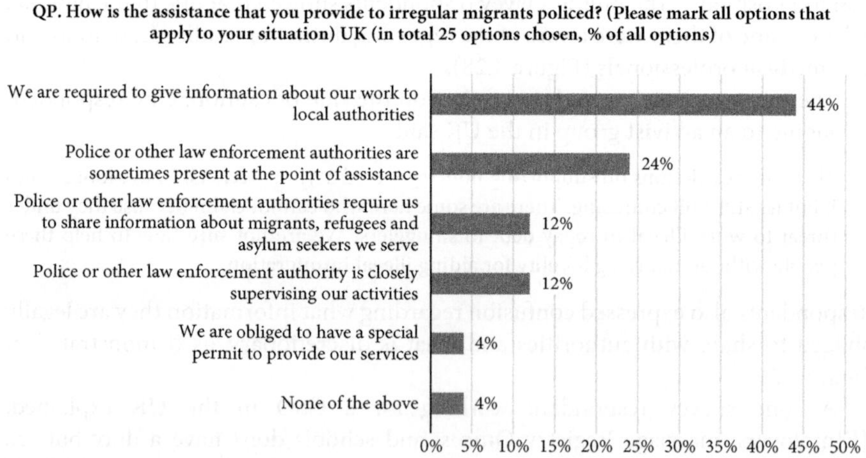


Source: CSA Online Survey (2017).

data-sharing Memorandum of Understanding, asking students for their country of origin as well as their address. 'This data could clearly be used for immigration control purposes', commented one interviewee who was part of a campaign calling on parents to boycott the census. '[I]n reality, parents didn't have to provide that information but the guidance made it look like they did. There were horror stories of teachers demanding kids bring their passports into school'.[74]

Other policing measures highlighted in the survey included individuals being required to show identification when accessing primary and secondary healthcare and registering for schools or colleges. Businesses have also been co-opted into working with the Home Office in immigration raids of irregular employers as a way of avoiding sanction. A range of activist groups called for the boycotting of the chain restaurant Byron Burgers in 2016, after London branches falsely invited staff to come for a training day when in reality they were collaborating in an immigration raid (O'Carroll 2016).

As was also reported in Italy, there was quite a strong spirit of defiance among UK-based survey respondents and interviewees in relation to whether the new reporting obligations in the 'hostile environment' would affect their work (see Figure 4.30). Seventy-four per cent of respondents said the work of their organisation was unaffected, although 16 per cent stated that it had impacted their work.

**Figure 4.30** Impact of reporting duties on humanitarian actors in the UK

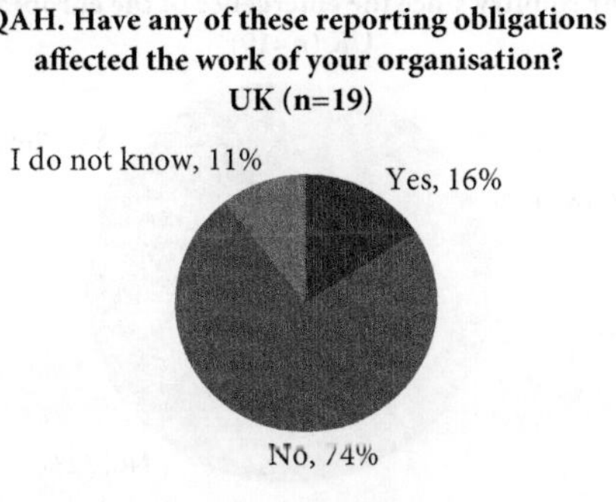


Source: CSA Online Survey (2017).

Respondents to the online survey largely saw laws that punish assistance to irregular migrants, asylum-seekers or refugees as part of a national rather than an EU agenda, or the majority were unsure (see Figure 4.31). Respondents were undecided about whether the policing of humanitarian assistance in the UK had increased with the so-called 'European humanitarian refugee crisis' (see Figure 4.32), but several interviewees traced the developments to before then, with the initiation of the 'hostile environment' under Theresa May's leadership of the Home Office. As one survey respondent belonging to an activist group in the UK commented, 'The "hostile environment" is being deliberately created by the UK government'. A respondent volunteering for a CSO in the UK (working in media) felt humanitarian work with migrants was 'stigmatised by the current Prime Minister [Theresa May, formerly Home Secretary]'.

[74] Interview with non-formal group (activists), 7 July, London, UK.

**Figure 4.31** Perceived origin of the policies 'criminalising' individuals and/or CSOs providing humanitarian assistance in the UK

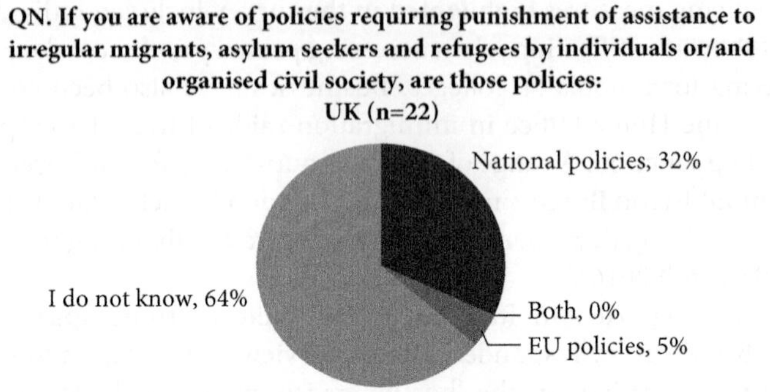


Source: CSA Online Survey (2017).

**Figure 4.32** Perceived change in policing humanitarian assistance in the UK

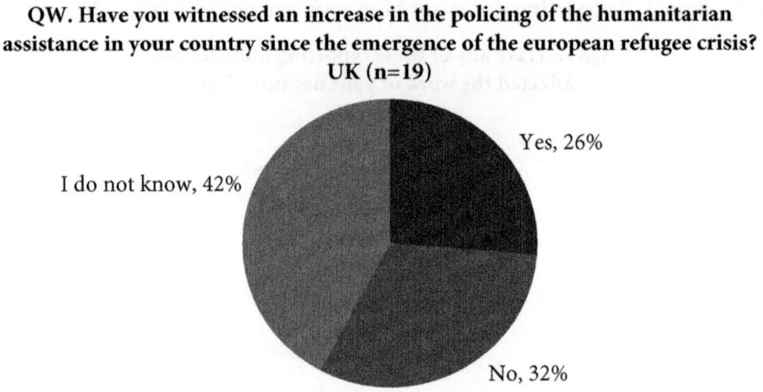


Source: CSA Online Survey (2017).

Around one-third of survey respondents knew personally of some cases where CSAs had been stigmatised, intimidated, accused or punished for assisting irregular migrants (see Figure 4.33). Many examples came from CSOs operating in Calais as well as in London, which are further discussed in the chapter 7.IV.

Incidents included people being fined for providing food without a licence in Calais (see chapter 5.II.B), and 'being stopped, questioned and searched and other low level police harassment both in Calais and at the border'. Unlike the 'hostile environment' in terms of policing irregular residence in the UK, the policing of service provision at the Calais border was said to have increased significantly since the start of the 'European humanitarian refugee crisis'. An individual volunteer in the UK (not affiliated with any organisation) who was operating at the UK border

**Figure 4.33** Awareness and proximity of policing humanitarian actors in the UK

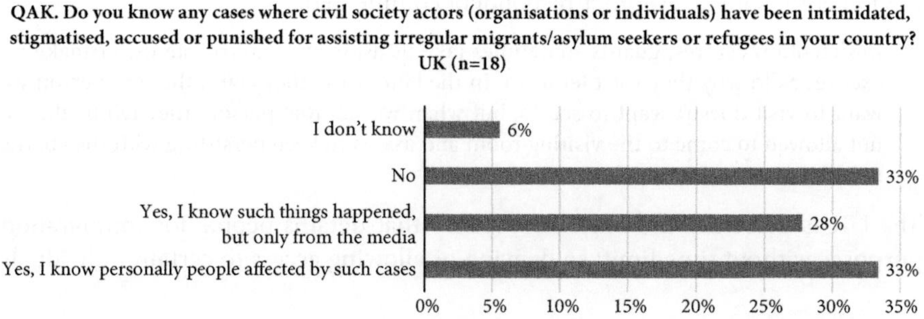


Source: CSA Online Survey (2017).

and Calais commented, 'Distribution wasn't monitored at all when [I] began volunteering in France. Now [it is] heavily policed, prevented, refugees are harassed and detained at point of support'. Another respondent belonging to an activist group in the UK similarly commented,

> In Calais we were constantly questioned by police – even just for our papers especially all our car papers and car searches, changes to access 'rules' – some fines for tyre wear etc. [J]ust to make the work more difficult.

Several survey respondents and interviewees raised the case of Rob Lawrie, a British army veteran who narrowly escaped jail under French law after smuggling an Afghan child to the UK to be with her family (Lusher 2016). This case raises the important issue of humanitarian actors who are citizens of one EU Member State being charged under the law of another Member State which may, as we have seen, differ significantly.

Another respondent belonging to an activist group in the UK knew personally someone currently under prosecution for trying to bring their disabled brother into the country. Again, it is important to stress that CSOs often include migrants themselves who may or may not be undocumented. Indeed, as mentioned above, the idea that those facilitating irregular entry or transit or residence may be migrants themselves without citizenship status is assumed in the wording of the penalties which include expulsion from the territory. Survey respondents echoed participants in the civil society focus group in commenting on how the UK media had targeted them. Smear campaigns, one respondent pointed out, can pose an existential threat by leading CSOs to have 'charitable status or grants withheld'.

CSOs also reported experiences of violence by UK police and French police when peacefully resisting immigration raids, as was also reported by the media (Addley 2014). One respondent working (in the media) for a CSO in the UK commented, 'People who stand up for the rights of migrants who are stopped by racist raids or even at targeted raids are often threatened by the police and immigration enforcement'. Another respondent commented,

> In detention centres, guards sometimes take us aside and interrogate us, or make up excuses as to why they can't let us in. In the latter case, they claim that the person we want to visit doesn't want to see us, but when we call that person, they tell us they're not allowed to come to the visiting room and ask us to keep persisting with the guards to be let in.

The UK is currently the only EU country that detains people for immigration purposes without time limit; so denying or allowing access to certain individuals

**Figure 4.34** Impact of policing of humanitarian actors in the UK on respondent's organisation

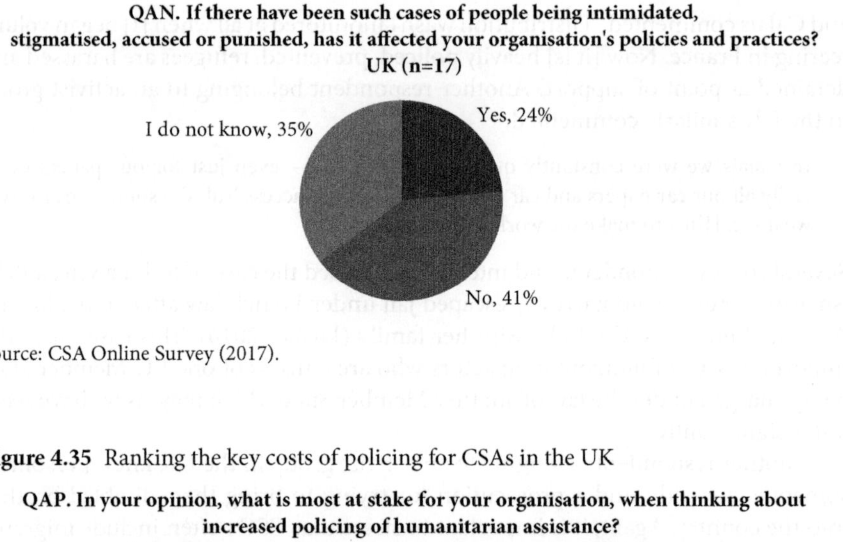


Source: CSA Online Survey (2017).

**Figure 4.35** Ranking the key costs of policing for CSAs in the UK

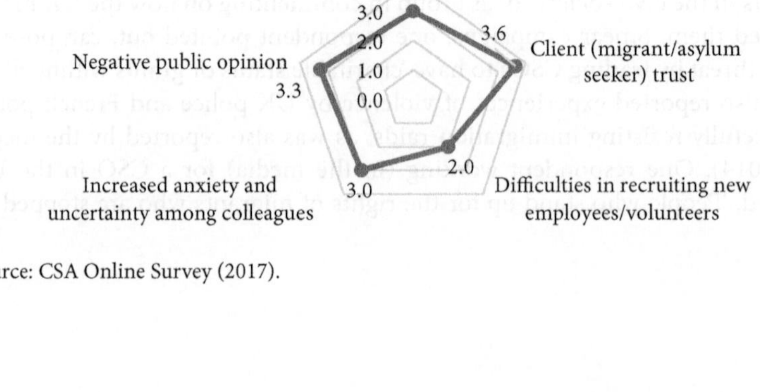


Source: CSA Online Survey (2017).

and organisations through visiting rights is an important tactic of policing and control (a similar dynamic was reported in Hungary). A respondent who was an individual volunteer in the UK pointed out that some volunteers from the UK had also physically been denied access to (Calais) France, in some cases on the grounds that they were under investigation for committing crimes (related to the provision of assistance to irregular migrants) in France.

Despite collected testimonies of various accusations, only one-fifth of the UK survey respondents said that their organisations' policies or practices had been directly affected by such practices (see Figure 4.34).

Figure 4.35 indicates that difficulties in accessing funding was the main stake for CSOs from the UK which responded to the survey when thinking about the increased policing of humanitarian assistance. This went along with issues of client trust, negative public opinion and anxiety and uncertainly among colleagues. As reported elsewhere (Carrera et al 2017), some CSOs engaged in what one survey respondent called a 'slight toning down of "militant" political profile' in recognition that the more their work was seen as political, and a challenge to authorities, the more it was policed.

# 5

# Effects of Countering Facilitation of Entry on Civil Society Actors Involved at External EU Sea and Land Borders

The remainder of this book studies the impacts of the EU's policy approach to countering migrant-smuggling outlined above, both in its normative and operational forms, on the work of CSAs. The analysis is structured around the provision of 'humanitarian assistance' in two main sites or stages: first, entry, including SAR (chapter five) and in/near the EU hotspot approach (chapter six) which lies in between the two; and second, in zones of transit and residence (chapter seven). Both categories of site are targeted by the EU Facilitators Package when it comes to intentionally assisting a third-country national to irregularly enter, transit or reside in an EU Member State. Each of these sites entails a number of specific challenges, depending on the kinds of controls employed by technologies in use to counter migrant-smuggling. and by the EU actors and nationals studied in chapters three and four respectively. The controversies surrounding assistance to migrants and refugees have been increasingly documented by the media (Open Migration 2017; Meret and Goffredo 2017).[1]

## I. Sea Borders and Search and Rescue

In Italy and Greece, for SAR cases, international maritime law instruments apply. The United Nations Convention on the Law of the Sea of 1982 and International Convention for the Safety of Life at Sea of 1974 require all shipmasters to rescue or assist 'persons in distress' at sea. Interviews in both countries with national border and coastguard authorities revealed a range of different interpretations concerning when people are regarded as in distress. Italian national border and coastguard authorities regard any unseaworthy vessel in the Central Mediterranean as being in distress, and therefore subject to SAR operations.[2] The Italian authorities

[1] For example a selection of articles at http://openmigration.org/en/web-review/the-10-best-articles-on-refugees-and-migration-162017/.

[2] Interview with national border/coastguard authorities, 9 November 2016, Rome, Italy; interview with national border/coastguard authorities, 27 June 2017 via Skype.

interviewed take into account overcrowding of the vessels and lack of crew and navigation skills to determine the distress situation. In addition, in Italy the failure to comply with this obligation would be regarded as an offence.

In the Aegean there are no high seas between Turkish and Greek islands, thus SAR zones are overlapping, making it unclear whose responsibility it is to rescue refugees and other migrants. In addition to this, Greek national border and coastguard authorities apply a different interpretation of when people are considered to be 'in distress'.[3] According to another official, 'If the boat is capable of sailing, it does not need to be picked up, thus we can accompany them to the shore'.[4] Another interviewee explained that in order to be rescued by the Hellenic Coast Guard, the vessel needs to call for help or be at 'immediate risk' of sinking.[5] The national authorities interviewed in Greece complained that smugglers are instructing asylum-seekers and migrants to risk their lives and to jump from the vessels in order to be rescued.[6] According to interviewed CSOs, the very unclear line between Greece and Turkey and the very narrow interpretation in Greek law of 'persons at risk' translates into the Aegean continuing to be a deadly route, despite the comparably short distance to the Greek islands.[7] UNHCR statistics show that despite the very sharp decrease in overall arrivals in the Eastern Mediterranean, the rate of dead and missing per 1,000 persons actually increased after 2015 (see Figure 5.1 and Figure 5.2, blue trend line). In 2015

**Figure 5.1** Trends of arrivals of persons via Central and Eastern Mediterranean

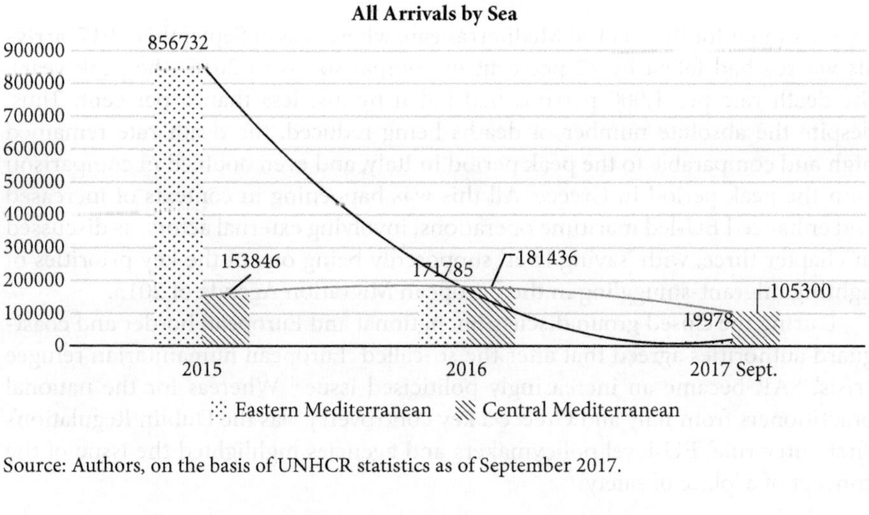


Source: Authors, on the basis of UNHCR statistics as of September 2017.

[3] Interview with national border/coastguard authorities, 9 June 2017, Lesvos island, Greece; interview with expert on border/coastguard authorities, 12 June 2017, Athens, Greece.

[4] Interview with national border/coastguard authorities, 6 June 2017, Athens, Greece.

[5] Interview with expert on border/coastguard authorities, 12 June 2017, Athens, Greece.

[6] Interview with national border/coastguard authorities, 6 June 2017 Athens, Greece; interview with national border/coastguard authorities, 9 June 2017, Lesvos island, Greece; interview with expert on border/coastguard authorities, 12 June 2017, Athens, Greece.

[7] Interviews with CSO providing legal assistance, 8 June 2017, Lesvos island, Greece.

(the peak year) in the Aegean, the death rate was only 0.9 per 1,000 persons; as of September 2017 it was 1.9 per 1,000 arrivals. Thus, we are presented with the conundrum that the death rate increased in the Aegean by 111 per cent in 2017 compared to 2015, whereas overall arrivals were reduced by 98 per cent.

**Figure 5.2** Trends of dead and missing per 1,000 arrivals of persons via Central and Eastern Mediterranean

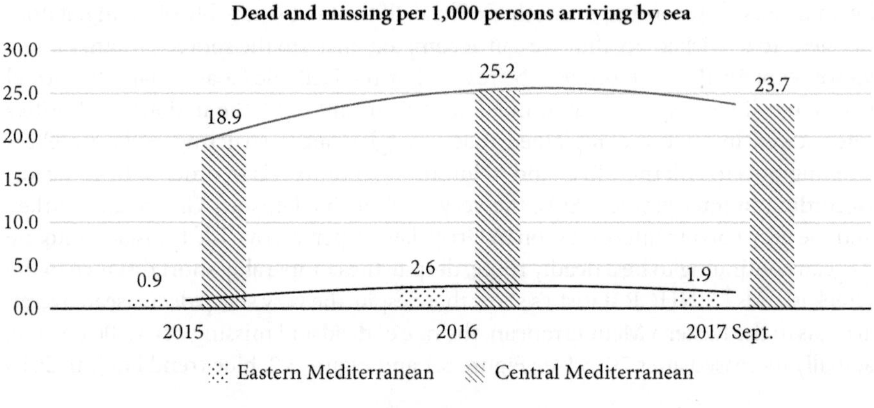


Source: Authors, on the basis of UNHCR statistics as of September 2017.

This is similar for the Central Mediterranean: whereas as of September 2017, arrivals via sea had fallen by 42 per cent in comparison with 2016 (the peak year), the death rate per 1,000 persons had fallen by just less than 6 per cent. Thus, despite the absolute number of deaths being reduced, the death rate remained high and comparable to the peak period in Italy, and even doubled in comparison with the peak period in Greece. All this was happening in contexts of increased and enhanced EU-led maritime operations, involving external actors, as discussed in chapter three, with 'saving lives' supposedly being one of the key priorities of fighting migrant-smuggling in the European Migration Agenda of 2015.

During the closed group discussion, national and European border and coastguard authorities agreed that after the so-called 'European humanitarian refugee crisis', SAR became an increasingly politicised issue.[8] Whereas for the national practitioners from Italy and Greece a key controversy was the Dublin Regulation's 'first entry rule', EU-level policymakers and agencies highlighted the issue of the concept of a 'place of safety'.[9]

[8] Closed-door discussion with EU and national actors representing coastguards, law enforcement and judiciary, 21 September 2017, Brussels.

[9] Closed-door discussion with EU and national actors representing coastguards, law enforcement and judiciary, 21 September 2017, Brussels.

## A. Italy: SAR in the Central Mediterranean Sea

In the Italian case, there are a number of actors involved in both SAR and anti-smuggling operations (see Annex 3, Figure A3.1). In light of amended Regulation 33 para 1 cl 1 of the Safety of Life at Sea Convention (SOLAS), the primary responsibility to ensure the disembarkation of rescued people stays with the state coordinating the SAR operation, namely the Italian Coast Guard. Italy is the state that must guarantee the disembarkation of the migrants rescued in the Central Mediterranean in a place of safety and similarly, and Greece for those rescued in its Aegean Sea waters. The exact points of disembarkation are decided at the strategic level by the National Coordination Centre (see Annex 3, Figure A3.1).

In the Central Mediterranean, none of the coastal states in the North African region can be deemed to be a 'safe place' for migrants, since they 'are currently either extremely reluctant or simply unwilling to properly host and process economic migrants and refugees from other parts of Africa who want to go to Europe' (European Commission 2017c). However, during interviews with EU agencies and some national officials, dissatisfaction was noted regarding the practice of systematically identifying Italy as a 'place of safety'.[10] One of the interviewees suggested that Tunisia or even Libya should be reconsidered as eligible places to disembark rescued migrants and refugees.[11] Nevertheless, the remaining Italian authorities interviewed were of the view that Italy should respect international laws and bring rescued people to Italian shores, and that the EU should better handle relocation schemes from Italy.[12] A discussant representing national border and coastguard authorities stressed that 'international and European cooperation and burden sharing are essential to manage the situation'.[13]

SAR at sea constitutes one of the main controversies in Italy regarding the effects of anti-smuggling policies on the impartiality and work of CSAs. The defining moment whereby civil society actors came to play an active role in the Central Mediterranean occurred during the transition between Operation Mare Nostrum (OMN) and the Frontex-led Joint Operation (JO) Triton. The end of OMN left an evident protection gap, which continued with the introduction of the Frontex Triton Operation, which in turn, as outlined in section I.B, was

[10] Preparation interview with EU agencies, 4 October 2016, via Skype; interview with EU agencies, 9 November 2016, Rome, Italy; interview with national border/coastguard authorities, 9 November 2016, Rome, Italy.

[11] Preparation interview with EU agencies, 4 October 2016, via Skype.

[12] Interview with national border/coastguard authorities, 8 November, 2016, Rome, Italy; interview with national border/coastguard authorities, 27 June 2017, via Skype.

[13] Closed-door discussion with EU and national actors representing coastguards, law enforcement and judiciary, 21 September 2017, Brussels.

never intended to replace OMN. OMN's operational area extended 400 nautical miles south of Lampedusa (Amnesty International 2014b), whereas JO Triton's operational zone was extended in July 2015 to 138 nautical miles south of Sicily. The operational zone for Operation Sophia meanwhile was 200 nautical miles from Sicily (European Commission 2017c). Thus, to close the gap, SAR NGOs entered the high seas closer to Libyan territorial waters. Nevertheless, this step remains challenging.

As of the beginning of July 2017, nine organisations (Jugend Rettet, Life Boat, Migrant Offshore Aid Station (MOAS), MSF, Proactiva Open Arms, Save the Children, Sea-Eye, Sea-Watch and SOS Méditerranée) with 13 vessels and one helicopter had entered the SAR humanitarian scene, which was previously the reserve of national and EU actors (Amnesty International 2017a). The contribution of CSAs to SAR was the cause of some unease among the national and EU officials interviewed for this research. During our Italy field trip in November 2016, national officials claimed that one specific CSO conducting SAR was said to be under investigation, as some of the volunteers involved in this CSO had an 'unclear past' and were therefore suspected of being 'smugglers'.[14]

Chapter three above explained how the mandate of EU agencies is increasingly focused on preventing and detecting cross-border crime and migrant-smuggling. One of the interviewees from a CSO conducting SAR in the Central Mediterranean explained that they aimed to cooperate closely with the Italian Coast Guard and to follow their orders because their common interest was saving lives at sea. However, misunderstandings arose when CSAs involved in SAR were asked to share information and pictures with Italian law enforcement authorities to help fight migrant-smuggling. Some CSA interviewees reported that they experienced this as a breach of their 'neutrality', which is a 'key principle' for the security of their operations. 'We are unwilling to be seen by smugglers as police officers, so as not to put our crew at risk', commented one CSO representative.[15] The respondent added that being conflated with police would deter migrants and asylum-seekers from coming forward with their health and protection needs.

Some organisations joined together under the umbrella group of Human Rights at Sea and developed, in February 2017, a Voluntary Code of Conduct for SAR Operations undertaken by civil society NGOs in the Mediterranean Sea. Among its guiding principles are the centrality of the principles of humanity, impartiality, neutrality and independence. It expressly states,

> The SAR operational aim is to save lives, not to focus on political comment, or undertake any other action that may void, or be perceived to void a neutral stance … NGOs SAR missions should act independently of governments, related military or any other

[14] Interview with national border/coastguard authorities, 9 November 2016, Rome, Italy; interview EU agencies, 9 November 2016, Rome, Italy.

[15] Interview with CSO conducting SAR, 10 November 2016, Rome, Italy.

> political ties, influences or pressures. No SAR NGO should be used or be allowed to be used as a political tool in order to serve other State and non-State actors' objectives which are not strictly humanitarian.[16]

The controversy surrounding SAR NGOs in the Mediterranean reached its peak with the December 2016 publication of an article in the UK's *Financial Times* (Robinson 2016), which brought to light a leaked confidential report by the EU border agency, Frontex.[17] The report raised concerns of possible interactions between SAR NGOs in the Central Mediterranean and smuggler groups operating in Libya. Rather than using the general term 'concerns' (as used in the official Frontex 2016 Annual Risk Assessment), a first version of the article referenced accusations of 'collusion' between NGOs and smugglers. The term was later employed by Carmelo Zuccaro, a prosecutor in Catania, who publicly accused CSAs of smuggling before national media (Albanese 2017).

In February 2017, Frontex made its concerns public in its Annual Risk Analysis report (Frontex 2017), justifying them in relation to the NGOs' proximity to Libyan waters and the increasing numbers of people rescued by NGOs monthly. The 2016 statistics illustrate, however, that Italian authorities rescued the greatest number of third-country nationals at sea (about 72,000 against the 46,000 rescued by NGO vessels). The labelling of SAR NGOs as a 'pull factor' for irregular immigration and smuggling networks diverted policymaking efforts to controlling the activities of CSAs at sea. The Frontex 2017 Risk Analysis report came with the implicit claim that gaining more control over SAR CSOs would reduce immigration flows from Libya.

The main result of these allegations was the adoption of an official code of conduct for SAR NGOs which the Italian government, supported by the EU, adopted on 31 July 2017. The code was not made public, and is reported to require separate negotiations with each organisation (see, eg, SOS Méditerranée 2017).[18]

Sea Watch publicly called the official code of conduct 'nonsensical, dishonest and illegal', and defiantly announced deployment of a second vessel (Sea Watch 2017). MSF, Save the Children and Sea Eye have consequently suspended their operations (Howden and Bode 2017), whereas the CSOMOAS signed the code but later announced that its vessel *Phoenix* would redeploy in Asia.

CSO interviewees were of the opinion that the code of conduct for NGOs sought to increasingly pass SAR responsibilities to the Libyan coastguard.[19]

[16] Human Rights at Sea (2017: 9).

[17] The leaked report is now available at www.documentcloud.org/documents/3531244-Frontex-Triton-Analytical-Report-December-2016.html.

[18] It is important to stress that this code is different from the Voluntary Code of Conduct developed by Human Rights at Sea.

[19] Follow-up interview with CSO conducting SAR, 3 July 2017, via Skype; follow-up interview with CSO conducting SAR, 22 August 2017, via Skype.

One CSO respondent expressed their fear that without NGOs being present at sea, more lives would be lost and asylum-seekers would not receive the necessary professional and specialised medical care and assistance. The same interviewee noted that even though the Catanian prosecutor had not charged any NGO with migrant-smuggling, 'the public defamation campaign was successful'.[20] For example, the accusations in the media also coincided with the period when Italian citizens decide on the charity to which to allocate a proportion of money from their tax returns. As a consequence of these developments, SAR CSOs reported a significant loss of financial support in Italy (though new donors joined from abroad, which helped to mitigate this existential threat). Moreover, an interviewee confirmed that organisations involved in SAR activities suffered attacks and threats on social media.[21]

Finally, SAR CSOs were the subject of explicit criminalisation. Prosecutors in Trapani opened a case against Jugend Rettet, a German organisation accused of migrant-smuggling and direct contact with smugglers (Dearden 2017b). Another case was opened against Nobel Peace Prize Nominee Mussie Zerai, an Eritrean priest, who helped to rescue thousands of individuals crossing the Mediterranean by transmitting their coordinates to the Maritime Rescue Coordination Centre (MRCC) in Rome. He is now under investigation in the Court of Trapani, on suspicion of abetting illegal immigration (Iqbal 2017). A CSA SAR volunteer interviewed in November 2016 mentioned that the priest and his supporters felt they were under suspicion for their activities; the Vatican lent them some protection.[22]

The shifting position of SAR NGOs from 2015 to 2017 shows how the policing modalities of i) suspicion/intimidation, (ii) disciplining and (iii) criminalisation were variably used by EU, statutory (including prosecutors) and private actors (including the media), with the effect of significantly reducing the presence of CSA at sea by 2017. Though it is beyond the scope of this chapter, we have also noted how CSAs engaged in SAR responded differently to these operational and existential threats. The next part of this chapter turns to the situation in Greece and the Aegean Sea, before turning to the situation on land at the Serbia-Hungarian border.

## B. Greece: SAR in the Aegean Sea

A key difference between the Aegean Sea and the Central Mediterranean is that there are no high seas between the Greek islands and Turkey. The operational SAR zones of Turkish and Greek authorities, namely the Hellenic Coast Guard, therefore overlap (see Figures 5.3 and 5.4). Interviewed national border and coastguard

[20] Follow-up interview with CSO conducting SAR, 3 July 2017, via Skype.
[21] Follow-up interview with CSO conducting SAR, 3 July 2017, via Skype.
[22] Interview with a non-formal group (volunteers and activists), 7 November 2016, in Rome, Italy.

**Figure 5.3** Helenic coastguard SAR zones

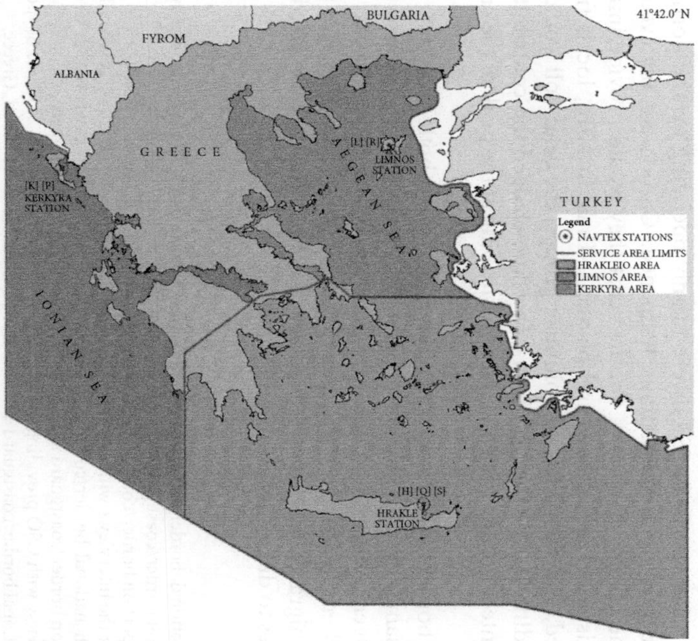


Source: Photo taken by authors during the interview in Athens, with interviewee's permission.

**Figure 5.4** Turkish coastguard SAR zone

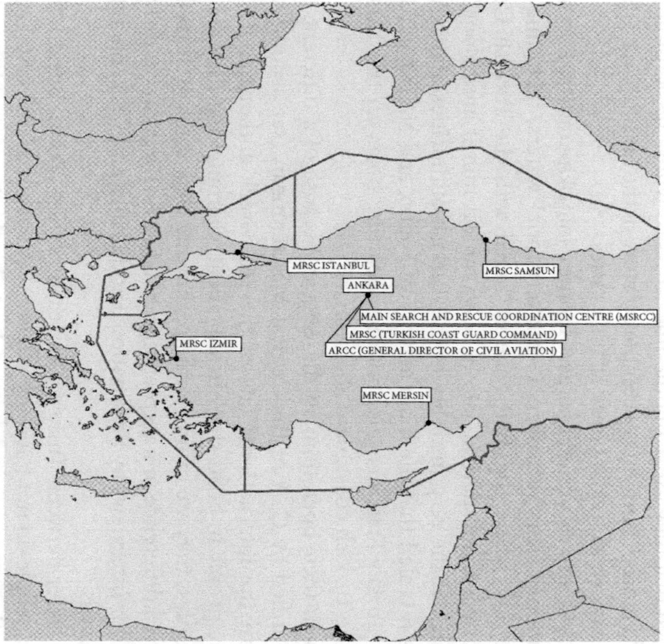


Source: Official website of Turkish Ministry of Transport, Maritime Affairs and Communications.[23]

[23] Turkish Ministry of Transport, Maritime Affairs and Communications, General Directorate of Marine and Inland Waters, Main Search and Rescue Co-ordination Centre (MSRCC), *SAR Co-operation Plan Between Search and Rescue Services and Passenger Ships, Annex B*, www.ubak.gov.tr/BLSM_WIYS/AAKKM/tr/Doc/Kurtarma.doc.

authorities explained that they use a 'middle-line' to assess whose responsibility is to rescue people.[24] Figure 5.3 provides a complex picture of the middle-line, whose distance from the eastern shores of Greek islands varies.

The Aegean Sea is also busier. The largest Frontex Joint Operation, Poseidon Sea, has an operational area that covers Greek territorial waters, including the 'above-the-middle line' where the SAR zone is shared with the Turkish Coast Guard. It does not cover the narrow (six or less nautical miles) area along the Turkish coast, which is the responsibility of the Turkish authorities and NATO (2016). Interviews revealed that the main activity of Fontex and NATO, particularly after the EU-Turkey Statement, is spotting departing boats on the Turkish side and alerting the Turkish coastguard about them.[25]

SAR CSAs began their operations in the Aegean because of a different type of gap to that identified by CSA in the Central Mediteranean (see section I.A). In accordance with the international law of the sea, Greek authorities do not 'proactively' rescue people in boats that are still afloat, claiming that they are not in need of rescue unless they are calling for help, showing clear signs of distress or are drowning. Such a difference in interpretation in Greece of 'persons in distress' was confirmed in our interviews by both national authorities and CSAs operating on the island of Lesvos.[26]

The stretch of water between Turkey and Lesvos is just 20 km, but dinghies can easily capsize; people do not have any safety measures, or as one CSO representive explained, they use toys and empty plastic bottles instead of life jackets and lifebuoys.[27] In Lesvos, SAR CSAs were mainly operating on the north of the island, where most disembarkations happened. CSAs were involved in patrolling both the sea and the coast. On the coast they would provide immediate medical assistance, dry clothes and blankets. Thus, in 2016, locals from Lesvos commented, 'If it wasn't for the volunteer groups, the death toll would be horrendous' (Wilding 2016). The Lesvos mayor acknowledged the contribution of CSOs and volunteer groups to saving lives and helping at the peak of the crisis (Wilding 2016).

The national border and coastguard authorities were both thankful and concerned at the same time. For example, one of the interviewees mentioned that NGOs and volunteers were using lights to signal the way for asylum-seekers in boats and direct them to Lesvos.[28] The same interviewee regarded this as 'a pull factor' for both migrants and their smugglers, therefore CSAs were asked by national authorities to discontinue this practice.

[24] Interview with national border/coast guard authorities, 9 June 2017, Lesvos island, Greece; interview with expert on border/coast guard authorities, 12 June 2017, Athens, Greece.

[25] Interview with expert on border/coastguard authorities, 12 June 2017, Athens, Greece.

[26] Confirmed during the interviews with CSO providing legal assistance, 8 June 2017, Lesvos island, Greece; interview with national border/coastguard authorities, 9 June 2017, Lesvos island, Greece; interview with expert on border/coastguard authorities, 12 June 2017, Athens, Greece.

[27] A follow-up interview with CSO providing social assistance in Lesvos, 14 July 2017, via Skype.

[28] Interview with national border/coastguard authorities, 9 June 2017, Lesvos island, Greece.

On the other hand, the national border/coastguard authorities regarded certain SAR CSAs, including the Hellenic Rescue Team and MOAS (active in the Aegean since 2014), as their 'trusted partners'.[29] However, MOAS was one among several CSAs that left SAR operations in the Aegean after a dramatic decrease in arrivals, following the entry into force of the EU-Turkey Statement. Interviewees from national border/coastguard authorities expressed dissatisfaction with some 'foreign NGOs' and initiatives run by activists or volunteers.[30] One of them pointed out the humanitarian implications of poorly monitored work, stressing that 'sloppy work at sea can do more harm than good'.[31]

In a similar move to the Italian case, discussed in section I.A above, the Hellenic Coast Guard, in cooperation with the International Maritime Rescue Federation (IMRF), introduced a vetting procedure for CSAs engaged in SAR activities in order to prove that they meet certain standards. As national border/coastguard authorities commented, NGOs had to coordinate with the Hellenic Coast Guard, so as not 'to duplicate the efforts in one area'.[32]

These efforts to control and police SAR CSAs through formal agreements were coupled with one clear case of formal criminalisation. Three PROEM-AID and two Team Humanity volunteers were accused by Mytilene's prosecutor's office of facilitating migrant-smuggling in January 2017. PROEM-AID is a Spanish organisation of professional firefighters and lifeguards; Team Humanity is a Danish humanitarian organisation. Thus the case again raises the issue of pan-European humanitarian mobilisation and foreign citizens being prosecuted under different interpretations of EU facilitation laws. Four of the five accused volunteers were made to pay €5,000 to be released on bail. The bail of the Team Humanity volunteer who was a captain of the vessel was set at a higher level (€10,000), and he was required to stay in Greece and report to a police station weekly (Safdar 2016).

The volunteers were accused by the Hellenic Coast Guard of migrant-smuggling after they towed a sinking boat to the Greek side, which allegedly was beyond the middle line and was therefore in a Turkish SAR zone. But the day the volunteers were arrested by the Hellenic Coast Guard they were not saving anyone:

> [A] military vessel [of the Hellenic Coast Guard] passed by too closely for comfort, sending waves crashing into the side of the small rescue boat [of Team Humanity]. 'Me and my crew were in shock, thinking, *Couldn't they see us?*' he [Aldeen, from Team Humanity] said. 'We had lights, and everything was clear'.[33]

Neither national authorities interviewed in June 2017 nor closed-door discussants from Greece were willing to comment on this case. One of the claims against the

[29] Interview with national border/coastguard authorities, 6 June 2017, Athens, Greece; interview with national border/coast guard authorities, 9 June 2017, Lesvos island, Greece.

[30] Interview with national border/coastguard authorities, 9 June 2017, Lesvos island, Greece; interview with expert on national border/coast guard authorities, 12 June 2017, Athens, Greece.

[31] Interview with national border/coastguard authorities, 9 June 2017, Lesvos island, Greece.

[32] Interview with national border/coastguard authorities, 9 June 2017, Lesvos island, Greece.

[33] Wilding (2016) (original emphasis).

volunteers was that they were found off the coast of Lesvos in possession of 'knives and an undeclared two-way radio' ('Volunteer lifeguards' 2016). CSAs interviewed in Greece, however, stated that knives are essential for SAR operations, for example for cutting ropes, leading to a perception that the authorities were clutching at straws in an attempt to 'criminalise' them.[34] One of interviewees noted that this formal criminalisation went together with disciplinary or intimidating measures, as police started to 'annoy' volunteers and activists, in particular foreigners, with identity checks, for example.[35] Media have also reported other cases of formal criminalisation, such as seven volunteers arrested in January 2017 'on suspicion of stealing lifejackets left behind by refugees' (The Local 2016). Similar experiences were shared during the focus group of CSAs which distinguished the difference in treatment of official well-established organisations and small groups of grass-roots activists.[36] It was also observed that the mood changed dramatically with the so-called EU-Turkey Statement:

> In recent months [as of May, 2016], a gradual hardening of the official attitude toward independent volunteers has become increasingly evident. Volunteers report that their efforts are now *routinely* met with *bureaucracy, suspicion*, and, in some cases, *prosecution.*[37]

One of the CSAs still operating in Greece in July 2017 explained during a follow-up interview that they were not doing SAR anymore, but rather were engaged in 'boat spotting' activities north of Lesvos.[38] According to this interviewee, the key safeguard for their operations is effective cooperation with the Hellenic Coast Guard. When the Hellenic Coast Guard rescues people, the organisation is authorised by them to assist persons with medical support or to bring them to Moria detention camp or to the local hospital, without risking the accusation of migrant-smuggling.[39] During the focus group it became apparent that cooperation with national authorities was seen as a 'safeguard' by some CSAs, and as an effort to 'control' them by others.[40]

While the involvement of CSOs in SAR has not reached the same level of media and political toxicity in Greece relative to the situation in Italy, interestingly, in Greece the Hellenic Coast Guard – not NGOs – was blamed by locals for bringing in the rescued migrants.[41] It was nevertheless apparent that EU agencies, particularly with the implementation of the EU-Turkey Statement, played a prominent role in and exhibited elements of the three modalities of policing those who move

[34] Interview with civil society organisation providing legal assistance, 6 June 2017, Athens, Greece; interview with civil society organisation providing legal assistance, 8 June 2017, Lesvos island, Greece.

[35] Interview with civil society organisation providing legal assistance, 8 June 2017, Lesvos island, Greece.

[36] Focus group with CSAs providing humanitarian assistance, 11 May 2017, Brussels, Belgium.

[37] Wilding (2016) (emphasis added).

[38] A follow-up interview with CSO in Lesvos, 14 July 2017, via Skype.

[39] A follow-up interview with CSO in Lesvos, 14 July 2017, via Skype.

[40] Focus group with CSAs providing humanitarian assistance, 11 May 2017, Brussels, Belgium.

[41] Interview with national border/coastguard authorities, 9 June 2017, Lesvos island, Greece.

and mobilise on behalf of migrants: i) suspicion/intimidation, (ii) disciplining and (iii) criminalisation.

## II. Land Borders and Humanitarian Assistance

Humanitarian assistance at the EU's external land borders seems, at first glance, a less complicated setting. Upon closer inspection, however, current research reveals that in the absence of land border international laws and norms comparable in clarity to International Maritime Law, it is even more difficult for humanitarian and human rights organisations to justify their contact with asylum-seekers or undocumented migrants. A plethora of academic research has raised the legal and practical issues of the enforceability of Article 30 of the Geneva Convention of 1951 (Bigo and Guild 2005; Guild and Minderhoud 2006) or Article 18 of the EU's Fundamental Rights Charter (Moreno Lax 2017). Thus asylum-seekers in this context are often treated and labelled as 'smuggled migrants'. EU law is clear that the Schengen Borders Code should not be applied to people crossing the border in an irregular manner to seek international protection (Carrera et al 2016b). Border procedures should also not hinder the obligation to provide shelter and food on the part of humanitarian organisations and various civil society actors in border contexts, in order to prevent the risk of destitution and hunger among refugees, asylum-seekers and undocumented migrants. While such humanitarian needs may not appear as imminent as the risk of drowning at sea, our research revealed that land borders also pose extremely grave and in some cases life-or-death situations of humanitarian need. This grey area and the margin of manoeuvre left to Member States by the EU's Facilitators Package have created very particular situations at the Hungary and UK borders.

### A. Hungary: Humanitarian Assistance at the Serbian Border

Since 2015, CSAs have played and continue to play a crucial role in the provision of humanitarian assistance to migrants and refugees seeking to enter or transit through Hungary via the Serbia-Hungarian border. While at the height of the European humanitarian refugee crisis in 2015, groups were operational on both sides of the border, since the erection of the anti-migrant border wall and the introduction of transit zones (see chapter 4.III), access to asylum-seekers on the Hungarian side has been heavily restricted, and most CSOs which have remained in the border area focus on assisting asylum-seekers who wait in camps on the Serbian side, where access is not guaranteed but is more readily available. Access to the refugee waiting camps on the Serbian border was easier for most CSOs, although some were very critical of the poor service provision, stressing that without the existence of humanitarian organisations, the residents would struggle to access basic needs such as clothing and hygiene products. The Red

Cross was a visible presence in a number of these camps, alongside informal activist groups.

CSAs were often the first and sometimes the sole actors responding to the scenes of humanitarian need which were widely reported in the summer of 2015 both before and after the construction of the border wall. This work was, and is, conducted by an expanding group of volunteers and professional service providers, many of whom came to work together for the first time – from reputed international NGOs, such as Médecins Sans Frontières, to grass-roots informal collectives and activist groups (both more political groups, and less explicitly political 'Refugees Welcome' groups) which sprung up in towns on both the Hungarian and Serbian sides of the border. As one Hungarian civil society actor put it in 2017:

> We are the only ones still doing any kind of work for these people. So there is practically nothing or bare minimum provided by the state and its institutions and authorities … If these organisations would shut down now these people would be left with nothing.[42]

It is beyond the scope of this research, but important to recognise that heightened attempts to stop people crossing the border – including disincentivising the presence of NGOs – coincided with a largely symbolic campaign internationally to deter migrants from coming even as far as the border. The Hungarian government placed advertisements in the Lebanese press in the summer of 2015, warning migrants and refugees of 'the strongest possible action' against anyone attempting to cross its borders illegally. 'Hungarians are hospitable, but the strongest possible action is taken against those who attempt to enter Hungary illegally', warned the adverts in publications *Al-Jumhuriya*, *An-Nahar* and French daily *L'Orient le Jour*. 'Do not listen to the people smugglers. Hungary will not allow illegal immigrants to cross its territory'. Hungary's advertisements in both Arabic and English came two weeks after Denmark placed similar adverts in Lebanese newspapers, in an attempt to stem the influx of asylum-seekers.

Specifically at the border, manifestations of the disciplining and intimidation of CSOs were primarily reported as taking the form of establishing physical distance between migrants and support groups. This primarily concerned the erection of the border fence and 'transit zone', but also the structure of the fence, which made it difficult for CSOs to provide assistance to those queuing for entry into the transit zones. With the erection of the fence, initially, a 'no man's land' was established between the Serbian and Hungarian sides, which made it hard for CSAs to provide assistance to those seeking entry into the newly established transit zones. From March 2016 to the winter of 2016 a significant informal camp of people seeking entry to the transit zones was established on the Serbian side. At the start of the erection of the wall and transit zones, there was no limit

[42] Interview with civil society organisation providing legal assistance in Hungary via Skype, 16 August 2017.

to the numbers coming in, but by 1 March 2016 Hungarian authorities stated they would only admit 50 people a day (see chapter 4.III). One month later the number was reduced to 30 and it continued to decrease through May 2016. In November 2017 it was reduced to 20. At the start of 2017 and until the time of the fieldwork it was 10.

One interviewee from an international organisation commented,

> The Hungarians who created this situation provided no help at all. There was no system at all as to who will have access, not by date of arrival or vulnerability. If you had muscles and you could fight your way to the revolving gate you could get through, other vulnerable people were left behind.[43]

Although since the winter of 2016, asylum-seekers seeking entry to Hungary have been mostly housed in a series of camps across Serbia, migrants at the border for many months were pushed back to conditions of squalor with limited statutory assistance on the Serbian side (Hungarian Helsinki Committee 2016). In April 2016, a census by the Hungarian Helsinki Committee revealed that approximately one-third of those waiting to access the transit zone in these conditions were children under 18 years old (Hungarian Helsinki Committee 2016). The report gave an impression of the poor humanitarian conditions:

> There are no toilets or any sanitary facilities in either area. Plastic bags with the UNHCR logo are strewn all over as remains of the food packages; even these can be put to further use though, by burning the bags to create a source of heat during the cold nights.[44]

UNHCR, along with Médecins sans Frontières (MSF) and volunteer groups, provided humanitarian relief to the migrants before they were able to lobby the Hungarian Office for Immigration and Nationality (OIN), which runs the transit zones and is in charge of asylum procedures in Hungary, to have the OIN distribute food packages each day. These packages were widely reported to be insufficient and distributed in a careless and inexpert way that provoked fighting. Meanwhile sanitation facilities were non-existent and then insufficient, with reports of people not showering for over 20 days. One report from the time documented the conditions:

> Women with children crowd under blankets as close as possible to the revolving entryway of the Tompa transit zone. Some people try to drink only small quantities of water so that they would not have to leave the queue even for a short period of time and lose their place. The HHC spoke to 3 Syrian families who were the closest to the revolving entrance and were expecting to be permitted entry the next day. When the HHC met these families in the open reception centre in Bicske on the following Wednesday, 27 April, the family said they were not granted access to the transit zone on Tuesday, the following day. So although they were the first in the queue, they still had to wait for 3 more days before being allowed access to the transit zone.[45]

[43] Interview with UN actor, 31 August 2017, Szeged, Hungary.
[44] Hungarian Helsinki Committee (2016: 2).
[45] Hungarian Helsinki Committee (2016).

Until the Serbian government responded with the establishment of nationwide camps where asylum-seekers were required to go in person to register their intent to apply for transfer to Hungary, thousands of asylum-seekers lived for months in squalid conditions at the border fence seeking entry into Hungary. The lack of provision of food and water was seen by some volunteers as a deliberate disciplinary tactic used to 'punish' the refugees and urge them to turn back. 'Without food or water and stuck in that no man's land it was in some ways inevitable that tensions would boil over', commented one interviewee. 'Women and children and elderly were starving.'[46] Several interviewees saw this deprivation of food and water as the spark that led to the so-called 'riot' on 16 September 2016 in which 10 migrants were arrested and one, Ahmed H, was charged with terrorism for protesting about the inhumane conditions.

Several CSAs interviewed for this research drew attention to this high-profile case, where anti-terrorism laws were inappropriately employed in an effort to deter irregular migration and silence opposition, in an explicit act of criminalisation. Following days of being stranded in the no-man's land between Hungary and Serbia, some refugees protested on 16 September. Ten asylum-seekers were arrested following the protest, including Ahmed H who was arrested on terrorism charges. In January 2017, Ahmed H was found guilty by the court in Szeged of using violence to force police into opening the border, considered an 'act of terror' under Hungarian law. He was also convicted of entering Hungary illegally. The 40-year-old is an EU resident of Cyprus, where he lives with his wife and children, and had the right to enter Hungary legally. He explained his actions as being in support of his elderly Syrian parents and relatives trying to seek sanctuary in Europe. His elderly parents were also arrested at the time for rioting. The ruling has been condemned by Amnesty International, among other international human rights watchdogs (Amnesty International 2017b) Again, the case demonstrates the intersection in the 'mobility society', between those who move and those who mobilise in support of migrants' rights.

### *i. Border Hunters and Hostility towards Migrants and the CSOs Helping Them*

At the time of fieldwork in 2016, 2,500 border hunters had been deployed at the Serbian-Hungarian border (see chapter 3.I.C). One CSO interviewee expressed concern about the recruitment of 'border hunters':

> Roughly 50 per cent of applicants failed the psychological or physical exam. The money seemed good but the conditions are awful – they have long shifts away from home. The weather is tough and it's pretty boring work, 12 hours a day on, off, on, off.

[46] Interview with non-formal group (activists) providing social assistance, 31 August 2017, Szeged, Hungary.

> On the Facebook page for recruitment people wrote comments like, 'Finally I can kill these intruders' and 'I can't wait to have a gun in my hand' and no one even moderated them.[47]

Several interviewees expressed concern that the escalation of police violence and hostility at the border and the lack of international scrutiny was having and would have a broader impact on social trust and democratic accountability in society as a whole. One member of a Hungarian CSO commented,

> In the past two years the general tone of the police in Hungary has changed. Also with citizens – their tone has changed. If they can beat up migrants without anything happening to them, with the entire body of Hungarian policy protecting them then they think they can do anything. They don't beat up ordinary citizens in Hungary, but the way they talk to you is horrifying … they are really rude, the tone is changing. This reminds me of communist Hungary. People were scared that the police had the power to do anything.[48]

An international organisation representative also expressed concern that the growing powers and militarisation of the police would have a broader effect on society:

> Violence at the border has become the law of the land especially since last summer. It's no longer the exception, it's the rule … Regardless of who is the target of such a hate campaign and smear campaign, it always hurts the social fabric. It's not rocket science to see the amount of hate that the government and the government sponsored media campaign have built up in last years, this whole image of Other and othering can easily turn against any other group in Hungary. It's a problem. If you look at question of violence at the border, the Hungarian police previously were not really known for its brutality. Every year there were a few exceptional cases but they were seen as exception.[49]

Of specific concern were the newly recruited 'border hunters':

> I wonder what is going to happen in few years' time. Those officers who have taken part in these acts of violence will go back to their original postings and communities where they will air or boast about it or lie about it and try to cope with what they have done on their own without the support of the police force. Will we see a normalisation of such violence beyond the border? How will they cope with that – it's a very serious issue which isn't even to do with migrants per se. These police officers [now at the border] will be the ones who stop me on the road or anyone else so that's very problematic … it has long-term consequences.[50]

This question of social trust is important to policing the mobility society. Generally, the presence of the Hungarian military at the border, which was granted new

[47] Interview with non-formal group (activists) providing social assistance, 31 August, Szeged, Hungary.

[48] Interview with non-formal group (activists) providing social assistance, 31 August, Szeged, Hungary.

[49] Interview with UN actor, 29 August, Budapest, Hungary.

[50] Interview with CSO providing legal assistance, 16 August, via Skype.

powers in 2015 (see chapters 3.I.C and 4.III), was seen to be less problematic by most of those interviewed since they were perceived to be more skilled and especially trained in working with foreigners. Interviewees said the army helped at the border with, among other functions, developing infrastructure, contributing heavy equipment and using its portable kitchens and containers to feed people in the transit zones.

### *ii. Lack of Access to Justice*

Some CSOs commented that the national police complaints mechanism is too slow (21 days). 'We no longer lodge complaints', one CSO commented, 'as it's not worth the ride'.[51] There were some reports of the Hungarian national authorities effectively responding to police complaints of violence. One CSO reported that out of 61 complaints reported by a consortium of CSOs, 11 investigations were ongoing. Two police officers had been fined, one for stepping on the face of a woman and another for kicking someone.[52] Both cases concerned criminal court fines sentenced through a normal criminal procedure. Huge barriers to justice remain, however, as migrants are often too scared to lodge claims for fear that it will affect their asylum application and prevent them from reuniting with families in Europe. Meanwhile, evidence is hard to obtain because the violence often happens off the record, video footage is often deleted and it is hard to prove it wasn't an 'accident'. One player explained the difficulties of taking such cases before justice and how the EU is failing to act on anti-migrant violence:

> We represent some people in criminal procedures against police but it's really hard to get a positive ending. We accompanied someone to hospital in Subotica to get a report of his broken skull but the thing is, people usually have their phones taken away so the moment they can first take a picture of themselves or have any kind of evidence is a few hours after the incident so they [the Hungarian police] are saying, 'Well, they got into a fight once we sent them back to Serbia'. It's hard to prove it is actually police. In this case we actually have a recording from the police as in some cases they actually record it, but the recording stops when they cross the border or before the beating. The investigation has gone on for ever … no one at the international level comes.[53]

Another formal monitoring mechanism that was widely reported to fall short in terms of offering transparency and accountability in relation to the border violence concerns the Ombudsman for the Convention against Torture (CAT). The appointment of the ombudsman was dismissed as a 'political appointment' by some CSOs and of limited use. One CSO reported,

> He won't do anything. He won't visit the transit zone, won't do anything about the riot which ended with 10 people charged with minor offences and one charged with

[51] Interview with CSO providing legal assistance, 28 August 2017, Budapest, Hungary.
[52] Interview with CSO providing legal assistance, 28 August 2017, Budapest, Hungary.
[53] Interview with lawyer, 31 August 2017, Szeged, Hungary.

> terrorism … He should visit all places of detention based on the optional protocol and CAT but he never goes.[54]

One civil society actor providing legal assistance commented that because NGOs' capacity and monitoring of work in relation to the borders and transit zones has been limited, the ombudsman – and also international monitoring bodies – are left with a poor evidence base on which to advocate. This lack of evidence was cited by CSOs as a deliberate consequence of the strategy of creating distance between asylum-seekers and NGOs pursued by the government at the border and within the transit zones.[55]

Meanwhile, the European Court of Human Rights continues to be an important though limited avenue to pursue cases of ill treatment of migrants and refugees around the border area. One current case concerns a person who died in the Tisa River and the allegation is that they were stoned by police.[56]

### *iii. Winter 2016 and New Camps in Serbia: 'The Lists', Smuggling and Possible Corruption*

Several CSAs commented on the important role played by the international media in drawing attention to the scene at the external Schengen border and putting pressure on the Hungarian government to allow aid to pass to the people there and for international organisations to step in and provide assistance. This makes recent restrictions on international and independent media in Hungary especially worrisome (see chapter 4.III). When conditions became unbearable in January 2017, people in the camps were moved to reception centres across Serbia. Interviewees for this research mostly saw the establishment of the camps across Serbia as a neutral move: it was obviously better than people being stranded next to the border seeking entry, but without more possibilities to legally enter Hungary it also did little to stop the smuggling.

Asylum-seekers were incentivised to stay in the camps by being told that only by registering in the camps would their names go on a 'waiting list' for access to the transit zones in Hungary. These transit zones were perceived as the gateway to the EU even among migrants who did not seek to stay in Hungary. The lists were the source of much concern on the part of all interviewees in Hungary and Serbia. As one international organisation commented, 'No one takes responsibility for the lists – it is a grey area.'[57] At one point, the lists were organised by community-appointed refugee community leaders; at other times in the course

[54] Interview with CSO providing legal assistance, 28 August 2017, Budapest, Hungary.

[55] Interview with CSO providing social assistance, 30 August 2017, Budapest, Hungary; focus group with CSAs providing humanitarian assistance, 11 May 2017, Brussels, Belgium.

[56] See for example the UNHCR's press release on the incident: www.unhcr-centraleurope.org/en/news/2016/unhcr-alarmed-at-refugee-death-on-hungary-serbia-border.html.

[57] Interview with UN actor, 31 August 2017, Szeged, Hungary.

of the research we were shown evidence of the involvement of Hungarian and Serbian camp leaders (which are run by Serbian National Immigration Authorities). While the actual mechanisms of how the list system operates and how individuals are chosen for transfer to the Hungarian transit zones from camps in Serbia remains opaque, it is clear that this lack of transparency leaves ample ground for possible corruption. Meanwhile, asylum-seekers' lack of faith in the list system means that many are turning instead to smugglers, who are readily available. Currently, the waiting time is estimated to be over a year for a family, and this is if the list system operates in a strictly chronological way, which it often does not appear to do in practice.

UN actors and representatives from international organisations also explained that they had sought to integrate criteria to identify especially vulnerable groups at the border, with limited success. We received several accounts of 'corruption' in relation to the lists, although none of these have been formally investigated. Several interviewees in Serbia reported the presence of smugglers outside and even inside the refugee camps.[58]

Several interviewees highlighted a notable lack of protection for victims of trafficking on the Serbian and Hungarian sides of the border. Although some interviewees from national and international organisations reported that vulnerable children were being 'fast-tracked' to the top of the list for entry into the transit zones, the way in which such 'fast-tracking' was operationalised was unclear. One story reported to us in the course of the field research concerned two unaccompanied minors who had been threatened by smugglers inside a waiting camp in Serbia. Fearing that the camp itself did not provide suitable protection for the boys (reported to be aged 10 and 11), a volunteer took them into their home and lobbied for them to be fast-tracked up the list. Through a process that is unclear, the boys were able to cross into Hungary legally the next day. It is unclear what protection they would receive on the Hungarian side and whether they would still be at risk from smugglers. Either way, the story highlights the lack of safeguarding and protection for unaccompanied minors in camps in Serbia who are awaiting entry into the transit zones.

As in the case of Calais, where a lack of coordination by authorities was believed to have led to chaotic rule and fears of corruption, some interviewees expressed concern that there was no clear authority in charge of the lists or rules according to which people were fast-tracked or positioned on the list and that there was a risk of smugglers infiltrating the process. UNHCR attempted to mitigate these effects by empowering refugee community leaders to fulfil this function themselves, although over the course of the fieldwork several cases were identified which were of concern in relation to unaccompanied minors being 'fast-tracked' up the list without scrutiny or any transparent process. In another reported case, a disabled

[58] Interview with national welfare authority providing social and medical assistance, 31 August 2017, Subotica, Serbia.

asylum-seeker was allowed access to the transit zone through the petitioning of an individual camp operator.

## *iv. Policing Access to CSOs on the Hungarian Side*

In Serbia, newly formed 'collectives' of individual volunteers and activists were able to operate without much interference and without formal registration, whereas on the Hungarian side of the border this was said to be possible but more difficult, since a range of new bureaucratic obstacles to registration were introduced for civil society from 2012 onwards. Without registering, it was impossible to get funds, and informal activist networks were wary of being targeted for illegally using funds. As such, for non-registered groups, all of their humanitarian actions had to be conducted via material donations. Volunteers were extremely wary of being seen to be involved in any exchange of money for fear of criminalisation. One volunteer explained that at the height of the border crisis in 2015, when thousands of asylum-seekers were coming through Szeged every day starving and in situations of dire humanitarian need, they had to turn down cash donations as a means to provide them with assistance time and time again for fear of getting into trouble with the government. Meanwhile, new criminal enterprises charged refugees extortionate fees for currency exchange.[59] 'We considered if we could help by providing some kind of free service but this would have just got us into trouble', said one CSO volunteer, 'perhaps some activists did it discretely, but I don't know'.[60]

The same volunteers were wary of being conflated with smugglers in public discourse and practice. Several times they sought to distance themselves physically from smugglers and had to 'self-police' heavily for fear of smugglers infiltrating their support groups. As one CSO volunteer put it, 'No one was aware of what the rules were, nothing was concrete. Not even the police knew what the rules were, but they were risk averse and erred on [the] side of caution'. This uncertainty was especially manifest in relation to the status of CSAs in assisting migrants upon entry and exit to Hungary.

On the Hungarian side, access to the transit zones was heavily policed with only formal members of the government-appointed 'Charity Council' granted access and funding to supply vital humanitarian services. Several long-standing and well-respected CSOs were banned from providing services in the transit zones even on a voluntary basis, including SOS Children's Village, Sirus Help and Cordelia Foundation, the last of which assists victims of torture. Several CSO interviewees and UN representatives expressed concern that without the expertise of these organisations, the level of humanitarian assistance provided in the camp

[59] Interview with non-formal group (activists) providing social assistance, 31 August 2017, Szeged, Hungary.

[60] Interview with non-formal group (activists) providing social assistance, 31 August 2017, Szeged, Hungary.

would be lacking. Several expressed the opinion that access to the transit zones and funding for services was being used as a policing and control tactic by the government.[61] 'Any organisation who criticises conditions will be denied access, as we were', commented one CSO interviewee.[62] This indeed appeared to be the case for several NGOs whose access was revoked following their issuing of public statements condemning conditions inside the transit camps.

The main policing tactic experienced by CSOs has been the reshaping and restructuring of civil society around groups with access and funding 'on the inside' and those denied access and funding 'on the outside'. Civil society in Hungary is composed of religious 'charitable' organisations and what are now known as 'internationally funded organisations'. In April 2017, the Hungarian Parliament adopted a draft law on NGOs which receive foreign funding. The draft law on NGOs was eventually passed in June (see chapter 4.III). Groups identified with 'foreign interests' were reported to include the Helsinki Committee, whose funding sources include the UNHCR and Open Society Foundation. Helsinki Committee lawyers had access to the transit zones drastically restricted and also reported more heavy policing within the transit zones. The fact that all documentation in the transit zones must be in Hungarian also poses an obstacle to legal assistance. Under new rules, asylum-seekers inside the transit zones must request in writing a visit by a named attorney. This must then be translated and sent – all of which takes time. The circulation of information is also policed through this language rule; bureaucratic delays are also a control tactic.

Whereas previously private lawyers were permitted to travel around the transit areas, they can now only meet with clients in particular containers and cannot inspect conditions themselves to collect evidence. Representatives from international organisations also commented on policing humanitarian workers in the transit zones, including bag searches and escorts.[63]

Some interviewed CSOs have been denied access to the transit zones altogether. Others suspect that those organisations who do have access are only allowed to maintain it on the condition that they remain silent regarding conditions inside the centres. A representative from a think tank close to the government stated that this was part of a deliberate strategy to keep civil society 'onside', based on best practices observed in Turkey. 'You can't just have organisations going around criticising the government without consequences', they commented.[64]

Civil society organisations present in the transit zones are part of the newly established Charity Council. This council includes five charities – all Christian in orientation, with the exception of the Hungarian Red Cross. Some interviewees expressed concern that religious organisations were being given priority for

[61] Interview with UN actor, 31 August 2017, Szeged, Hungary.

[62] Interview with CSO providing social and medical assistance, 30 August 2017, via Skype.

[63] Interview with UN actor, 31 August 2017, Szeged, Hungary; interview with lawyer, 31 August 2017, Szeged, Hungary.

[64] Interview with government-affiliated think tank, 30 August 2017, Budapest, Hungary.

government funding for services and access for political reasons, despite not having the requisite expertise in children's or migrants' rights.[65] Specific gaps in humanitarian provision which were repeatedly raised included services for children, pregnant women and survivors of torture.

## *v. Disciplining and Intimidation*

While previously in the transit zones independent (non-governmental) lawyers were able to move around more freely and visit the living quarters of their clients, their visits now take place in a separate container, to which they are escorted by a guard. This was reported to be intimidating, but also posed obstacles to conducting research on cases regarding poor living conditions. Bag checks were also seen as a tactic used to intimidate lawyers.

Several interviewees saw the physical layout of the transit zones as a form of disciplinary regime in itself. The transit zones are divided into sub-sections, dividing families, for example, and unaccompanied minors aged over 14 years. Residents are unable to move between these sections. This splitting of the camp poses a practical obstacle to access to services, because if a service provider visits one part of the camp they are not accessible via the other areas. This means that access to activities and healthcare can be restricted.

The very structure of the transit centre – floodlit and surrounded by barbed wire – serves as a physical manifestation of mistrust and fear.

Asylum-seekers within the transit centre experience this criminalisation. The monitoring role of UN organisations has played an important role in challenging certain disciplinary practices, such as the handcuffing of residents when leaving the transit zone to receive medical care. This practice was reported to have a direct impact on access to medical care, since individuals reported refusing to seek out medical assistance, even when urgent, because they did not want to undergo the humiliation of being handcuffed.[66]

Asylum appeals are conducted over video link, which restricts access to the outside world. Poor conditions in the transit zones as well as the long waiting times meant that many individuals – including the very vulnerable – chose to leave for Serbia. Some CSOs reported this as the individuals effectively being forced out.

There were no reports in our research of police being explicitly violent towards civil society volunteers, but there were several reported cases of disciplining or intimidation by both Hungarian and Serbian authorities. In Serbia, volunteer groups reported being warned to stay away from transiting migrants, although they suggested some lenience was shown during the winter when conditions were especially dire and, in the words of one volunteer, 'It would have been

[65] Interview with UN actor, 31 August 2017, Szeged, Hungary; interview with CSO providing social and medical assistance, 30 August 2017, via Skype.

[66] Interview with UN actor, 31 August 2017, Szeged, Hungary.

inconvenient to have a build-up of frozen bodies at the border'.[67] One volunteer active on both sides of the border reported being verbally threatened by police, explaining,

> Serbian police don't like me much – they were tolerant in winter time – they have power to shut us down, even though what we do is not illegal in any way. They made me come to police station the other day for two hours because they said my driving licence wasn't real – they know me on first-name terms and they knew it was real. I go to hospital with people. The only time I was ever personally threatened was by border police on Serbian side and one guy was quite nice other guy said, 'You would rather see a ghost than see me again on this border'. It seemed so nominal I didn't think to report it.[68]

On the Hungarian side, volunteers were also often repeatedly asked to show identification.

Policing and surveillance was reported to be the most prominent modality of criminalisation at the Hungary-Serbian border and took a range of forms which intersected and changed between 2015 and 2017. Before the erection of the fence, police were present surveilling the border area, although there was not the same sort of 'insecuritisation'. With the building of the fence, 'insecuritisation' rapidly increased and all manner of words, discourses and semantic drifts of suspicion were employed to justify the increased policing and militarism of the border. Enhanced policing measures included a new 'smart fence', police dogs and the deployment of Frontex officers (see chapter 3.I.C). At the border, CSAs reported other examples of increased policing of their work, including frequent searches of their vehicles and questioning when crossing the border.

## *vi. Civil Society and Violence against Migrants at the Border*

CSAs have played a particularly key role over the past two years at the Hungarian-Serbia border in monitoring, responding to and treating incidents of violence by border police, including through dressing wounds, providing first aid and taking victims of violence to hospitals. This has been in the absence of sufficient scrutiny from more national and international actors (see chapter 3.I.C). A significant feature reported by CSOs operating at the border was their role in responding to and recording incidents of police violence. Incidents of police violence have been recorded by a range of international, national and informal CSOs operating inside Hungary and Serbia. Incidents of such violence reported over the course of the research included the following:

— Beatings with fists and implements, leaving marks and wounds.

— Bites by police dogs, including upon children.

[67] Interview with non-formal group (activists) providing social assistance, 31 August 2017, Subotica, Serbia.

[68] Interview with non-formal group (activists) providing social assistance, 31 August 2017, Subotica, Serbia.

- Tactics of torture and humiliation, including taking people's shoes and clothes in the height of winter and requiring them to walk back across the border in the snow.
- Sexual violence.
- Islamophobic humiliation, including smearing asylum-seekers with pig's blood, forcing people to lie face first in the snow and walking dogs over their backs, and taunting them with bacon.

One civil society volunteer referred to some of the cases of violence she had seen as 'torture'.[69]

CSOs reported that perpetrators of the violence used a range of tactics to avoid attempts to pursue recourse to justice through legal avenues. This included officers not wearing identification numbers, violence taking place out of the way of cameras, and the short time for which the footage collected by CCTV at the border fence is held. The uniforms of the various actors present at the border were also reportedly hard to distinguish, meaning that victims were unable to identify the perpetrators of the violence as being military, police or vigilante groups.

Many asylum-seekers were unwilling to report violence to the police, for fear that it might affect their asylum claim and because of a lack of trust in the authorities. As one lawyer commented, 'Why would you report violence to someone from the same institution that beat you up in the first place?'[70]

Because of this mistrust, those subject to violence were also reluctant to seek out medical treatment. Numerous cases were reported where untrained volunteers were thus in the position of administering not just first aid but fundamental and life-saving care. As one volunteer put it, 'I came to take a photo and learnt how to disinfect a wound and dress dog bites'.[71]

As referenced in chapter 3.I.C, more than one interviewee from international organisations as well as national NGOs reported an impression that the presence of international forces, including Frontex officers and civil society groups, served to interrupt the violence and a protective function. NGO groups reported cases of violence directly against Frontex as well as the ombudsperson monitoring the Convention against Torture, and in both cases it was reported that the response had been minimal. This was in part because the investigations were conducted by the Hungarian authorities themselves, and because of the absence of possibilities for independent monitoring by civil society groups who were denied access to the border zones or monitoring of patrols. NGOs attempted to pursue both domestic and European accountability functions regarding human rights abuses suffered by migrants but with mixed success (see chapter 3.I.C).

[69] Interview with non-formal group (activists) providing social assistance, 31 August 2017, Subotica, Serbia.

[70] Interview with lawyer, 31 August 2017, Szeged, Hungary.

[71] Interview with non-formal group (activists) providing social assistance, 31 August, Szeged, Hungary.

### *vii. Criminalisation*

Disciplinary and policing measures were coupled with formal criminalisation of irregular border crossings from the start, but, in some ways in contrast to other contexts, in Hungary these tended to focus on migrants themselves, rather than civil society actors seeking to assist their crossing. The case of Ahmed H (see above) shows the importance of not drawing too thick a line between CSOs and migrants advocating for themselves since, in speaking out, Ahmed H could be seen as enacting advocacy as part of an unorganised group.

As mentioned above, activist and NGO groups at the border have not been subject to fines and penalties. That said, some volunteers and religious actors were fined at the Hungarian-Austrian border for transporting migrants. The Hungary campaign has focused much more on publicly shaming of CSOs and removing access and funding or making them conditional on compliance with non-disclosure rules.

### *viii. Impacts of Crackdown on CSOs at Hungarian-Serbia Border*

Several interviewees commented that pushbacks at the Serbia-Hungary border simply served to raise prices and redirect smuggling flows, leading asylum-seekers to use the services of smugglers to cross through Romania into Hungary. Meanwhile, at the time of fieldwork, informal groups were still trying to cross the border, staying in make-shift camps supported by residual volunteers. Although, as one activist lamented, 'It seems for most of the world the attention has shifted, conditions for these migrants remain dire'.[72] Recent reports by the Helsinki Committee draw attention to specific risks to children (Hungarian Helsinki Committee 2017a) and survivors of torture (Hungarian Helsinki Committee 2017a and Voynov et al 2017).

For those living near the border, the militarised fence impacted their living standards, contributing to unease and insecurity among society more broadly. This is, as we identify below, a key aspect of the policing of the mobility society (see chapter eight). One case reported in the research concerned a couple who had recently moved to Rozke, a village outside of Szeged, only to find their peace shattered by the erection of the border fence next to their house. The alarm and three-language warning would go off throughout the night, set off sometimes by animals. Police and military vehicles also reportedly caused disruption throughout the night during their patrols. A respondent reported that when the couple tried to launch a legal case for compensation on the grounds that they were unable to sell their house, the court ruled that contrary to the house being devalued, its value had actually increased, given its status as the most protected house in Hungary.[73]

[72] Interview with non-formal group (activists) providing social assistance, 31 August 2017, Subotica, Serbia.

[73] Interview with non-formal group (activists) providing social assistance, 31 August 2017, Szeged, Hungary.

## B. Humanitarian Assistance at the Calais Land/Sea Border

The northern border of France is the main European land/sea border and entry point for irregular migrants and asylum-seekers crossing into the UK from other parts of Europe. It also marks an external EU Schengen border with high levels of operational border control on both the UK and French sides, since the UK is not a party to the Schengen agreement on the free movement of people within the EU. The UK and Ireland, while both EU Member States, do not participate in the border and visa aspects of the Schengen agreement and continue to operate border controls with other EU Member States.

In this section, we refer to the northern France/UK border as a 'land/sea border', although we recognise that this term is problematic in several respects. The term 'land/sea border' is used in recognition of the fact that most irregular crossings and smuggling operations at the UK/France border take place through smuggling in private or haulage vehicles which board trains crossing the Channel Tunnel or via vehicles in ferries which cross the Channel.

The English Channel has been a historic site of controversy concerning migrant-smuggling between the two nations. Before the 'refugee crisis' sparked an increase in the population seeking to cross the border between 2015 and 2016, previous controversies arose following the building of the Channel Tunnel train service, which opened for service in 1994, and the creation of juxtaposed border controls. The tunnel is operated by rail and runs for 50.45 kilometres, linking Folkestone in Kent (UK) with Coquelles in the Pas-de-Calais region, near Calais (northern France).

Meanwhile, the sea route across the channel has long been a major shipping route for trade to and from the UK, as well as one used by passengers travelling for pleasure or business. Several private ferry companies regularly operate across this route between Calais and Dover, but also other routes such as between Cherbourg (France) and Portsmouth (UK). The channel is just 20.6 miles wide at its narrowest point between France and the Kent coast, but the crossing is extremely hazardous, with strong sea currents and huge cargo ships navigating the congested waters. Three main strategies are employed by migrants or asylum-seekers to reach the UK: (i) stowing away, (ii) false documents and (iii) boats.[74]

### *i. Specificities and the EU's Non-Intervention in Smuggling across the Land/Sea Border*

The situation at the UK-France border is distinct from the other three case studies in terms of the almost complete lack of operational support provided by EU Home Affairs actors over the course of 2015 and 2016 – this includes Frontex, which

[74] A significant proportion also enter the country via airports, although there is not sufficient space to discuss this phenomenon further in the scope of the section which focuses on the land/sea border.

had no operational presence at the border. Europol and Eurojust, meanwhile, support the UK and French national authorities in the investigation of relevant smuggling cases.[75] International organisations also play a limited operational role. At the time of fieldwork in 2017, UNHCR had one staff member in charge of the region, whose role was mainly coordination and monitoring. Occasionally, UNHCR has intervened in strategic litigation. Meanwhile, the International Organization for Migration (IOM) has offered its services to support Dublin III transfers, but at the time of fieldwork their role remained minimal and they had no presence.[76]

Instead of relying on the support of EU and international actors, France and the UK built on past experience of responding to build-ups of migrants in northern France seeking to cross irregularly into the UK, by adopting their own bilateral approaches to address smuggling over the sea border.

In the absence of external support, the French government continued a trend pre-dating the 2015 crisis, by deploying police units from across the country. At times, the UK government contributed directly both through the deployment of personnel and financial contributions. In 2015–16, the UK contributed an estimated £80 million in Calais to efforts to manage migratory pressures in northern France, £250,000 of which was for a specific anti-trafficking project, along with an additional £36 million to clear the Jungle camp and £2 million to build a wall (Safe Passage 2017). A recent report from the CSO Safe Passage comments,

> In contrast to the investment in securitizing the border, the Home Office seconded just one member of staff to France to process family reunion claims, though one-sixth of the people in the Jungle was a child trying to reach their family.[77]

In terms of staff deployment, the UK reportedly seconded just one Home Office official to process Dublin family reunion claims in northern France; and for a limited duration it deployed over 50 Home Office staff to assess the Dublin family reunion eligibility of some 1,900 children, who were redistributed from the Jungle camp to 70 specialist temporary French-run children's centres, following the camp's 2016 demolition.

Field research for this book revealed a common understanding that there has been a notable absence of effective law enforcement in northern France. Several trends were identified. First, in the absence of strong national or European law enforcement, private actors were increasingly required to take on the duties of border guards: for example, lorry drivers doing checks for stowaways and facing financial penalties if any were found.

[75] Interview with EU agencies/ official, 24 August 2017, The Hague, the Netherlands.

[76] Interview with UN actor, 22 August 2017, via Skype; interview with CSO providing social and legal assistance, 4 July 2017, London, UK.

[77] Safe Passage (2017: 3).

Secondly, civil society played a fundamental role in stepping up to protect migrants from the dire humanitarian conditions in the camps of northern France and in redirecting them away from smugglers towards one of a limited number of safe and legal pathways across the channel. To date, over 1,000 child refugees have been supported by CSOs in reuniting with families in the UK through their support in operationalising the Dublin III scheme or through the separate pathway (Dubs) established for unaccompanied minors following the Jungle's 2016 demolition. Immigration Act section 67 – known as the 'Dubs' amendment – was passed by the UK Parliament in May 2016. The amendment was spearheaded by Lord Alf Dubs, who himself had arrived in the UK as a refugee as one of 10,000 children brought over on the *Kindertransport*. The original intention of the amendment was to grant sanctuary to 3,000 of the 91,000 unaccompanied child refugees who arrived in Europe in 2015–16. In early 2017 the Home Office nevertheless announced that the number of children that would be transferred under the scheme would be 480, just 0.5 per cent of the total number of children to arrive in Europe.

At the time of fieldwork, only 200 children had been transferred under the scheme, all from France during the Calais 'demolition' process. Legal action has been taken against the government by the CSO Help Refugees, on the basis that local authorities were not properly consulted about the scheme, and offers of spaces went unaccounted for (Safe Passage 2017).

## *ii. Policing and National Actors*

Both the UK and French governments have invested substantial financial resources in securitising the Calais port and border. These have included the erection of a five-metre-tall border fence with barbed wire and security camera equipment. A fence has also been constructed along the motorway near the port. The UK government was reported to have invested £3 million in heartbeat and carbon dioxide detectors and dog searches for UK-bound lorries in France in addition to £7 million in a new 'control and command centre' and the deployment of 500 extra British and French police (BBC, 2016).

From 2014 onwards, there were reports of police using more extreme measures to control migrants trying to access lorries, including the use of tear gas and the deployment of more officers. In September 2014, Gilles Debove, the Calais area delegate for the French police union, reportedly explained that tear gas was being used to stop 'mass onslaughts' on vehicles about to cross the channel. 'The other day, two to three hundred migrants tried to get into a lorry park and we fired tear gas to scatter them because there are too few of us to control situations like this any other way', he was reported to have commented (Chazan, 2014).

While some CSOs have criticised the French and UK authorities for heavy policing in northern France, our research also showed another side to the story. Civil society interviewees had mixed reactions to the lack of external support. Some argued that the level of support and the notable absence of international actors, eg, Frontex, had led to a breakdown in order, which meant that they were unable to deliver vital humanitarian assistance in certain camps. As one CSO interviewee commented, 'In the absence of the rule of law, under the smugglers, the law of the jungle really did prevail.'[78] CSOs were split over whether more police was the solution to this disorder. The more politically activist groups tended to be on one side (not wishing for a greater presence of the authorities in northern France, for fear that they might target, rather than protect, the work of CSAs and the migrants). More established NGOs, meanwhile, tended to be on the other side (they felt that greater police or even Frontex presence could help them to restore order in the camps and deliver their vital humanitarian functions). There was a consensus among interviewed international actors and CSOs in Calais that the UK government's financial investment in the French side had often been unsuccessful, including their attempts to fund anti-trafficking initiatives remotely.[79]

### *iii. Private Actors*

We saw in section II.A that at the Hungarian-Serbian border, in the absence of a significant force of EU actors like those present at the Greek-Italian sea border, the Hungarian government recruited new forces and the military to control the situation. In contrast to these two different approaches, at the northern France border, UK and French anti-smuggling operations' primary strategy was to co-opt private companies into border control policing. Fence-building and securitisation similar to that of the Hungarian border was, as mentioned above, a secondary strategy.

As stated above, the English Channel is key to business into and out of the UK and as such, a range of private actors operate at the border. These actors have faced what one representative of a private company called 'a double yoke' in the context of the fight against migrant-smuggling at the border. Firstly, they are affected by the operations of smugglers; secondly, they are required to participate in anti-smuggling operations and face significant penalties for failing to effectively conduct these additional duties (see chapter 4.IV).

It is clear from the above that private actors are required to play an important role in anti-smuggling operations at the France-UK land/sea border. Several representatives of CSOs and international organisations interviewed for this research saw this as part of a broader trend of devolving the powers of border guards to private, everyday actors on the part of the UK government (see chapter 4.IV). Some saw this trend as motivated by resource restrictions while others saw it as a more ideological move linked to the creation of a 'hostile environment' for irregular migrants (see chapters 4.IV and 7.IV).

[78] Interview with CSO providing social assistance, 5 July 2017, via Skype.

[79] Interview with CSO providing social and legal assistance, 4 July 2017, London, UK; interview with UN actor, 22 August 2017, via Skype.

## *iv. Cooperation between National Government and Private Companies*

Key private actors involved at the border include Eurotunnel, haulage companies and ferry companies. The British government has taken some measures to try to bolster anti-smuggling infrastructure; however, in our fieldwork, these efforts were widely reported to be insufficient. Private actors have called for more French police, the deployment of military to support security, better procedures to assess asylum claims in France to avoid people seeking to arrive across the channel, and other measures.[80]

One interviewee explained that private companies have called for the French military to be involved in policing anti-smuggling in the region. There was a perception among some private actors that just the visible presence of soldiers might act as a deterrent. Responses to the legal penalties faced by private companies including haulage vehicles are discussed in chapter 4.IV, but it should be noted here that among some private actors, the location of the border in France under the Le Touquet treaty was seen as part of the problem, since British authorities had limited sovereign authority to act. The same interviewee, working for a professional body representing the private sector, commented,

> What British authorities tend to say is 'We sympathise with what you're saying … we know it's happening, however we're not the French police or government. This is France and they must be in charge of their own borders and policing' … The absolute starting point is that you can't deploy British police to police in France.[81]

Private actors were also vocal in calling for the dismantling of the Jungle camp in Calais. One interviewee nevertheless expressed dismay at the lack of alternatives, following the camp's dismantlement in 2015:

> You need to tackle the underlying cause of the problem. They did dismantle it but without assigning a new place. What we've seen since is the dispersal, not so much big camps, although there is one sizable camp. Instead, people traffickers disperse along the main approach to the road to Calais and that's where we're now seeing new road blocks and attempts to slow traffic down as people seek to gain access to lorries.[82]

In June 2017, a van driver was killed when he crashed into a tailback on a motorway near Calais, where UK-bound migrants had blocked the road with tree trunks to slow lorries down.[83]

In summary, in the context of northern France, the UK and France adopted their own bilateral approach. There was evidence of CSOs working closely with the authorities to create safe and legal routes for child migrants, however there was also evidence that this relationship of collaboration became more strained when

[80] Interview with professional body representing the private sector, 11 July 2017, via Skype.
[81] Interview with professional body representing the private sector, 11 July 2017, via Skype.
[82] Interview with professional body representing the private sector, 11 July 2017, via Skype.
[83] www.telegraph.co.uk/news/2017/06/20/van-driver-dies-migrants-block-calais-road-tree-trunks/.

CSOs resorted to strategic litigation to force authorities to act more quickly and with more resources. As in other border sites, such as Ventimiglia, there were also reportedly some tensions among CSAs operating in Calais in terms of those that were willing to work with the authorities and those that were not; and concerning the strategic prioritisation of children and what the fates would be of adult migrants in Calais following the demolition of the Jungle camp.

Significantly, in comparison to other case studies in this volume, despite the well-documented humanitarian catastrophe unfolding – with poor camp conditions, insufficient state capacity and migrants frequently dying trying to reach Europe through smuggling – there was a very notable absence of EU actors. As one CSO participant in our focus group put it, 'In Calais both the French and the UK put politics over people'. The UK government did not comply with resettlement quotas, but rather upon demolition of the main Jungle camp in Calais it introduced its own criteria for resettling a small number of unaccompanied minors. The role of international organisations in Calais has also been small. While IOM leant its support to facilitating some of the transfers of unaccompanied minors, UNHCR and IOM were also criticised for not doing more sooner to improve the squalid camp conditions.

## *v. Collaboration between CSOs and National Authorities*

The solutions proposed by some CSOs overlap with those suggested by private actors to solve the humanitarian situation in northern France. Efforts by CSOs focused primarily on providing humanitarian assistance to migrants in refugee camps in the Calais region, but also, importantly, on seeking to dissuade people from crossing by giving them access to legal channels to seek sanctuary in the UK from France. No kind of 'hotspot' resettlement system was in place. Instead, what emerged was a system that one UN actor described as 'picking the lowest lying legal fruit'[84] – supporting those entitled to family reunification under the Dublin III procedure to reunite with family members in the UK through legal processes in France (see above).

Four of the children who died trying to cross alone into the UK in 2015 had a legal right to cross the channel and be reunited with their family members, yet chose to employ the services of smugglers instead, or take risks themselves, because of the Dublin III system not being operational in practice or because of a lack of trust in the system and delays in the system. 'We knew that making the broken system work would put smugglers out of business and save lives', said one CSO interviewee.[85]

As well as providing life-saving humanitarian aid, CSOs thus played an important strategic role in making legal routes operational in practice – working for the most part alongside authorities and police.

[84] Interview with UN actor, 17 August 2017, via Skype.

[85] Interview with CSO providing social and legal assistance, 4 July 2017, London, UK.

Some tensions between these two roles – as a humanitarian provider and operational aid working with the authorities – nevertheless emerged. One CSO involved in lobbying the government to improve Dublin III procedures commented that their relations with authorities began to break down once they pursued legal action against the UK and French governments.[86]

In view of the imminent dismantling of the Jungle camp, a July 2016 census conducted by the British NGO Help Refugees recorded the camp population in Calais to be 7,307 migrants, of which 761 were minors. The population reportedly reached some 10,000 after the UK voted to leave the EU in June 2016, because of rumours around the camp that the border would be closed (*The Economist*, 2016). At the same time as CSOs sought to improve Dublin III transfers, CSOs thus wrought a parallel campaign to resettle other vulnerable unaccompanied minors in the camp in the UK, in a deal reminiscent of the one stuck after the closure of the former Sangatte refugee camp in northern France.

The 2016 border 'crisis' between England and France echoes a smaller-scale but equally politically fraught episode which took place in the late 1990s when informal refugee camps began emerging in and around Calais. In 1999, the Red Cross opened a refugee camp with the approval of the French government to provide humanitarian assistance to migrants there. The camp was located in a warehouse in Sangatte, around half a mile from the entry of the Channel Tunnel. Originally intended for 600 people, by 2002 it was said to house some 2,000. Conditions were documented as being poor.

Then French Minister of Home Affairs, Nicolas Sarkozy, announced the definitive closure of the camp at Sangatte on 30 December 2002,[87] in exchange for a promise from the British government to accept 1,000 Kurdish refugees and some 250 Afghans, who would all receive a work permit for three months. This deal would satisfy 80 per cent of the refugees and migrants lodging in Sangatte at that time. The remaining 300–400 would receive a residence permit in France. In 2016, the UK and French applied a similar logic in responding to the demolition of the Jungle camp by agreeing to 'split' the population of unaccompanied minors between the two countries. This move took place under the pressure of a coalition of CSOs on both sides of the channel.

Eventually, the UK (which did not comply with EU resettlement quotas) thus introduced its own bilateral criteria for resettling unaccompanied minors from the camp. CSO interviewees were critical of the government's 'poor management of this process which led to hundreds of minors arriving at the last minute without beds to sleep in.'[88]

At the time of fieldwork, 950 children had been transferred to the UK with the support of CSOs: 750 through expedited Dublin procedures and 200 through the separate (Dubs) agreement which followed mainly the demolition of the Jungle

[86] Interview with CSO providing social and legal assistance, 4 July 2017, London, UK.
[87] https://en.wikipedia.org/wiki/Nicolas_Sarkozy.
[88] Interview with national welfare authorities providing social assistance, 6 July 2017, London, UK.

camp. Importantly, following the operations in France, CSOs are rolling out their collaboration with government authorities to speed up Dublin III transfers for vulnerable children to other parts of the EU, including Greece and Italy.[89]

UK efforts to resettle children from Calais to the UK were framed by UK CSOs as a modern-day *Kindertransport*, which sought to honour Europe's past tradition and learn from mistakes. Lord Alf Dubs, a former *Kindertransport* refugee himself and former British Member of Parliament lent his own name to the Bill seeking to facilitate the safe passage to more unaccompanied minors from Europe to Britain. As Heidi Allen, the Conservative MP who tabled the amendment, stressed in Parliament, the amendment was not just about helping child refugees, but also about the principle of 'European solidarity' (Allsopp 2017b).

The idea that providing safe and legal resettlement routes for asylum-seeking children in the EU was a 'pull factor' was nevertheless soon raised by other UK politicians (Jackson 2017). Partly in response to political pressure, the UK government shut down the so-called 'Dubs scheme' in 2017 and refused to work with NGOs to provide 'safe and legal routes' for unaccompanied minors from Calais to come to the UK, on the grounds that it constituted a 'pull factor'. Opposition MP Yvette Cooper, Chair of the UK's Home Affairs Select Committee, explicitly stressed that far from stopping a 'pull factor' for irregular migration, in abandoning the scheme the government was reopening a market for traffickers and smugglers to transport children illegally from Calais to the UK. Referring to the then ongoing parliamentary inquiry into the issue, she insisted on the need to listen to and work with NGOs on the ground:

> There is a big gap between what the government has said, and the evidence we heard from local councils and from organisations like Unicef who are working with child refugees. This is too important to get wrong when children's lives and futures are at risk … Ministers have said that they need to end the Dubs scheme in order to prevent trafficking, but Save the Children and others have said this will make child trafficking, abuse and exploitation worse.[90]

Some CSOs suggested in the course of this research that in increasing their scrutiny of NGOs, certain government and EU actors were trying to distract attention away from policy failures and find a common 'scapegoat'. Common critiques levelled in this regard include that: i) EU and statutory actors lack standards for effective policy delivery; ii) statutory actors have no standardised frameworks for measuring the effectiveness of their policies; and iii) that there is therefore a lack of evidence regarding the impacts of policies and standards being met (see Allsopp 2017a for more on this).

CSOs, like governments, have different ideas about what makes 'effective' policy and what these minimum standards should be. In a radio debate on the BBC's Moral Maze, a representative of an NGO working to operationalise

[89] http://safepassage.org.uk.
[90] Jackson (2017).

Dublin III's family reunion provisions in Calais challenged that with four children having died between 2015 and 2017 trying to cross to the UK illegally (all of whom had a full right to lawful family reunion), and thousands more perishing in the Mediterranean, the obligation to evidence the claimed humanitarian justification for deterrence ('pull factor') is both extremely heavy and unmet.[91] In his words, 'In our logic, no child should die to deter others from coming'. This position was echoed by submissions from UNICEF UK, Save the Children and the International Rescue Committee to the aforementioned UK Home Affairs Select Committee Inquiry into the Situation of Unaccompanied Minors in Europe (UK House of Lords 2016).

### *vi. Effects on Civil Society Actors Providing Humanitarian Assistance in Calais*

A number of challenges of policing, disciplining and intimidation, and criminalisation were reported in terms of the provision of humanitarian assistance in northern France. CSAs were a mix of French and British civil society organisations and informal activist groups who mobilised in response to the crisis. As noted in chapter three, the role of EU actors and the international community was minimal at the Calais border.

Legal challenges brought by French CSAs resulted in court orders that forced the French authorities to ensure the provision of water points, showers, one hot meal a day, toilets and rubbish collection via contracted agencies in the Jungle camp in Calais. In addition, the Centre Jules Ferry, run by La Vie Active, was established by the state to provide secure shelter and limited services to mothers with young children – normally between 200 and 400 people at any one point. In the main camp, meanwhile, CSAs provided the bulk of direct humanitarian assistance, particularly the distribution of tents and sleeping bags, shelter-building programmes, and the distribution of food and clothing. There was an informal women and children's centre and a community theatre, while the only legal advice services available in the Jungle were all provided by CSAs.

Both British and French states were clear that, since the development of services and access to legal pathways from Calais was seen as likely to constitute a pull factor to the area and result in increased migrant presence (see chapter 4.IV), their principal policy objective was the dispersal of people from the Calais area and the maintenance of the border's integrity. One CSO worker commented, however, that of more concern was the 'push factor' driving refugees to the UK:

> There was an issue of trust with the French authorities … if someone chooses to stay in France they have to go via the authorities and if your only experience of being in France

[91] Interview with a representative of a civil society organisation providing legal assistance in Calais, France, 4 July 2017.

> is being in Calais and being pepper sprayed every single night and chased by the police, well the kids don't know the system and police violence deters the kids from staying in France.[92]

CSAs were in agreement in the focus group that push factors were rarely discussed but were as crucial to the anti-smuggling debate as any potential 'pull factor'.

It was reported that the division of responsibilities between the different French authorities was unclear to both migrants and CSAs. Indeed, one CSO reported,

> In July 2016 we took these lists with the names and details of about 400 unaccompanied children to the French authorities all over Calais – the Prefecture, the police, the mayor, the public prosecutor, just trying to get them to receive the data because under French law when alerted to the presence of an unaccompanied child public agencies become responsible for protecting them. Well, barely a single agency would receive the lists, we were practically thrown out of the police station who agreed to take the list 'informally' only, no receipt was given, no officers would give their names or confirm any formal process had been initiated. It was unbelievable that they would refuse to receive intelligence about unaccompanied children in their jurisdiction.[93]

The lack of clear allocation of responsibilities among public authorities was a major barrier to CSO effectiveness. Meanwhile, as at the Serbian-Hungarian border, CSAs reported that efforts to monitor and pursue challenge to cases of abuse by public authorities and police violence were hindered by ambiguity over the roles of these organisations and indeed their personnel. 'Often the police would hide their numbers or wouldn't give you their names', commented one CSO representative.[94]

Prior to the destruction of the main Jungle camp in Calais in October 2016, CSAs reported significant levels of policing of their operations, with regulations brought into effect to prevent hot food distribution and the arbitrary closure of key access points, along with low-level disciplining and intimidation through the deployment of large numbers of heavily armed French officers whom CSAs reported behaving in an intimidating and unaccountable fashion.[95]

Another major role played by CSAs at the French-UK border, as they did at the Serbian-Hungarian border, was in providing medical assistance, including for major injuries. One CSO interviewee explained,

> Theoretically there is a clinic that serves refugees, but realistically we're seeing very poor access to healthcare. The clinic is really limited in what it can do, they don't have capacity to do more and they don't have transport provision between the clinic and the hospital so the refugees are left to get themselves there.[96]

[92] Interview with CSO providing social assistance, 5 July 2017, via Skype.
[93] Interview with CSO providing social and legal assistance, 4 July, London, UK.
[94] Interview with CSO providing social assistance, 5 July 2017, via Skype.
[95] Interview with CSO providing social assistance, 5 July 2017, via Skype; interview with CSO providing social and legal assistance, 4 July 2017, London, UK; interview with UN actor, 17 August 2017, via Skype.
[96] Interview with CSO providing social assistance, 5 July 2017, via Skype.

A volunteer who had taken a migrant in this position to hospital after he had suffered a facial fracture (allegedly caused by a strike from a police baton) reported that she feared that the act of taking the migrant in her car could be a criminal offence. Similarly, a CSO reported that having secured successful Take Charge Requests to see 14 minors transferred from Calais to Britain to be reunited with their family, those 14 minors were left in the Jungle for over 10 weeks. The CSO had undertaken legal casework in France and Britain to secure the transfers and yet, as they described,

> The only part of the process the states actually want to be in charge of is the physical transfer. That one job, and they left those kids waiting there 10 weeks. So we wrote to them, saying if they didn't do the transfers within the next week or two, that we ourselves would put the kids on the train. We were told this would be illegal and we would be stopped.[97]

A representative from the IOM reported that it had offered to facilitate this transfer process and was still in discussions with the government.[98] Meanwhile, IOM was contracted to facilitate transfers to the UK from Greece under the Dublin III Regulation.

A key concern for CSAs was ambiguity over the idea of 'facilitation' (see also chapter 4.IV). A UK NGO which went to Calais to give workshops, to make migrants aware of the legal situation in the UK, was confused as to whether their work could be thus considered. An interviewee from the CSO commented,

> There's a lot of confusion over anti-smuggling and how it intersects with aid and activism, people seem to think the whole facilitation of entry rule doesn't apply if there's no profit but it's all up in the air. There's a real confusion, many are over-cautious.[99]

The organisation had to seek legal advice prior to their workshops, but even then the lawyers consulted reportedly gave differing opinions.

A final barrier concerning the provision of humanitarian assistance in northern France concerned the actual lack of police enforcement in some areas. One UK CSO operation providing legal and social support in Calais reported,

> We were unable to operate in Dunkirk, we couldn't give the kids legal advice on how to reunite with their families in Britain using the EU Dublin III provisions because the camp was so heavily organised by traffickers that we'd be beaten up, as would any children we spoke to. We had to work through a complicated network of intermediaries to get even basic advice to the children.[100]

Another UK-based NGO providing legal advice commented,

> The Refugee Info Bus in Dunkirk was run with an iron grip by the smugglers. MSF was trying to get in there too – the smugglers represented a physical danger to service

[97] Interview with CSO providing social and legal assistance, 4 July 2017, London, UK.
[98] Interview with UN actor, 22 August 2017, via Skype.
[99] Interview with CSO providing social assistance, 11 July 2017, London, UK.
[100] Interview with CSO providing social and legal assistance, 4 July 2017, London, UK.

> providers. The police had no control and were disinterested. Everyone knew who the smugglers were, but there's no data gathering – the smugglers were left to it.[101]

It's clear that in northern France some CSAs managed to work with state authorities, principally where they acted as agents of the state providing court-mandated services. However, other CSAs seeking to expand humanitarian provision or to open legal pathways for transfer from northern France to Britain faced a full range of barriers, from low-level harassment and intimidation, to policing efforts principally organised through controlling access and distribution within the camp, criminalisation and fear, and ultimately failure to uphold even basic conditions of the rule of law necessary for CSAs' activities to be conducted with a bare minimum of physical safety for those involved.

[101] Interview with CSO providing social assistance, 11 July 2017, London, UK.

# 6

# Humanitarian Assistance in the Context of the EU Hotspots Approach

The main EU operational efforts in the Mediterranean Sea have mainly focused on preventing and reducing cross-border criminality and countering migrant-smuggling from North Africa and Turkey. This has come with a similar focus at points of entry or disembarkation through the implementation of what has come to be known as the 'hotspots approach' in Italy and Greece. Hotspots mark the second stage of a migrant journey – upon arrival, and in the context of Italy and Greece – upon disembarkation. EU Home Affairs agencies are present in new 'Migration Management Support Teams'. These carry out border control and identification (screening) tasks, but their focus is heavily concentrated on fighting migrant-smuggling and in identifying smugglers among those disembarked.

Until recently, the hotspots were not based on any formal EU legal act or piece of legislation, but came in the form of a Commission communication. Their existence and implementation therefore took place in a legal vacuum with profound accountability challenges. The European Commission explained in Annex 2 of its Communication on 'Managing the refugee crisis: immediate operational, budgetary and legal measures under the European Agenda on Migration' that 'hotspot' should be understood simultaneously an area, approach and operational framework. Specifically, it stated,

> A 'hotspot' is an *area* at the external border that is confronted with disproportionate migratory pressure … The approach is an operational concept to maximise the added value of this support through *Migration Management Support Teams*. This is an *operational framework* for the Agencies to concentrate their support on the spot where it is most needed, to coordinate their interventions and to cooperate closely with the authorities of the host Member State.[1]

In Italy, there are publicly available Standard Operational Procedures (SOPs) applicable to Italian hotspots (Italian Ministry of the Interior 2016). Interviewees representing national authorities, EU agencies and UN actors have referred to this document as the main tool clarifying the mandates of each actor involved.

[1] European Commission (2015: 2) (emphasis added).

However, a similar SOP does not seem to exist in the five Greek islands (Samos, Chios, Kos, Lesvos and Leros), besides the Joint Action Plan for Implementation of the EU-Turkey Statement (European Commission 2016c). Field research conducted in Greece revealed that EU agencies have changed their roles in the hotspots after the entry into force of the EU-Turkey Statement in March 2016 (Council of the EU 2016). According to CSOs operating in Lesvos, EASO representatives were tasked with supporting national authorities to speed up asylum procedures and identifying persons eligible for returns to Turkey in accordance with the 'one for one approach'.[2] Meanwhile, UNHCR's role shifted from managing the reception of asylum-seekers to being tasked with supporting conditions at closed detention centres.

The EU Regional Task Forces (EURTF) in Catania, Italy and Piraeus, Greece were established as part of the hotspot approach. Initially, they were seen as 'joint operational headquarters with representatives of all three agencies [Frontex, Europol and EASO]' (European Commission 2015: 2). Eurojust is engaged in the activities relating to anti-smuggling, however, it is not physically present in the hotspots or permanently present in the regional taskforce. In the case of Italy, EUNAVFOR Sophia is represented at the EURTF. In addition, our field research highlighted that in each of the five Greek islands there are Turkish and DG Home Affairs representatives tasked with overseeing the implementation of the EU-Turkey Statement.

Thus, one of the main effects of 'the EU hotspots approach' has been the focus on 'identification' and fingerprinting of irregular immigrants and asylum-seekers, but also the investigation (information gathering and exchange) by EU and domestic law enforcement authorities to find smugglers among the disembarked. Hotspots are operational in Italy and Greece with some important variations in actors and practice, outlined in chapter three above.

## I. Italy: Hotspots in Southern Sicily

Every third-country national who is rescued at sea and brought to Italian territory should be taken to a hotspot and registered there. As of September 2017, there were four hotspots in Italy (Lampedusa, Pozzalo, Taranto and Trapani). In the first Progress Report on Relocation, the European Commission (2016) called for a 100 per cent identification rate. The implementation of this rule has been difficult in practice, with some arrivals not passing through the allocated hotspots. Among those who enter via the hotspots, 97 per cent are fingerprinted (European Court of Auditors 2017). Previously this figure was 60 per cent (Amnesty International 2016).

[2] Interview with CSO providing legal assistance, 6 June 2017, Athens, Greece; interview with CSO providing legal assistance, 8 June 2017, Lesvos island, Greece.

Hotspots are 'closed' detention facilities. Thus CSOs (beyond those INGOs formally participating in their implementation, such as UNHCR, IOM and some medical organisations) have difficulties gaining access. Our research revealed that CSAs need to request a permit directly from the Italian Ministry of Interior, which can be refused at any time on security or other grounds. When the authors of this chapter requested such permission before relevant Italian authorities, for example, it was denied on the basis that our presence would obstruct work at the hotspots, and we were asked to contact them again in December or June, when there are almost no arrivals. Restrictions of access limit to a very large degree the accountability of what is happening in the hotspots. This was also often mentioned as an obstacle by the online survey respondents.

Officially, persons should be placed in hotspots only for identification and registration for up to 72 hours, and minors should not stay there at all. In practice, our Italy fieldwork confirmed cases of people staying for two weeks and also of minors overstaying the time limits.[3] Another interviewee was critical of the living conditions, pointing to examples of men, women and minors sharing rooms with limited access to toilets and bathrooms.[4] An interviewee from a social and legal CSO explained that adults are not allowed to go out, though minors can. Because they are denied access to provide services inside the hotspot in Pozzalo, their organisation's operations are restricted to meeting and assisting the minors outside the hotspot.[5]

The field visit to Italy coincided with the publication of an Amnesty International (2016) report on forced fingerprinting practices in the hotspots. This caused a media scandal (eg, Nielsen 2016) and was one of the central issues addressed during interviews. An interview with a medical CSO[6] as well as interviews with UN actors[7] confirmed the self-silencing or censoring effect of including some CSAs in the logic of hotspots. Despite widespread support for the Amnesty report findings, none of the CSOs and UN agencies working in the hotspots wanted to speak about this issue. A national authority representative interviewed for this research meanwhile called the Amnesty International report 'a collection of lies', adding 'that none of organisations working with us have witnessed anything like that'.[8]

[3] Interview with CSO providing medical assistance, 8 November, 2016, Rome, Italy; interview with CSO providing social assistance, 9 November 2016, Rome, Italy; interview with CSO providing social and legal assistance, 11 November 2016, Catania, Italy; interview with non-formal group/activists, 11 November 2016, Catania, Italy; interview with CSO/volunteers providing medical assistance, 12 November 2016, Syracuse, Italy.

[4] Interview with non-formal group/activists, 11 November 2016, Catania, Italy.

[5] Interview with CSO providing social and legal assistance, 11 November 2016, Catania, Italy.

[6] Interview with CSO providing medical assistance, 8 November 2016, Rome, Italy.

[7] Interview with UN actor, 9 November 2016, Rome, Italy; interview with UN actor, 10 November 2016, Catania, Italy; interview with UN actor, 11 November 2016, Catania, Italy.

[8] Interview with national border/coastguard authorities, 8 November 2016, Rome, Italy.

Interviewees from several CSAs not directly involved in the implementation of hotspots confirmed the report's findings, having heard from their clients about malpractice in hotspots during identification and fingerprinting, and also of cases of police and Italian authorities using physical and psychological violence as a tactic to force fingerprinting.[9] One CSA interviewee cited the practice of promising something to the migrants in exchange for them giving their fingerprints.[10]

The dependency of the CSAs on government permission to access hotspots, and for many their dependency on government funding for their activities, constitutes a disincentive to 'speak out' about injustices or humanitarian concerns. Our interview experience confirmed a hesitancy to discuss hotspot conditions, even among UN actors such as IOM and UNHCR. This situation can be understood as a disciplinary modality of policing: a way of imposing constraining circumstances which limit what civil society and UN actors can do and say.

## II. Greece: Hotspot in Lesvos Island

During our field research in Lesvos, several negative accounts were provided regarding the effects of anti-smuggling policies on the work of CSAs, with negative effects reportedly increasing pursuant to the introduction of the EU-Turkey Statement and its accompanying hotspots. Open reception camps in five Greek islands were turned into de facto detention facilities.[11]

According to interviewees with EU agencies and UN actors, 'geographical limitation' became a new criterion for the readmission of irregular immigrants and asylum-seekers to Turkey: only individuals from the islands, but not from mainland Greece, could be 'readmitted' in light of the statement.[12] Turkish authorities accepted to rapidly return all migrants who irregularly crossed from Turkey to the Greek islands and did not apply for asylum there. Asylum-seekers whose applications were found to be unfounded or inadmissible also fall under the return scheme established by the EU-Turkey Statement (European Commission 2016b; European Commission 2017). UNHCR and well-established UN actors and CSAs initially sought to challenge the decision (Middle East Eye 2016). Yet while they were finally 'convinced', as one EU agency representative put it, to continue cooperation in the detention camps,[13] many CSAs left the camps or the island

[9] Interview with CSO providing social assistance, 9 November 2016, Rome, Italy; interview with CSO providing social and legal assistance, 11 November 2016, Catania, Italy; interview with non-formal group/activists, 11 November 2016, Catania, Italy; interview with CSO/volunteers providing medical assistance, 12 November 2016, Syracuse, Italy.

[10] Interview with CSO providing social and legal assistance, 11 November 2016, Catania, Italy.

[11] Interview with CSO providing legal assistance, 8 June 2017, Lesvos island, Greece.

[12] Interview with the UN actor (a), 9 June 2017, Lesvos island, Greece; interview with the UN actor (b), 9 June 2017, Lesvos island, Greece; interview with the EU agency/official, 8 June 2017, Lesvos island, Greece.

[13] Interview with the EU agency/official, 9 June 2017, Lesvos island, Greece.

altogether, in disagreement with the legality and morality of the deal and in fear of being 'instrumentalised'.[14] The EU-Turkey Statement had the effect, in the words of one focus group participant, of 'dividing civil society groups' into those willing to work with the deal and those unwilling to compromise.[15]

As of June 2017, the European Commission's DG European Civil Protection and Humanitarian Aid Operations (ECHO) funding for civil society via UNHCR was also ending. The main message from national authorities in Greece to humanitarian CSAs thus seemed to be: 'Thank you for your help, your job is done.'[16] ECHO funding was replaced with DG Home Affairs funding. This effectively meant that many of the services provided by CSAs were taken over by local municipalities. Our fieldwork revealed concerns about their readiness to pick up this work without the support of CSAs. An interviewee representing one of the UN actors in Lesvos reported concerns, for example, about the sanitary and hygiene services at the Moria detention camp following the transition.[17] Laundry, cleaning and waste removal were previously organised by local and foreign CSAs; after the local municipality took over the responsibility, at the time of the interview, the toilets had not been cleaned for two weeks, rubbish had not been removed from the camp and people had no clean clothes.[18] Similarly, as of 23 October 2017, 109 civil society organisations started to demand that people be removed from the Greek islands which had been turned into closed detention camps. According to the Open the Islands campaign (2017), the outrage started when '[s]ix people who were seeking refuge and protection in Europe died in Moria last winter, their deaths linked to inhumane winter living conditions. Their families are still waiting for answers from the authorities as to how and why their relatives died, and for those who are responsible to be held accountable'.

Civil society organisations and UN agencies interviewed were critical of the conditions in the camps and at the time of our field trip, levels of frustration were rising.[19] According to one of the UN actors, asylum-seekers were spending up to 25 days in Moria, whereas they are supposed to be there only up to 72 hours.[20]

The EU-Turkey Statement reportedly led to confusion among migrants about who could be 'trusted' and led to protests and attacks on the EASO and UNHCR – two organisations whose mandate is to serve and protect refugees

[14] Interview with CSO providing legal assistance, 6 June 2017, Athens, Greece; interview with CSO providing legal assistance, 8 June 2017, Lesvos island, Greece; a follow-up interview with CSO providing social assistance in Lesvos, 14 July 2017, via Skype.

[15] Focus group with CSAs providing humanitarian assistance, 11 May 2017, Brussels, Belgium.

[16] Interview with CSO providing legal assistance, 8 June 2017, Lesvos island, Greece.

[17] Interview with the UN actor (b), 9 June 2017, Lesvos island, Greece.

[18] Interview with the UN actor (b), 9 June 2017, Lesvos island, Greece.

[19] Interview with the UN actor (a), 9 June 2017, Lesvos island, Greece; interview with the UN actor (b), 9 June 2017, Lesvos island, Greece; interview with CSO providing legal assistance, 8 June 2017, Lesvos island, Greece.

[20] Interview with the UN actor (b), 9 June 2017, Lesvos island, Greece.

and asylum-seekers.[21] On the other hand, according to several interviewees, law enforcement authorities, including Frontex and Hellenic Coast Guard, were 'respected' by asylum-seekers and migrants, for being open about their mandate and what they do.[22] This development is indicative of the importance of keeping the mandates clear. Maintaining trust with clients is vital for the efficiency and safety of the work of CSAs.

For example, UNHCR (2017) publicly declared that 'from 1 January until 5 September 2017, the total recorded contributions for Greece amount to 202.9 million USD'. Of that amount, $200.3 million came from the European Commission's DG Home and DG ECHO. In light of the lack of preparations for winter in Kara Tepe camp, the UNHCR received some public criticism for becoming overly dependent on the European Commission's funding:

> It must be an international record to depend so highly on a single donor, making this a very politicized response and UNHCR the operational arm of the EU's shortsighted policies. Reliance on any single donor is considered bad practice among humanitarians, because it ties their action to the politics of the donor, stripping it of its independence.[23]

Interviewees from national border/coastguard authorities and EU officials claimed that many CSAs left due to dramatically decreased arrivals following the EU-Turkey Statement and thus it was only logical to cut the funds available.[24] In June 2017, 20 to 70 people arrived daily. Interviewees from CSAs and UN actors nevertheless provided a more nuanced picture of the reduced role of NGO and state authorities' willingness to take control of activities, citing episodes of increasing suspicion, intimidation and disciplining, in particular of foreign NGOs.[25]

The policing of CSAs in Greece manifested directly as an obligation to register, and indirectly to be 'coordinated'. Respondents to the online survey representing CSAs providing legal assistance indicated 'prohibitive requirements for the registration of NGOs' in a context lacking information on how to do so, in particular due to language constraints for non-Greek speakers. An interviewee representing a CSO in Lesvos explained the need to register both individual volunteers and organisations.[26] A survey respondent explained, 'If these requirements of

[21] Interview with CSO providing legal assistance, 8 June 2017, Lesvos island, Greece.

[22] Interview with national border/coast guard authorities, 9 June 2017, Lesvos island, Greece; interview with CSO providing legal assistance, 8 June 2017, Lesvos island, Greece.

[23] Rantsiou (2017).

[24] Interview with EU agency/official, 8 June 2017, Lesvos island, Greece; interview with national border/coastguard authorities, 9 June 2017, Lesvos island, Greece; interview with EU agency/official, 9 June 2017, Lesvos island, Greece.

[25] Interview with CSO providing legal assistance, 6 June 2017, Athens, Greece; interview with CSO providing legal assistance, 8 June 2017, Lesvos island, Greece; interview with the UN actor (a), 9 June 2017, Lesvos island, Greece; interview with the UN actor (b), 9 June 2017, Lesvos island, Greece; a follow-up interview with CSO in Lesvos, Greece, 14 July 2017, via Skype.

[26] Interview with CSO providing legal assistance, 8 June 2017, Lesvos island, Greece.

registration were not met, the NGO and volunteers would be acting in violation of the [Greek] law and policies requiring registration'. An interviewee from a CSO reported the intimidation experienced by activists squatting in Lesvos who, though often known to be EU citizens, were frequently asked about their migration status by police.[27] These bureaucratic measures and controlling tactics were perceived as an obstacle for the provision of humanitarian assistance.

According one EU agency, all the NGOs working in Lesvos were expected to attend coordination meetings organised by UNHCR.[28] All the actors interviewed, from UN and EU agencies to national authorities and CSAs, repeated the mantra about the 'importance to avoid overlaps and to be coordinated with other actors'. Whereas better coordination sounds a very well-intended and legitimate public policy aim, some of the CSAs attending these meetings saw such coordination as an 'upper hand'.[29]

An interviewee from an EU agency mentioned that they were also attending such meetings and gathering information about the number and activities of different NGOs and activists.[30] A statutory actor meanwhile expressed a similar need to monitor the work of CSAs, stressing that 'there are NGOs and "NGOs"!'[31] In this context, official calls for coordination emerged as a subtle form of policing civil society.

CSOs acknowledged cases of activists in disagreement with EU policies, doing what they felt to be humanitarian and morally right in helping migrants to leave the island in order to reach their family members in another EU Member State.[32]

In the hotspots, many CSOs, volunteers and UN actors thus came to work alongside national and EU authorities and increased monitoring of the law enforcement work. Meanwhile, several interviewees representing CSOs explained that they had been arbitrarily denied access at hotspot gates after witnessing and reporting mistreatment of migrants and refugees by the law enforcement authorities.[33] These CSOs felt 'unwelcomed to the camps', or even 'not allowed to enter camps on "security" concerns'.

Cases of intimidation also took place beyond the camps. One CSO interviewee claimed they were intimidated by the local police while having dinner in a café: 'They took me out and threatened me'.[34] Another CSO interviewee said

[27] Interview with CSO providing legal assistance, 8 June 2017, Lesvos island, Greece.
[28] Interview with EU agency/official, 8 June 2017, Lesvos island, Greece.
[29] Interview with CSO providing legal assistance, 8 June 2017, Lesvos island, Greece.
[30] Interview with EU agency/official, 8 June 2017, Lesvos island, Greece.
[31] Interview with national border/coastguard authorities, 9 June 2017, Lesvos island, Greece.
[32] Interview with CSO providing legal assistance, 6 June 2017 Athens, Greece; interview with CSO providing legal assistance, 8 June 2017, Lesvos island, Greece.
[33] Interview with CSO providing social assistance, 7 June 2017, Athens, Greece; interview with CSO providing legal assistance, 6 June 2017, Athens, Greece Interview with CSO providing legal assistance, of June 2017, Lesvos island, Greece.
[34] Interview with CSO providing social assistance, 7 June 2017 Athens, Greece.

that they were taken into police custody pursuant to an attempt to report police mistreatment cases.[35] The same interviewee mentioned that they were threatened with a financial audit alongside being subject to heightened scrutiny and the outright cutting of access to the hotspots (thus losing contact with their clients). Their efforts to alert the UN actors were said to be even more counterproductive, due to overly close links between local law enforcement, EU agencies and international organisations.

As in Italy, then, in Greece the dependency of CSAs on government permission to access hotspots, and limitations related to funding, posed a barrier to humanitarian interventions and advocacy on behalf of migrants and asylum-seekers. Other modalities of policing included intimidation and disciplinary measures, though no cases of outright criminalisation of CSAs were reported in relation to the hotspots.

[35] Interview with CSO providing legal assistance, 8 June 2017, Lesvos island, Greece.

# 7

# The Effects of Countering Facilitation of Residence: Access to Services and Rights

## I. Italy: Cases of Rome and Ventimiglia

CSAs in Rome reported that the policing of their work aiding migrants and asylum-seekers transiting through or residing in Italy had evolved significantly, from a climate of tolerance to one of more hostility, from 2015 to 2017. At the beginning of the so-called 'European humanitarian refugee crisis', CSAs interviewed in Rome reported that they had been largely left to their own devices. One volunteer from Baobab Experience, a CSO composed of volunteers who provided shelter and food to some 55,000 irregular migrants and asylum-seekers between summer 2015 and spring 2016, explained, 'The police and the authorities pretended we weren't there … [they were] happy for us to do it, and that [the migrants] would basically move on and not be Italy's problem'.[1] Their work, the interviewee explained, was perceived to decrease the pressure on the municipality, which was unable to accommodate the growing number of asylum-seekers coming up from the south. In the initial period, police and immigration authorities even referred asylum-seekers to the Baobob Experience centre.[2] Moreover, the group received strong support from the local community and local, national and international press, which served a 'protective' function.[3]

CSAs in Rome reported that the policing of their operations became more acute with the evolving debate over SAR operations and with the establishment of hotspots in the south per the EU-Turkey Statement. One CSA interviewee reported that this pressure was perceived to come from 'above' – at the EU level – rather than below – at the level of the local community, which was more supportive.[4] Other interviewees pointed out a direct link between crackdowns on

[1] Interview with CSA (volunteers) providing social assistance, 31 January 2017, Rome, Italy.

[2] Follow-up interview with CSA providing social assistance (volunteers) in Rome, 23 September 2017, via Skype.

[3] Interview with CSA providing social assistance (volunteers), 31 January 2017, Rome, Italy.

[4] Interview with CSA providing social assistance (volunteers), 31 January 2017, Rome, Italy.

their operations and terrorist incidents in Europe. Following the Bataclan terror attack in Paris on 13 November 2015, for example, Baobab Experience was raided by police, and migrants without identification were rounded up in riot vans to be fingerprinted (Giannoli and Lucente 2015). This demonstrates that the work of CSAs is impacted not just by the anti-smuggling agenda but by a broader set of securitisation and anti-terrorism priorities which often justifies the involvement of a wide range of EU Home Affairs agencies (see chapter three above). This sentiment also echoes the analysis of Ticktin and Feldman (2010) on the nexus of humanitarian governance and security. The visible raids were reported to undermine social trust among some sectors of the population, and parts of the media became more hostile (see also Allsopp 2017a).[5]

Other policing measures reported in our research included the posting of riot vans and police cars near migrant support operations, and volunteers being frequently asked to present their identification. Meanwhile, formal criminalisation measures included the issuing of penalties and fines for the offence of 'occupation of public land' (*occupazione di suolo publico*) following the erection of tents and in one case relating to a plastic gazebo to provide shelter from the rain following the closure of the Baobab Experience centre by the Rome municipality on 6 December 2015. The centre currently operates in an abandoned car park. They frequently move the location of their camp at the request of the police, and occupations have been met with tear gas; escalating police violence is also reported (Camilli 2017). Baobob Experience has sought to protect itself from dissolution by maintaining an active media presence and public profile and by registering as a legal entity. One representative interviewed in the research explained this as a means to secure funding (including from EU sources) to protect its ongoing existence as well as an element of legal protection.[6]

This policing of the mobility society in Rome has come with humanitarian risks, the same interviewee explained: 'Where the collective is prevented from providing these services, the migrants either end up in the street or are forced to turn back to smugglers for assistance … bringing it into the public sphere is a form of protection'. They thus make a clear differentiation between their work and that of 'smugglers'.

One of the observations reported by CSAs in Italy was that the more political mobilisation is associated with the humanitarian assistance provided to migrants, the more authorities police and seek to discipline a group's operations. The experiences of solidarity activists providing food and shelter to irregular migrants and refugees in Ventimiglia demonstrate this link between political mobilisation and policing. While the media has largely treated Baobab through the lens of charity (see, eg, Ruetenik 2016), in Ventimiglia, the provision of assistance to irregular

[5] Interview with CSA providing social assistance (volunteers), 31 January 2017, Rome, Italy; follow-up interview with CSA providing social assistance (volunteers) in Rome, 23 September 2017, via Skype.

[6] Interview with CSO providing social assistance (volunteers), 31 January 2017, Rome, Italy.

migrants was always highly politicised.[7] The presence of various self-identified 'No Borders' groups from across Europe was, one CSA interviewee argued, 'used as a justification for a more general crackdown on humanitarian work', including similar tactics to those observed in Rome (posting of riot vans and police around the camp and service delivery stations, dispersals of camps, identification checks etc).[8] The media also reported on the new levels of policing and violence, including the confiscation of food and medicines, and incidences of sexual violence allegedly committed against activists (Gulia 2017).

One interviewee who had volunteered in Ventimiglia understood the need for activist groups and more informal camps as a direct response to the breakdown of trust between migrants and more formalised NGOs: 'Because of the policing and militarisation of the [formalised NGO-run] camp', they commented, 'some migrants were put off using the NGO services'.[9] The dismantling of one of the informal camps, the Balzi Rossi camp, in September 2015, at the time host to some 150 migrants and supporters, included 12 riot vans and some 250 officers from Italy's various police branches. Arrests followed clashes between activists and police. Surrounded by police in riot gear, some migrants facing identification and return to the hotspots of the south reportedly resorted to throwing themselves from the rocks in an attempt to swim away via the sea (Gulia 2017).

On 3 July 2015, a Ventimiglia mayor's office ordinance banned the provision of food to irregular migrants without authorisation under penalty of a €200 fine. On 10 August 2015, a French organisation was stopped and held by the police for breaking this ordinance. In another incident, a volunteer explained they had a cooking stove confiscated: 'We bought huge pots of steaming rice and stew and were handing it to the migrants and the police came and it was like we were smuggling Kalashnikovs not rice!'[10]

As in Rome, the offence of occupying public ground was used to discipline the work of some CSAs. Some volunteers and activists were also formally criminalised through the issuing of papers banning them from the area (over 60 *foglio di via* were reportedly issued in one year, encompassing various distances). Individuals were fined and occasionally arrested for physically blocking tent evictions and identifications, and several individuals were stopped when accompanying migrants on a train or at a train station and arrested for the crime of facilitating irregular entry and stay (Gulia 2017).

While the support of the local community was deemed to be an important asset in shielding the work of Baobab Experience from harassment and intimidation, solidarity activists in Ventimiglia reported that the lack of such local (and especially local media) support left them more exposed. One volunteer explained

[7] Interview with non-formal group (activists) in Ventimiglia, 20 February 2017, via Skype.
[8] Interview with non-formal group (activists) in Ventimiglia, 20 February 2017, via Skype.
[9] Interview with non-formal group (activists) in Ventimiglia, 20 February 2017, via Skype.
[10] Interview with non-formal group (activists) in Ventimiglia, 20 February 2017, via Skype.

that this lack of support was fostered by authorities as a disciplinary tactic to discourage their work. The authorities 'deliberately tried to stop us meeting with the local people as well as with migrants', one activist explained, 'and even confiscated information flyers'.[11] The same interviewee spoke of feeling 'intense stress, anxiety and paranoia' when trying to help people under the constant watch of police. While some activists in Rome and Ventimiglia were willing to admit that they deliberately broke the law, they felt that the way that they were treated by the police was intimidating and unjust.[12]

The Italian cases demonstrate the variation in both the way in which CSAs operate and position themselves politically in providing humanitarian assistance, and the way in which the police and authorities have responded to them over time in sites of transit and residence. Alongside policing modalities of intimidation and disciplining, administrative offences or penalties have been used to criminalise organisations and groups providing support.

## II. Greece: Case of Athens and Thessaloniki

Interviews confirmed the existence of a similar situation to that described in Italy, in Greece where the context became more tense following the EU-Turkey Statement, not only in the islands but also inland.[13] Thessaloniki has de facto become a place of residence and destination for asylum-seekers and migrants, who cannot move further. This has raised tensions in the local communities. One CSA interviewee mentioned attacks on activists and squatters in Lesvos, Athens and northern Greece.[14] A volunteer in Greece meanwhile submitted a worrying account of such intimidation by law enforcement in Thessaloniki to our online survey:

> There is an abandoned building where many undocumented migrants and refugees live. They are from Pakistan and Afghanistan and many have been denied access to camps due to their nationalities and the belief that 'they are not refugees'. Volunteer groups provide basic assistance (food, medical assistance, legal assistance) to the people of the building. Police come almost every day and detain volunteers for a few hours 'to check their documents', take the plates off the volunteer's cars and the ambulance and ultimately do everything to make the volunteers' work as difficult as possible.

[11] Interview with non-formal group (activists) in Ventimiglia, 20 February 2017, via Skype.

[12] Follow-up interview with CSA providing social assistance (volunteers) in Rome, 23 September 2017, via Skype; interview with non-formal group (activists) in Ventimiglia, 20 February 2017, via Skype.

[13] Interview with CSO providing legal assistance, 6 June 2017, Athens, Greece; interview with CSO providing social assistance, 6 June 2017, Athens, Greece; interview with CSO providing social assistance, 7 June 2017, Athens, Greece; interview with CSO providing legal assistance, 8 June 2017, Lesvos island, Greece.

[14] Interview with CSO providing social assistance, 7 June 2017, Athens, Greece.

In Greece as in Italy, policing measures are therefore multimodal at the point of assistance during transit or residence. Similarly, a famous squat in Athens called 'City Plaza' went through a challenging period:

> Since then the solidarity initiative has, for more than 500 days, provided free and decent housing to over 1700 people in the center of Athens, irrespective of their nationality and residence status. These people are housed in the hotel's 120 rooms, 350–400 persons at a time, a third of whom are children.[15]

The City Plaza squat came about after the hotel was bankrupted. Former hotel owners, instead of selling the building and getting some money to cover their unpaid salaries, decided to let the migrants and refugees in:

> All of this might seem like a miracle when you consider that City Plaza's funding depends exclusively on donations from individuals and solidarity groups and is run on an entirely voluntary basis. But … it started as a counter-formation against EU-Turkey Statement (Squat.net 2017).

Interestingly, politicisation and employment of the right-wing narratives concerning migration in Greece and particularly the EU-Turkey Statement mobilised a number of citizens to express their disagreement on how migrants and asylum-seekers are treated. Threats hang over the squat:

> An eviction order was published by the state prosecutor in April 2017, ordering the police to carry it out but it first has to overcome the broad solidarity movement of City Plaza, and so far, the Greek government has appeared to tolerate Plaza and the other refugee housing squats. Nevertheless, this is more a political issue than an operational one and concerns a balance of power.[16]

During the field research trip in Athens, City Plaza was attacked. One of the interviewees confirmed that both refugees, asylum-seekers, migrants and City Plaza volunteers are constantly under threat of being evicted.[17]

## III. Hungary: Budapest and Szeged

The response to migrants in Hungary can be divided according to those staying for a period or transiting through the country at the height of the so-called 'European humanitarian refugee crisis' between 2015–16, and the more limited population resident in the country, primarily in the capital, Budapest. Both responses have nevertheless been defined by a hostile and unwelcoming rhetoric to asylum-seekers and refugees and cumulative restrictions on their rights and access to

[15] Squat.net (2017).
[16] Squat.net (2017).
[17] Interview with CSO providing legal assistance, 6 June 2017, Athens, Greece.

services. One interviewee identified 2012 as the turning point when the laws began changing and there emerged a 'Hungarian solution to migration'.[18]

## A. Access to Rights during Short-Term Residence or Transit

At the height of the European refugee response, Hungary was a major transit country for those seeking to move to northern Europe, primarily to Germany and Sweden. A range of CSOs responded quickly to the need to provide humanitarian aid for this transiting population. This assistance was often provided at transit hubs, including Szeged train station and Budapest central station at Keleti.

'Back in 2015, it [aiding irregular migrants] wasn't an issue', commented one CSO volunteer who was part of an informal activist group.[19] Throughout 2015 this group provided a range of not-for-profit services to transiting migrants including, among others, helping them access shelter, charging phones, giving them directions, helping them access transport links and even helping to transport individuals and families across the border to Austria.[20] At that time the Hungarian government was also facilitating people to move through the country to Austria. CSOs reported that prior to the erection of the wall and new powers to push irregular migrants back from across the whole Hungarian territory in spring 2017, the government's strategy vis-à-vis combatting migration was a 'let them go' strategy.

After the government stopped migrants departing on trains and stopped buses to Austria at the start of September 2015, almost 2,000 people signed up to form a convoy to drive migrants stranded in Hungary over 300 miles to Vienna, Austria, fearing that smugglers would jump in. The action was framed by organisers as an alternative and direct response to the tragedy of migrants dying in criminal smuggling operations. They wrote on Facebook:

> Our relief operation is the only effective way to prevent more deaths in trucks at the moment … We urgently ask political leaders not to impede the process of this action, which seems to be the only right thing to do at the moment: spare no effort to save lives!

CSOs interviewed for this research explained that even at this point, the CSOs were largely left to their own devices. For around a year these kinds of 'humanitarian convoys' were in operation from Hungary to Austria. Another CSO interviewee commented that although this act of transporting someone across the border into Austria was in breach of the law, few people were stopped in practice. Some were made an example of. In some instances, CSO interviewees reported that the police

[18] Interview with non-formal group (activists) providing social assistance, 30 August 2017, Budapest, Hungary.

[19] Interview with non-formal group (activists) providing social assistance, 30 August 2017, Budapest, Hungary.

[20] Interview with non-formal group (activists) providing social assistance, 30 August 2017, Budapest, Hungary.

deliberately provoked activists or migrants in an attempt to get them to react: 'That was part of the government communications campaign', said one volunteer providing sanitation and social assistance, adding, 'to create and film a few clashes here and there for the public media'. The clash between stranded migrants and police and vigilante groups in Budapest's Keleti station in August 2015 was cited by more than one CSO.[21]

After March 2016, humanitarian groups in Budapest and Szeged nevertheless both revealed that they had sought out legal advice and training for their staff and volunteers to be sure of how the new laws targeting irregular migration and smuggling affected their work. This confusion about what kind of facilitation was punishable under Hungarian law became more manifest after 9 March 2016, when a 'crisis situation' which had first developed in Hungary's southern territories on 15 September 2015 in response to mass migration, was extended to the whole national territory. Another important turning point was in July 2016, when the Hungarian police became obliged to automatically escort back to the external side of the border fence any migrants who were apprehended within eight kilometres of the wall. By means of a subsequent decree, this emergency situation was kept in place at least until September 2017,[22] when it was expected to be continued.[23] Meanwhile, the zone for pushbacks of irregular migrants out of Hungarian territory was extended in April 2017 to the entire Hungarian territory. At the time of our fieldwork, CSOs were seeking legal advice as to how the new changes affected their operations; however, most appeared relatively resolved to continue their support where they could.

Local and national governments were also reported to be using intimidating and disciplining tactics to dissuade humanitarian assistance. Examples of such intimidation or disciplining cited in the research included authorities in Budapest closing down an important organising hub for CSOs assisting migrants in spring 2017, on the grounds that they had found people there using marijuana.[24] After a long appeals process, at the time of fieldwork, it had recently been agreed that the hub would be reopened.

## B. Services for Those Resident in Budapest

Some CSOs interviewed for this research contended that the government's hostile environment is intended to eventually push out even those who claim asylum

[21] Interview with non-formal group (activists) providing social assistance, 30 August 2017, Budapest, Hungary.

[22] www.helsinki.hu/wp-content/uploads/HHC-Info-Update-New-Asylum-Bill-15.02.2017.pdf.

[23] www.independent.co.uk/news/world/europe/refugee-crisis-hundreds-of-volunteers-join-convoy-to-take-asylum-seekers-from-hungary-to-austria-as-10486170.html.

[24] Interview with non-formal group (activists) providing social assistance, 30 August 2017, Budapest, Hungary; interview with CSO providing social assistance, 29 August, Budapest, Hungary.

in Hungary. Between April and June 2016, Hungary enacted legal amendments with a crucial detrimental impact on asylum-seekers and refugees. It also declared its intention to close all refugee camps across the country. A 2015 report by the Helsinki Committee summarises these changes, claiming Hungary is 'no country for refugees' (Hungarian Helsinki Committee, 2015).

The important changes to those resident in Hungary are the following. The amendment of the Asylum Government Decree (in effect from 1 April 2016) terminates the monthly cash allowance for asylum-seekers (HUF 7,125/€24) and the school enrolment benefit previously provided to child asylum-seekers. The Amendment of the Asylum Act (in effect from 1 June 2016) terminates the integration support scheme for recognised refugees and beneficiaries of subsidiary protection introduced in 2013, without replacing it with any alternative measure, and introduces the mandatory and automatic revision of refugee status at minimum three-year intervals following recognition or if an extradition request is issued (previously refugee status was not limited in time, yet it could be withdrawn at any time). It also reduces the mandatory periodic review of the subsidiary protection status from five to three-year intervals following recognition; reduces the maximum period of stay in open reception centres following the recognition of refugee status or subsidiary protection from 60 days to 30 days; and decreases the automatic eligibility period for basic healthcare services from one year to six months following the recognition of refugee status or subsidiary protection.

As a consequence, refugees and beneficiaries of a subsidiary protection status in Hungary are now obliged to move out of the reception centre where they are accommodated one month after the grant of their status and will not receive any targeted support for their integration (financial benefits, housing allowance, language courses, etc).

These provisions may immediately force the few who actually get international protection in Hungary into homelessness and destitution.[25] Meanwhile, the issue of how few asylum-seekers actually receive protection in Hungary was raised by multiple national and international actors. 'Recognition rates are one of lowest in Europe, even for Syrians', commented one UN representative.[26]

Some CSO and international organisation interviewees suggested that by creating a hostile environment, even for those who are legally allowed to stay in Hungary and had considered staying may be tempted to seek out the services of smugglers to move elsewhere, thus promoting irregular secondary migration within the EU.

Other measures by which the government was recorded to be constructing a 'hostile environment' included dissuading certain human rights advocacy

[25] www.helsinki.hu/wp-content/uploads/HHC-Hungary-asylum-legal-amendments-Apr-June-2016.pdf.

[26] Interview with UN actor, 29 August 2017, Budapest, Hungary.

NGOs from going into public schools to teach about the rights of refugees.[27] Some schools self-police and are worried about accepting invitations, even from well-established groups such as Amnesty International, for fear of seeming 'too political'.[28] A marked shift was noted by one CSO, from the previous successful collaboration between migrant-support CSOs on topics including documenting hate crime and promoting employment for new refugees, to the current hostile climate.[29]

The creation of a 'hostile environment' for asylum-seekers entering into Hungary is mirrored in policies which hinder integration and actively promote 'zero migration' from outside neighbouring states. As one representative of a national Hungarian NGO commented,

> How do we expect them [refugees] to successfully integrate and start a new life here when the entire environment extremely hostile? The whole support set up is important for smuggling because the lack of support fuels secondary migration elsewhere in Europe. It's therefore a European issue.[30]

In terms of social cohesion and social trust, the same respondent opined, 'I think already this has horrible long-term consequences'.

Prior to the new laws, a range of integration support was available for asylum-seekers and refugees in Hungary. The number of asylum-seekers and refugees in Hungary has always been relatively small compared to other EU Member States, with the population concentrated in Budapest. Integration support included housing, language school and a small financial package. Integration work was conducted by a range of civil society organisations such as Menedék – Hungarian Association for Migrants.

In the course of fieldwork a number of challenges to integration were raised by the new policy. Social support for Hungarian nationals is already relatively minimal, social benefits being tied to involvement in public goods work. One issue raised was that in order to participate in such programmes, knowledge of the Hungarian language is often a requirement – a substantial bar for refugees, given the cuts to language provision. This might encourage them, one interviewee commented, into situations of irregular work or slavery.[31] Other issues raised included lack of financial means to pay rent and unwillingness of landlords to rent to refugees. A range of CSOs are seeking to plug these gaps by providing services including housing and language classes for free, as well as support with work integration, however there is extremely limited government funding available for these NGOs. Indeed, some of these NGOs described facing an existential financial threat. This financial insecurity is coupled with reputational damage experienced

[27] Interview with CSO providing social assistance, 29 August 2017, Budapest, Hungary; interview with CSO providing social assistance, 30 August 2017, Budapest, Hungary.
[28] Interview with CSO providing social assistance, 30h of August, 2017 Budapest, Hungary.
[29] Interview with CSO providing social assistance 29 August 2017, Budapest, Hungary.
[30] Interview with CSO providing social assistance, 29 August 2017, Budapest, Hungary.
[31] Interview with CSO providing social assistance, 30 August 2017, Budapest, Hungary.

as a result of the government's anti-NGO campaign and zero-migration policy. As one NGO worker commented, 'People think that organisations working with refugees or migrants in any capacity are smugglers'.[32]

Some positive examples of efforts to foster integration were highlighted. A UN agency is currently engaged with a national CSO on a pilot programme to train the Budapest Citizens Advice Office in dealing with the problems commonly faced by newly arrived refugees and migrant communities more generally. But it is uncertain where medium- and long-term funding for this initiative can be secured.[33]

International organisations seem keen to support initiatives in this area in recognition of the current gap, which they clearly see as a major risk factor both for the well-being of refugees and the success of social integration on potential secondary migration. There is strong evidence that the aforementioned conditions and the challenges associated with integration drive secondary migration to areas of Europe with more receptive social and labour market contexts, alongside the pull posed by family and social networks elsewhere. In somewhat of a vicious circle, Hungarian authorities already seem to justify the lack of integration support on the basis of high levels of secondary migration. As one interviewee from a think tank that advises the government said, 'Why would the government invest in people who don't want to stay in Hungary to begin with? It's throwing money away'.[34] However, this lack of support itself is identified as a major driver of that secondary migration. This circular debate was raised repeatedly in interviews with domestic and international NGOs, and appears to have stalled conversations around the need for integration support and a level-headed approach to managing the risks of secondary migration. This vicious circle creates a market for smuggling operations, with several interviewees commenting that they have seen large numbers of smugglers around the refugee camps and that it was common knowledge among staff in the centres that residents were likely to disappear at any time. There appeared to be a distinct lack of policies addressing the protection needs of unaccompanied minors and victims of trafficking.

The anti-refugee rhetoric was confirmed in an October 2016 referendum in which Hungarian citizens were asked to express their opinion on the EU migrant relocation quotas.[35] Orbán defined the relocation system an abuse of power. In response to Hungarians' vote against quotas and other immigration enforcement measures, the EU took formal action by launching infringement procedures.[36]

[32] Interview with CSO providing social assistance, 30 August 2017, Budapest, Hungary.

[33] Interview with UN actor, 29 August 2016, Budapest, Hungary.

[34] Interview with government-affiliated think tank, 30 August 2017, Budapest, Hungary.

[35] www.politico.eu/article/janos-ader-hungary-referendum-on-eu-migrant-relocation-in-october/.

[36] On relocation see http://europa.eu/rapid/press-release_IP-17-1607_en.htm; other infringement procedures are reported below in pertinent sections. For the first one of these measures related to asylum policies see http://europa.eu/rapid/press-release_IP-15-6228_en.htm.

Migrants have also been demonised in a range of public campaigns. In May 2015, the government launched a National Consultation on Immigration and Terrorism. The introduction to the questionnaire stated:

> The questions are the most important issues, as these are in contradiction with the rules of the European Union in force today, these are silly rules, in force today, which paralyse the Member States. The common European asylum policy norms, a system of law that we have developed, is more an obstacle than a help. It would be better if the Member States could decide on their own as per their specialties how they want to stop the refugee waves. Should we get this possibility, then we Hungarians would be able to solve our own problems as well.

In parallel with the consultation, a billboard campaign, including slogans such as 'If you come to Hungary you cannot take Hungarian jobs', was conducted. Also, before declaring a crisis situation in September 2015, the government issued a statement that framed the issue in the following terms:

> We believe that what is at stake at present is Europe, the European lifestyle, and the survival or disappearance of European values and nations or their alteration beyond recognition. We must not let this happen, as then we would lose our identity; without a firm identity, there can be no success – either in economic or cultural senses.[37]

Several smaller CSOs who provide support to asylum-seekers and refugees have closed down in the last two years because of lack of access to funding and reputational harms. They also face new bureaucratic pressures such as filing longer annual reports.[38] These various conditions make it increasingly difficult for CSAs to provide assistance and services to those transiting through or resident in Hungary in the longer term. All CSO interviewees were of the opinion that because of the new law allowing pushback of irregular migrants from anywhere in the whole Hungarian territory, it is increasingly unlikely that vulnerable undocumented migrants will come forward to authorities or even CSOs to report abuses and humanitarian needs.

Finally, the public and media discourses in Hungary and militarisation of the external Schengen border also impacts social trust. Media outlets controlled by the government frequently ran stories about the border and policing efforts, including successful pushbacks of migrants. A public advertisement aired to coincide with the referendum on whether Hungary should accept EU refugee resettlement quotas showed images of the border with lines of migrants queuing up to enter. This was said by some to foster a climate of social mistrust.[39] As discussed above, NGOs were framed by some media outlets as being complicit with the smugglers.

[37] The statements of this section are available in UNHCR report, *Hungary as a Country of Asylum* (2016).

[38] Interview with CSO providing social assistance, 29 August 2017, Budapest, Hungary.

[39] www.youtube.com/watch?v=2cWZo5iSUxA.

## IV. The UK: 'Hostile Environment' in London

As outlined in chapter 4.IV, the creation of a 'hostile environment' for irregular residing migrants in the UK, as in Hungary more recently, has been a deliberate and explicit policy intention of the government for some years, the aim being to deter migrants from irregularly entering the UK. One CSO explained how they had changed the nature of the social support they provide to migrants as a result of the changing context:

> Our work changed from anti-deportation campaigns to what we do now, which is helping people access rights in the community. We figured there's no point trying to stop people being deported if they have no legal right to stay since these days, life as an undocumented person is pretty unliveable. You can survive but you can't be part of society … the government has been scarily successful [with creating a 'hostile environment'].[40]

Also as discussed in chapter 4.IV, amendments to successive immigration bills in recent years have increasingly criminalised the act of irregular migration. Meanwhile, the immigration detention estate has expanded, which means that thousands of irregular migrants are detained indefinitely without access to civil society support in one of 11 detention centres. Over 30,000 migrants are held in immigration detention under Immigration Act powers every year.[41] As in Hungary, access to asylum-seekers and other migrants is therefore reported as a key tactic of control and policing of civil society. Some CSOs reported arbitrary access requirements for detention centres, and journalists are not allowed into UK immigration detention. Legal assistance is also strictly controlled and contracted out. The Global Detention Project reports that 'the United Kingdom has one of the largest immigration detention systems in Europe, confining up to 4,000 people – including children – in detention every day under Immigration Act powers' (Global Detention Project 2016).

CSOs have played an important role in reforming detention and putting more asylum-seekers in the community, where they have greater access to services. In 2010, a coalition of CSOs successfully lobbied for a time-limit of 72 hours on the detention of children.[42] Meanwhile, more recently, strategic litigation by CSOs including Detention Action has been successful in overturning the detained fast track, which automatically detained certain categories of asylum-seekers. In January 2017, the UK High Court ruled that the UK's 'detained fast track' process used for asylum appeals from 2005–14 was unlawful and beyond the power of the Home Office, and that more than 10,000 asylum-seekers were treated unfairly.[43]

[40] Interview with CSO providing social assistance, 11 July 2017, London, UK.

[41] www.aviddetention.org.uk/immigration-detention/what-immigration-detention.

[42] www.theguardian.com/politics/2010/dec/16/nick-clegg-shameful-detention-children-end.

[43] www.theguardian.com/uk-news/2017/jan/20/uk-high-court-rules-10000-asylum-seekers-treated-unfairly-detained-fast-track.

As with civil society successes in bringing unaccompanied children from Calais to Britain through safe and legal routes, the courts and strategic litigation were a key weapon for civil society in removing asylum-seekers from harmful conditions and upholding migrants' access to their human rights.

In addition to criminalisation of irregular migration, successive immigration bills have also placed greater duties on service providers to police the immigration status of recipients. In some cases, as for landlords, the consequences of failing to perform these checks may include a fine or prison sentence (see chapter 4.IV). In other cases, such as for GPs and schools, there appears to be more discretion, although, as one CSO interviewee put it, 'It's really, really not yet clear how the new NHS checks will pan out'.[44] Police meanwhile are generally understood by CSOs to have a proactive duty to report irregular migrants, but, again, interviewees and survey respondents gave examples of localised practices where more discretion was employed, and the legal situation at the time of writing remains ambiguous.

Following a fire at Grenfell Tower, a social housing block in West London, in June 2017 in which at least 71 individuals lost their lives and hundreds more became destitute,[45] under pressure from the opposition the government announced a firewall[46] for any irregular migrants affected by the fire and offered to grant them a one-year amnesty status (this amnesty was recently turned into a permanent one).[47] The need for the sudden firewall (despite there being no published statistics on whether anyone has taken up the offer of amnesty) suggests that provisions for undocumented migrants to access services or report crimes are not in place.

A CSO with decades of experience which provides services to migrant victims of domestic violence, among other services, commented on the ambiguity surrounding their local policing situation in terms of protecting undocumented female victims of crime:

> We want to know how are police deciding to report [an undocumented crime victim] or not … because we're getting mixed messages and we still don't know the protocol. It seems it really depends on the police officer there. We're trying to check with different police officers but we have different versions of the rules. It depends who you approach, the answer you get … you have resources but police use them at their discretion … if you approach the police as an undocumented woman you may be turned down, you may be offered a great tool of support, it's really polarised, there's no standard procedure.[48]

[44] Interview with CSO providing medical assistance, 6 July 2017, London, UK.

[45] www.independent.co.uk/news/uk/grenfell-tower-fire-victims-list-dead-presumed-killed-71-people-sir-martin-moore-bick-inquiry-a7945866.html.

[46] A term meaning a separation between the mandates of the basic service provision and border controls (see Chapter 9).

[47] www.standard.co.uk/news/london/amnesty-for-illegal-immigrants-affected-by-grenfell-tower-fire-extended-for-three-months-a3624381.html.

[48] Interview with CSO providing social and legal assistance, 16 August 2017, London, UK.

The key issue for many CSOs providing services to irregular migrants is not whether there should be a firewall – which there appears to be consensus on – but 'at what level the firewall can and should be set'.[49] CSOs were understanding that in criminal prosecutions at some point identification became inevitable but that 'the first thing a migrant reporting abuse shouldn't be asked is for a passport'.[50] One CSO was relatively optimistic about the possibilities of piloting a project in London with the support of the new London Metropolitan Police Victim's Commissioner. They are working together with the commissioner and London universities to map different types of undocumented women and their vulnerabilities in accessing services. Again, the issue of stratification of social rights according to legal status and who is entitled to what is of determining significance (see chapter 4.IV).

There are many different types of status and different barriers at different stages. Women who have spousal visas and victims of domestic abuse, for example, under certain conditions, can access indefinite leave to remain (ILR) under the destitute domestic violence (DDV) concession rules. Confusion within this landscape creates real challenges to the provision of critical services. Another CSO worker explained,

> There's this pernicious narrative that undocumented women don't have any rights but they do have the right to support when they are victims, but in many cases it's not implemented … yes, we need to talk about what rights they don't have but also make sure authorities and police and the women themselves know what rights they do have.[51]

Several UK CSOs cited the localisation agenda and growth of privatising and contracting out social services as compounding the problem of accountability. 'You have G4S doing this, Circo doing that, here is a trained police officer, here is a "community police officer", here is an NGO working on a government contract … it's tricky to keep people accountable in [this] fragmented landscape'.[52]

The UK government and NHS Digital, which stores NHS patients' data, published a deal[53] in January 2017 to give the Home Office easier access to migrant patients' personal information.[54] This allows immigration officials to access patients' personal details, such as addresses, and then to track down, arrest, detain and deport them. According to the Department of Health, the Home Office made 8,127 requests for data in the first 11 months of 2016 alone.[55] This led to 5,854 people being traced by immigration teams. CSOs working in the field of healthcare reported that new charges and document checks being introduced in

[49] Interview with CSO providing social and legal assistance, 16 August 2017, London, UK.
[50] Interview with CSO providing social and legal assistance, 16 August 2017, London, UK.
[51] Interview with CSO providing social and legal assistance, 16 July 2017, London, UK.
[52] Interview with CSO providing social and legal assistance, 7 July 2017, London, UK.
[53] www.doctorsoftheworld.org.uk/news/medics-mobilise-against-nhs-patient-data-sharing.
[54] www.buzzfeed.com/jamesball/trumping-donald-trump?utm_term=.qudY8bJPv#.cqk0Y7MeK.
[55] www.theguardian.com/uk-news/2017/jan/24/nhs-hands-over-patient-records-to-home-office-for-immigration-crackdown.

the NHS as well as data-sharing agreements between the NHS and Home Office were having the effect of putting irregular migrants off accessing services. One interviewee from a government advice organisation said that they knew of cases where a lack of awareness about what they were entitled to in terms of benefits and rights, coupled with a fear of being reported to authorities, had stopped parents from taking their children to hospital for treatment until the need became acutely severe.[56] A medical CSO commented,

> We're very concerned that confidential healthcare information just isn't confidential anymore and that the Home Office is being very active in using healthcare information for non-healthcare related purposes. I think the direct effect is sinister but what is potentially much more sinister is the way if this becomes pervasive it will be a very active discouragement for the seeking of health care … the combination of their fear of their information being shared with the Home Office and the fear of being given a bill for antenatal care is probably quite effective at increasing the hazard to an unborn child … Meanwhile, communicable diseases are being left untreated which is a good example of the broader impact on society as a whole.[57]

Such penetration of border enforcement activities into the healthcare system is rapidly growing. The NHS complied with 8,000 requests for data checks in 2016, a threefold increase on the number in 2014 when the Home Office was granted powers to request otherwise confidential patient data. Doctors have been at the frontline of resisting such measures through the new organisation Docs Not Cops, which has staged protests and civil disobedience.[58] The *British Medical Journal* has also spoken out against the new measures and data-sharing agreement.[59] The international charity Doctors of the World continues to provide a free, volunteer-run health service in its London clinic and support migrants to register with GPs without interference from authorities. Despite having the right to register with a GP, migrants without papers are frequently turned away by receptionists or doctors unaware of the rules.[60]

While this penetration of policing powers into the public sector grows, its character is varied and fragmentation proves to have far-reaching consequences in the hostile environment. In immigration detention, healthcare is now contracted out to private doctors. 'Ironically, they may be exempt from having to report to the Home Office', explained one CSO interviewee who provides social care and legal support in detention, because such medical staff will not be bound by the NHS Home Office data-sharing agreement.[61] Further

[56] Interview with national welfare authority providing social and medical assistance, 12 July 2017, London, UK.
[57] Interview with CSO providing medical assistance, 6 July 2017, London, UK.
[58] www.docsnotcops.co.uk.
[59] www.bmj.com/content/356/bmj.j911.
[60] Interview with CSO providing medical assistance, 6 July 2017, London, UK.
[61] Interview with CSO providing social and legal assistance, 7 July 2017, London, UK.

contrasts emerge in this where service delivery is fragmented and compartmentalised: in detention, for instance, migrants can access free secondary healthcare services – such as psychiatric care – for which they would be charged while outside immigration detention.

Despite the hostile environment policy objectives, some CSOs reported opportunities to open access to services back up at a local level. One is, for instance, engaging in some pilot work with a local bank to secure access to banking services for irregular migrants, despite banks now being prohibited from offering such migrants bank accounts. Beyond this, the same CSO has another project looking into driving licences based on best practice from parts of the US which have implemented the 'Safe Drivers Bill'. For some CSOs, progress lies at the city level and through 'leaning in' to powers of discretion at the local level.[62] But, as highlighted above, this discretion is also widely reported to be at the root of many humanitarian problems. In Yarl's Wood detention centre, undercover investigations led by the media have revealed evidence of private guards using their discretionary powers to exploit migrant women, including for sexual favours.[63]

Challenging and subverting the hostile environment agenda is however far from simple. More than one CSO which engages in both service provision and advocacy commented that at times, campaigning against the 'hostile environment' and for more access to services for irregular migrants could have the effect of simply 'doing the government's propaganda for them'.[64] One volunteer commented,

> The last thing we want is to start putting people off, for example, sending their kids to school because of the new data sharing agreement with the Home Office, but at the same time people need to know because there is a genuine risk there – it's difficult.[65]

Other CSOs reported that they felt working with migrants was becoming a more reputationally toxic area, like in Hungary. 'There is a media threat', one medical CSO commented. 'We have to be as squeaky clean as we can and be very mindful of Charity Commission guidelines … all small organisations are vulnerable in one way or another'.[66]

Several CSOs reported a sense that civil society efforts to support migrants in the UK are increasingly split between organisations in receipt of government money, which were unwilling to speak out, and those which are independent and prepared to do more advocacy work. It was raised as a concern that in a context where more and more areas of civil society are implicated in border policing

[62] Interview with CSO providing social and legal assistance, 3 July 2017, London, UK.
[63] www.channel4.com/news/yarls-wood-immigration-removal-detention-centre-investigation.
[64] Interview with CSO providing legal assistance, 7 July 2017, London, UK.
[65] Interview with non-formal group (activists), 7 July 2017, London, UK.
[66] Interview with CSO providing medical assistance, 7 July 2017, via Skype.

and control, the expertise of the migration rights sector is becoming diffused. Meanwhile, several CSOs reported that, as in Hungary, contracts for services are often awarded on criteria that do not place migrants' best interests at heart and which often push out the more critical voices with the most experience.[67]

## A. Social Trust

The new landlord-conducted 'right to rent' checks detailed in chapter 4.IV have been shown to impact all categories of migrants, including those with documents and a legal right to rent. British citizens without passports have also been affected, demonstrating the wider consequences of such policing for social trust.[68] One non-white CSO worker reported she had personally been reported to police after her brother-in-law came to stay with her:

> Some London boroughs have made it a condition that you cannot offer multiple occupancy – you cannot rent a room unless you go through them and gain a licence in [X] where I live. We had my brother-in-law staying and someone thought he was a tenant and reported us. The Council wrote to us and said you have to get a licence if you're subletting and we said what are you talking about, this is my brother, he's visiting and we're not charging. I think the idea was to crack down on rogue landlords pulling people in and harbouring but it can go to extremes too.[69]

CSOs in the UK have complained that their service delivery is increasingly co-opted by the work of border control, threatening, on a practical level, the bonds of trust between service providers and the migrants, but also the independence of civil society.[70] The effect of dissuading migrants from accessing services also has broader consequences for society as a whole. As a representative from an international medical NGO based in the UK said,

> [W]hat we're seeing is a normalisation of civil society being expected to play a role in immigration. Even if it's not explicit that it's a policing event, it's your responsibility to be concerned as well about someone's immigration status. Whereas the doctors we speak to would say 'actually it's not, I'm not interested in the person's immigration status, I want to treat the patient. And … that's been replicated … with landlords, in schools to a certain extent as well … [A]lthough what you might hear from a politician

[67] Interview with CSO providing social and legal assistance, 5 July 2017, London, UK; interview with CSO providing social and legal assistance, 3 July 2017, London, UK; interview with CSO providing social and legal assistance, 7 July 2017, London, UK.

[68] www.theguardian.com/uk-news/2016/nov/14/british-citizens-without-passport-struggling-rent-property-immigration-checks.

[69] Interview with CSO providing social and legal assistance, 5 July 2015, London, UK.

[70] Interview with representative of civil society organisation providing medical assistance, 6 July 2017, London, UK; interview with representative of civil society organisation providing social, medical and legal assistance, 10 July 2017, London, UK; interview with representative of civil society organisation providing educational assistance, 7 July 2017, London, UK; interview with government organisation providing legal and social assistance, 12 July 2017.

> is that the intended impact is to dissuade, about making it a hostile environment, from our perspective the hostile environment isn't persuading people from staying in the UK or from not coming to the UK, what it's doing is making sure you have greater health inequalities because people are getting more sick and not accessing any care … it increases the risk of exploitation … criminals taking advantage of marginalised people and thriving off this niche area which has been created.[71]

Previous studies have shown that a degree of trust is important for compliance with enforcement on the part of irregular migrants and those who assist them.[72] In the Netherlands, it is reported that local authorities' obligation to report irregular migrants who make use of the new special night shelters has dissuaded them from accessing the service and left them sleeping rough (Carrera et al 2015: 57). A representative of an NGO which provides health and social care in London reported that concerns about potential obligations to share data with government officials regarding clients meant they were less likely to collect the data in the first place, which has consequences for funding and monitoring their work.[73]

One positive example concerns a CSO which has been working alongside police to collect data on hate crimes affecting the migrant community post-Brexit.[74] CSOs in the focus group were keen to stress that while some data-sharing with authorities is problematic and can put clients at risk, not sharing other data – such as data on abuse and hate crimes – serves to just sweep issues under the carpet. One focus group CSO said, 'Firewall isn't just about creating a safety net where you're not going to go straight to immigration enforcement, but also to turn down the barriers and record what is happening'.[75] The latter has impacts on the social security of society as a whole.

Meanwhile, in immigration raids, to avoid accusations of racial profiling, police now are reported to demand papers from more and more of those present. Recent research suggests that a greater number of raids on businesses is having the impact of intimidating black and minority ethnic staff and 'putting off' customers and harming business.[76]

The 'hostile environment' is also creeping into education. From September 2016 parents, guardians and carers in England have been asked to state if their children are foreign nationals. The Department of Education has an agreement to send details of up to 1,500 children a month to the Home Office.[77] Another

[71] Interview with civil society organisation providing medical assistance, 6 July 2017, London, UK.

[72] See, eg, A Ellermann 'Street-level democracy: how immigration bureaucrats manage public opposition' (2006) 29(2) *West European Politics*, 293.

[73] Interview with civil society organisation providing social, medical and legal assistance, 10 July 2017, London, UK.

[74] Interview with CSO providing social and legal assistance, 16 August 2017, London, UK.

[75] Interview with CSO providing social and legal assistance, 16 August 2017, London, UK.

[76] www.opendemocracy.net/beyondslavery/alice-bloch-sonia-mckay/sanctioning-employers-does-not-prevent-exploitation-and-unfree.

[77] www.theguardian.com/uk-news/2016/dec/15/pupil-data-shared-with-home-office-to-identify-illegal-migrants.

new civil society activist group, Against Borders for Children (ABC), has emerged to challenge these measures.[78] Although the new data-sharing is optional, the guidance does not make this clear.[79] An activist commented on the wider impact on social trust:

> It's made a lot of people angry. EU migrants, British parents with British kids who see this as divisive and unnecessary. We had one Jewish parent who sent us a copy of a letter they sent to their school saying this reminds me of what happened to my family.[80]

The same CSO received reports that the poor guidance in the new census had made some traumatised refugee children fearful of going to school since, for example, in Eritrea schools are sometimes used as places of army recruitment.[81]

Meanwhile, EU migrants with a legal right to be in Britain are also being targeted under anti-homelessness measures, on the grounds that rough sleeping is a breach of EU Treaty Rights. Following eight anti-homelessness raids in London, a reported 133 rough sleepers were detained, while 127 people were deported in under a year in Westminster alone.[82] The 'collaboration' of certain anti-homelessness NGOs in these measures has been widely criticised by the migrant support organisations and human rights monitors.[83] Some argued that it is better that they are there in a monitoring function, whereas others have argued that their presence condones the measures and that they may be motivated by new managerialism and meeting targets for government-funded schemes.[84] This also has wider European diplomatic impacts. Brexit and the consequences of the 'hostile environment' being rolled out to EU nationals was raised by several interviewees and in the focus group. As a CSO providing social assistance to migrants commented,

> If you're thinking about us having to Brexit, that is going to be more and more an issue and more pronounced as EU nationals are now going to have to be part of that environment of having to prove they are allowed to be in the country and what they have rights to.[85]

Another CSO interviewee commented on the lack of valuable evidence on smuggling that the UK government is failing to capture because of the absence of a firewall. Speaking of a case where a migrant had been systematically abused by smugglers following arrival in the UK, the interviewee said, 'I was thinking that's

[78] www.schoolsabc.net.

[79] Interview with CSO providing legal assistance, 7 July 2017, London, UK.

[80] Interview with non-formal group (activists), 7 July 2017, London, UK.

[81] Interview with non-formal group (activists), 7 July 2017, London, UK.

[82] https://corporatewatch.org/wp-content/uploads/2017/03/CW%20rough%20sleepers%20investigation.pdf.

[83] See, eg, https://corporatewatch.org/wp-content/uploads/2017/03/CW%20rough%20sleepers%20investigation.pdf.

[84] Interview with CSO providing social and legal assistance, 5 July 2017, London, UK.

[85] Interview with CSO providing social assistance, 11 July 2017, London, UK.

amazing intelligence that could be used but they are not going to get any of that because there is no firewall'.[86] Europeanising civic activity holds some promise for the development of alternative practice. One CSO has a programme on safe reporting for women victims of domestic violence which is part of the European Step up for Migrant Women Campaign coordinated by WAVE (Women Against Violence Europe).[87]

[86] Interview with CSO providing social and legal assistance, 5 July 2017, London, UK.
[87] Interview with CSO providing social and legal assistance, 16 August 2017, London, UK.

# PART III

# Conceptualising the Effects of EU Anti-Migrant-Smuggling Policies on Civil Society

# 8

# The Three Faces of Policing the Mobility Society in the EU

The preceding chapters of this book have illustrated and provided evidence on the multifaceted effects of EU policies aimed at countering the facilitation of entry and residence of irregular immigrants in Italy, Hungary, Greece and the UK. The examination of the criminalisation of entry, transit and residence in these four EU Member States has revealed a complex web of practices, instruments and actors affecting directly or indirectly CSAs actions and activities related to the phenomenon of migration and asylum. Our research has revealed a set of broader policing dynamics beyond examples of formal criminalisation and which encompass different manifestations of pressures, limitations/restrictions or coercion over CSAs' activities.

The academic literature has acknowledged and advanced frameworks of analysis for studying restrictions to non-governmental organisations. Van der Borgh and Terwindt (2012) for instance have identified a typology of policies, laws and measures which may have restrictive or constraining effects on civil society 'humanitarian environment or operational space'.[1] There is no widely or commonly accepted definition of what that 'civil society space' actual is or entails. There is however a well-rooted understanding that whatever those spaces are, an environment enabling and safeguarding the principles of neutrality and independence are critical for ensuring that CSAs can effectively conduct their humanitarian mandates and accountability activities.[2]

[1] Van der Borgh and Terwindt (2012: 1068) advance the following concept of 'operational space of NGOs': 'their capacity to function as an organization and to perform the key tasks of the organization, in accordance with the principles protecting civil society that are embedded in international law'. See also Jordan and Van Tuijl (2006), who distinguish five categories of the most commonly used tactics by governments, including: to challenge credibility, co-opt or corrupt, challenge legality, disturb operations and intervene beyond the rule of law.

[2] According to the Office for the Coordination of Humanitarian Affairs Policy Development and Studies Branch, 'Humanitarian Operating Environment' as follows: 'A key element for humanitarian agencies and organizations when they deploy, consists of establishing and maintaining a conducive humanitarian operating environment, sometimes referred to as "humanitarian space". The perception of adherence to the key operating principles of neutrality and impartiality in humanitarian operations represents the critical means by which the prime objective of ensuring that suffering must be met wherever it is found, can be achieved. Consequently, maintaining a clear distinction between the role and function of humanitarian actors and that of the military is the determining factor in creating an operating environment in which humanitarian organisations can discharge their responsibilities

Independence is particularly central for CSAs promoting human rights protection and documenting human rights violations by states. The role of CSAs and citizens' movements in exposing risks of abuses and actual breaches of fundamental human rights, and in mobilising to secure effective redress and access to justice, has remained central in upholding the democratic rule of law. Neier (2012) has provided a historical account of the emergence of an international human rights movement since the 1970s and how an essential part of this movement has been making concerns and findings about human rights abuses internationally known. The construction of the European Communities, and the subsequent European Union, has taken place with a deep understanding and commitment that CSAs constitute a key component of accountability of governments' lawfulness and of potential abuses of individuals' rights and liberties.[3] Article 12.1 of the EU Charter of Fundamental Rights enshrines the right to freedom of assembly and of association in civic matters, which has been interpreted to be of core importance for CSAs.[4] Particularly in the context of foreign affairs or external relations policies, the European Commission has expressly stated:

> An empowered civil society is a crucial component of any democratic system and is an asset in itself. It represents and fosters pluralism and can contribute to more effective policies, equitable and sustainable development and inclusive growth. It is an important player in fostering peace and in conflict resolution. By articulating citizens' concerns, civil society organisations (CSOs) are active in the public arena, engaging in initiatives to further participatory democracy. They embody a growing demand for transparent and accountable governance.[5]

both effectively and safely. Sustained humanitarian access to the affected population is ensured when the receipt of humanitarian assistance is not conditional upon the allegiance to or support to parties involved in a conflict but is a right independent of military and political action'. Refer to Office for the Coordination of Humanitarian Affairs Policy Development and Studies Branch (OCHA), *Glossary of Humanitarian Terms in relation to the Protection of Civilians in Armed Conflict*, (New York, United Nations, 2003) 14–15.

[3] See for instance European Commission, *The Commission and Non-Governmental Organisations*, Commission Discussion Paper (2000). The European Economic and Social Committee (EESC), set up in the early 1950s, is a consultative body in the EU representing 'civil society'. It presents itself as contributing to 'strengthening the democratic legitimacy and effectiveness of the European Union by enabling civil society organisations from the Member States to express their views at European level'. See www.eesc.europa.eu/en/about. For more information on the Committee refer to Arts 301–304 of the Treaty on the Functioning of the European Union (TFEU). See also European Economic and Social Committee 'The Civil Society Organized at European Level – Proceedings of the First Convention', Brussels, 15–16 October 1999. The participation of civil society in promoting 'good governance' in the EU is acknowledged in Art 15 TFEU. See also Art 11.3 Treaty on European Union. Data and evidence provided by civil society have been given an express role in the context of public consultations in the EU Better Regulation Guidelines and the evaluation of EU policies on the ground. See European Commission, 'Better Regulation Guidelines', Staff Working Document, SWD(2015) 111 final, Strasbourg, 19.5.2015, and European Commission, 'Better Regulation Toolbox', http://ec.europa.eu/smart-regulation/guidelines/docs/br_toolbox_en.pdf.

[4] Refer to F Dorssemont 'Article 12: Freedom of Assembly and of Association' in S Peers et al (eds), *The EU Charter of Fundamental Rights: A Commentary* (Oxford, Hart Publishing, 2014), 341.

[5] The EU's engagement with civil society has been particularly active in foreign affairs and accession process. See for instance European Commission, *The Roots of Democracy and Sustainable Development: Europe's Engagement with Civil Society in External Relations*, COM(2012) 492 final, Brussels, page 3.

The literature has identified a mix of 'limitations' affecting CSAs. These include for instance physical harassment and intimidation, preventive and punitive criminal measures, administrative restrictions, stigmatisation as well as limiting spaces of dialogue (Van der Borgh and Terwindt 2012). This book has taken as its starting point of analysis the EU, and particularly the EU's approach in countering smuggling and its effects on CSAs. How do the wider set of limitations and restrictions affecting civil society manifest themselves in our field or areas of investigation? When studying the effects of anti-migrant-smuggling over the role and activities of civil society actors in the EU a number of preliminary considerations need to be taken into account. The first one relates to the need to locate policies and actors/agencies aimed at countering smuggling into the wider matrix of EU border policies, particularly in the context of the so-called 'Schengen system'. The expulsion and anti-smuggling-driven rationale guiding current EU migration policies is symptomatic of a deeper dilemma characterising this phenomenon and the role that 'Europeanisation' dynamics (Guiraudon 2000; Block and Bonjour 2013; Bonjour and Vink 2014; Bigo 1996) have played in migration management policies and the establishment of a common EU external border during the last three decades. Indeed, as Guild (2006a: 407) reminds us, the concept of 'smuggling' of persons can only be understood within a context of a 'border' and a set of border management tools and practices. Smuggling in the EU depends therefore on the existence of a common EU external border among the Schengen system participants.

Since its first steps, the European integration process has had an ambivalent relationship with mobility by non-EU nationals. The materialisation of the free movement of persons for EU citizens and the abolition of internal border controls under the remits of the Schengen system have constituted key factors behind the increasing role of and contributions by the EU in the management of migration and the consequent co-creation of 'irregularity' in the EU. Since the first intergovernmental steps of European integration in the area of irregular immigration and the adoption of the Schengen Implementing Convention in 1990,[6] EU Member States have been keen to cooperate and transfer to the EU powers related to policing irregular migration, particularly when it comes to expulsion and repatriation of irregularly present third-country nationals.

According to this same Communication, 'The concept of CSOs embraces a wide range of actors with different roles and mandates. Definitions vary over time and across institutions and countries. The EU considers CSOs to include all non-State, non-for-profit structures, non-partisan and non-violent, through which people organize to pursue shared objectives and ideals, whether political, cultural, social or economic. Operating from the local to the national, regional and international levels, they comprise urban and rural, formal and informal organisations. The EU values CSO's diversity and specificities; it engages with accountable and transparent CSOs, which share its commitment to social progress and the fundamental values of peace, freedom, equal rights and human dignity'.

[6] Convention Implementing the Schengen Agreement of 14 June 1985 on the Gradual Abolition of Checks at their Common Borders, 19 June 1990, OJ 2000 L 239/13, which entered into force on 1 September 1993.

Freedom of movement within the Schengen area was discursively linked to insecurities such as 'irregular immigration' and 'crime' which were expected to result from the establishment of the internal border-free area. Indeed, while Schengen was originally inspired by freedom of circulation, it has also played a fundamental role in the co-creation of non-EU mobility as insecurity and 'irregular immigration'. A set of 'flanking or compensatory measures' were progressively designed and added to that framework since the beginning of the 1990s, which were aimed at preventing and policing irregular immigration.

Bigo (1996) has studied the ways in which the creation of Schengen and EU free movement was underpinned by a discursive component driven by police and security professionals, who argued that the abolition of internal border controls would constitute a major security deficit. These served to legitimate EU policies focused on crime and security. EU anti- migrant-smuggling policies and actors need to be understood and read in light of this background. They have been given increasing salience during the so-called 'European refugee crisis' as part of the wider 'EU toolkit of migration management'. This toolkit is composed by a matrix of laws, institutions/agencies and technologies focused on a strengthened external borders and visa policies, penalising carriers, employers and smugglers and facilitating expulsion and repatriation (Guild 2006b; Carrera and Hernanz 2016).

Policing is therefore the lifeblood of the EU Schengen system. This is so both regarding its origins and subsequent legal and institutional developments, including the setting up of the EU External Borders Agency, Frontex (now called the European Border and Coast Guard). It is therefore against the background and policing dynamics surrounding the EU Schengen external border, and the more recent European refugee crisis, that we have investigated the EU's approach in countering migrant-smuggling and its implementation in the four countries examined. Our research has revealed the following three modalities or 'faces' of policing.

First, intimidation and suspicion. This modality has been shown to encompass non-formal law enforcement and policing practices on CSA activities taking place through surveillance (preventive measures), indirect pressure and intimidation. Intimidation practices may take the form of open verbal and even physical attacks and harassment. They also entail a logic of suspicion through political and/or media discourse and semantic drift creating links or accusing CSAs of being linked with smuggling networks or constituting 'pull factors' of migrant-smuggling.

Second, disciplining. This second modality of policing covers practices such as calls for more centralised coordination and making registration (or adherence to a 'code of conduct') mandatory for conducting activities lawfully. They also entail increased demands for financial accountability and transparency regarding funding sources, particularly 'foreign' donors, or cutting or limiting funding (including both subsidies and tax provisions). It may entail accusations that CSAs endanger stability owing to influence by foreign donors, or even framing them as quasi-terrorist organisations. This modality also covers policies limiting venues of dialogue/input in policy debates and proposals, as well as limiting access to information regarding implementation of government policies.

Third, formal criminalisation. This modality fits with the use of traditional criminal justice and/or criminal justice-like approaches to facilitation of entry/residence, including penal sanctioning, as well as preventive justice approaches focused on prevention. CSAs may be declared suspect of criminal activities, or even face criminal prosecution or penalisation, or other 'administrative' sanctions such as fines or financial penalties.

In some cases one modality may lead to another in a cumulative or escalating fashion. Features of each modality may also manifest variably over time and are highly dynamic in nature. Moreover, the lines between them might often become blurred. Some of the above-mentioned limitations or modalities may take more visible forms, such as enacted laws or legislation that impact – to varying degrees – CSA spaces. They may also show different modes of combination depending on the national, regional and local contexts under study. Our research demonstrates the existence of various CSA operational spaces and venues, which show features going beyond purely domestic spheres of action.

There is a complex set of processes and dynamics at stake through which CSAs are brought under the spotlight of one or several policing modalities. There is also a wider variety of ways in which each of these actors experience, witness or perceive the effects of countering smuggling policies, depending on mandate, perspective/focus of activities and end-users. The actors behind the design and implementation of each of these modes of policing also vary. National governments and other domestic power holders (such as different law enforcement authorities) play a crucial role through formal or informal tactics, legal/policy and financial instruments and means. Our research demonstrates that EU actors and agencies are increasingly active and involved in the domestic dynamics of policing CSAs.

The kind of CSAs which experience more limitations and restrictions are those which are involved, engaged or politically active in the monitoring of public policies and the provision of humanitarian aid, rights and human dignity to migrants and asylum seekers. Three kinds of CSAs are most vulnerable to 'policing dynamics' or have been affected most visibly by EU anti- migrant-smuggling policies: first, CSAs engaging in search and rescue in the Mediterranean Sea; second, those assisting irregular immigrants and asylum-seekers in accessing fundamental rights and basic services and social support (such as shelter and food); and third, claim-making CSAs advocating for immigrant and asylum-seeker rights to be upheld and holding states' policies – and human rights violations – accountable and justiciable.

Restrictions on funding may play a central role in attempts to police civil society. A typical example which emerges from our research has been limiting the availability of financial support in an attempt to ensure uncritical service provision and limiting accountability of human rights violations. Some governments under study use funding as a way of silencing CSAs. By financing selectively only some CSAs mainly focused on service provision, the official (yet often unspoken) expectation is that CSAs self-discipline themselves by becoming 'quasi-implementing agents' of domestic migration management policies.

These policing modalities have important and as yet under-researched consequences. These relate not least to issues of social trust in liberal democratic regimes and the EU as a whole. Social trust can be understood here as the trust which is necessary for the safe and effective delivery of humanitarian services and human rights to those in need. It also relates to the trust invested in the autonomous activities by CSAs and in civil society as a whole in its function as a safeguard in keeping governments accountable in their compliance with human rights legal obligations and democratic rule of law principles.

Figure 8.1 represents how the three modalities of 'policing' take place or are constructed across what can be called 'the facilitation and humanitarian assistance continuum', which covers CSA contributions at the three main sites assessed in this book, which move around the EU Schengen border: first, that of entry (including in the cases of Italy and Greece SAR and at the ports of entry – EU hotspots), and second, those of transit and residence, which entail service provision and access to justice and rights. As seen in chapters five, six and seven, the three modalities of policing manifest themselves across this continuum.

**Figure 8.1** Policing the mobility society: a continuum of sites and modalities

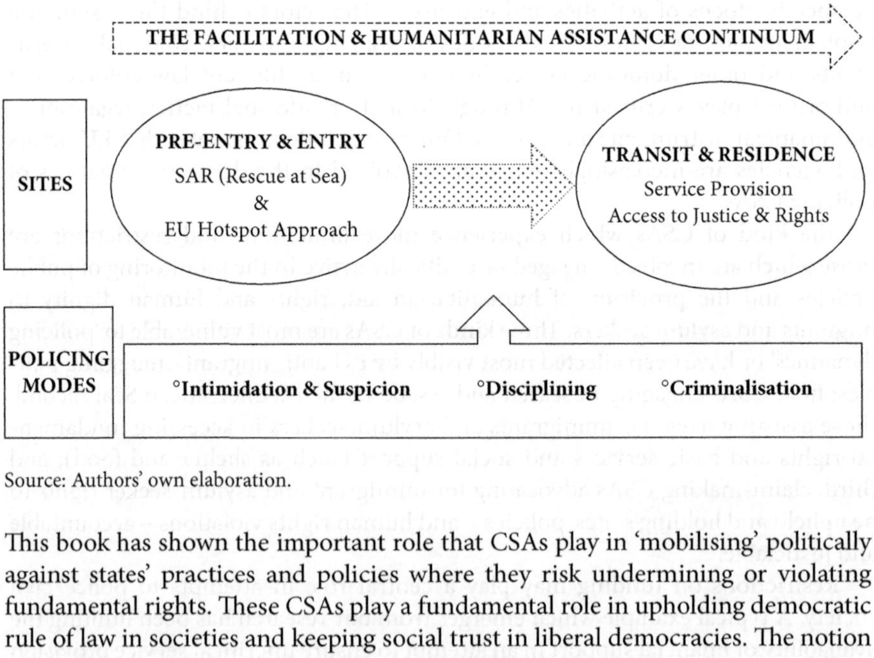


Source: Authors' own elaboration.

This book has shown the important role that CSAs play in 'mobilising' politically against states' practices and policies where they risk undermining or violating fundamental rights. These CSAs play a fundamental role in upholding democratic rule of law in societies and keeping social trust in liberal democracies. The notion of 'mobility society' aims at capturing the diverse set of actors and citizens falling under the rubric 'civil society'. It also facilitates a better understanding of the finding in our research that the effects of anti-migrant-smuggling policies seem to be more visible and felt by CSAs which are 'filling gaps' in service provision and critically monitoring and making accountable the societal effects and inefficiencies left by state and EU policies. These CSAs play a key role in ensuring access to justice and rights for irregular immigrants and asylum-seekers.

More and more voices refer to an increasingly 'shrinking space of civil society' in the EU. Our notion of 'mobility society' moves beyond engaging in substantiating whether the operational spaces for CSAs are 'shrinking' or not.[7] The term 'shrinking civil society space' has found particular appeal as an attempt to capture the latest 'global trends' or challenges to civil society organisations and individuals. According to Youngs and Echagüe (2017: 5),

> The shrinking space phenomenon is getting worse. The global clampdown on civil society has deepened and accelerated in recent years. Over a hundred governments have introduced restrictive laws limiting the operations of civil society organisations (CSOs). Many regimes deploy a range of other – formal and informal – tactics to disadvantage CSOs. Restrictions on civil society are intensifying in non-democratic but also democratic countries.

All too often, claims about 'shrinking space' have been criticised because of a lack of reliable data or consistent methodology demonstrating 'a point in time' or a clear 'trend' that shows the operational spaces for CSAs and human rights movements have significantly shrunk in comparison to a recent past (Brassard-Boureau and Hubert 2010). Such a conclusion would indeed require a detailed historical account of developments substantiating 'shrinking' dynamics in their venues and sites of activities over time. This falls outside this book's scope and objectives.

Our analysis provides evidence that the operational spaces for CSAs had originally increased in response to the European humanitarian refugee crisis in countries like Greece and in the central Mediterranean Sea. Policy and legal developments during 2016 and 2017 proved, however, that the conditions under which CSAs provide humanitarian assistance, access to justice and human rights monitoring in the four countries under assessment have been increasingly under pressure and consequently constrained and limited. This has been the result of a mix between old and new modes of policing – particularly those resulting from EU interventions – which have affected especially the role and activities of the three kinds of CSAs highlighted above, ie, those delivering humanitarian assistance, human rights protection and accountability.

The concept of 'mobility society' offers a more comprehensive tool for incorporating both the restrictions and limitations to which CSAs may be exposed, but also their 'agency' as actors with the capacity of redirecting and mobilising their

[7] Refer for instance to Amnesty International 'Human Rights Defenders under Threat: A Shrinking Space for Civil Society' (London, 2017); or E Aho, 'Shrinking Space for Civil Society: Challenges in Implementing the 2030 Agenda' (Forum Syd, 2017).

activities and strategies in light of the three emerging faces of policing modalities. These acts of resistance or 'mobilising and advocacy strategies' have included, under the four EU Member States investigated in this book, engaging in 'strategic litigation' before relevant ombudspersons or courts; bringing the issue before the attention of relevant international and regional human rights monitoring bodies, or international media; rejecting compliance with demands of centralised registration, codes of conduct or budgetary (foreign-origin) exposure; or refusing to receive certain governmental funding or to participate in the implementation of specific projects.

The political context within which CSAs operate plays a key role in determining the room for manoeuvre regarding mobilisation. As Jordan and Van Tuijl (2006: 7) have rightly underlined,

> An NGO will be in a much better position to address accountability demands in an environment that is free, democratic and conducive to civic action, as opposed to a situation in which an authoritarian regime is repressing the basic freedoms of association, assembly and expression.

Policing may also lead CSAs to self-control, self-silence and self-discipline, corresponding with a sort of restructuring of social behaviour by 'CSAs' (Foucault 1980).

Other consequences of policing modalities may include damaging effects over CSAs reputation and credibility, stigmatising their role with a veil of suspicion and untrustworthiness, or limiting their capacity and agency to engage freely in policy activities and spaces of dialogue and deliberation on public policies and their implementation. This book has provided a wealth of information regarding the various ways in which EU anti-smuggling policies are changing and influencing policing modalities in national and local contexts of the countries under examination.

The phenomenon of increased policing of NGOs that has accompanied the EU response to the 'European refugee crisis' can be understood as part of a fundamental tension of liberal democracy and nation states writ large at the EU level. This tension is encapsulated by the three-part question: (i) who has the power to include and to exclude; (ii) under what conditions; and (iii) how is this power policed? The resulting picture is one where policies aimed at countering smuggling are increasingly targeting the 'disloyal citizen' who assists the 'excluded' – those who do not belong. In the facilitation and humanitarian assistance continuum, CSAs may be framed as committing a crime against the state and the EU community, eg, smuggling or irregular entry, transit or residency.

The processes at stake show a sort of snowball effect over the wider boundaries of society which transcend the traditional foreigner-citizen divide. The division between 'insiders' and 'outsiders' becomes ever-more blurred (Miller 2003). The logics at stake behind the notion of policing the mobility society can also be interpreted as an attempt to delimit who is a real member of 'the society' defined as the group of loyal citizens and legal residents – including civil society actors and individuals – deserving inclusion, security and rights. Some 'insiders' are 'policed by association' and labelled as 'smugglers' by complicity.

International humanitarian law recognises a general duty to act to save fellow human beings in need, and that human rights are universal. Other protections are included, for example in the 1999 UN Declaration on Human Rights Defenders. Yet the boundaries of where this duty begins and ends are often contested in the EU. Meanwhile, as Feldman and Ticktin (2010: 12) have argued, 'Human rights and humanitarian perspectives on how best to protect human life can mandate conflicting courses of action'. We have seen that in the fight against migrant-smuggling in the EU, the official rhetoric of 'humanitarian reason' (Fassin 2011) has been often used by some national governments, European institutions and agencies to justify stringent anti-smuggling laws and an increased set of policing dynamics and practices over CSAs in the Mediterranean and across the EU to avoid the risk of 'facilitation' or 'pull factors' of irregular immigration and smuggling crimes. EU-led anti-smuggling operations are justified as necessary to protect EU Member States from terrorism and organised crime, but also as a form of 'saving migrants from themselves' by deterring them from taking unsafe journeys and risking their lives.

The frequent deaths of migrants seeking safe passage both to and within the EU in real time is a price that many statutory actors appear willing to pay to deter future migrants. Meanwhile, NGOs assert the humanitarian nature of their acts as justification for critiquing and, in some cases, disobeying increased policing and new anti-smuggling regulations and laws. The unprecedented focus to control the actions of some CSAs by EU and Member State actors, coupled with a lack of clear legal protection for citizens to provide humanitarian assistance and access to rights to irregular migrants and asylum seekers, has made the EU, for one of the first times, an arena of democratic deliberation and critical civic engagement. Civil society has awoken across borders to contest policies and laws which it believes to be contrary to the 'core principles' and human rights obligations of both the EU and its Member States.

We have argued elsewhere that 'the increasing involvement of the EU and its actors in irregular immigration is likely to displace mistrust on the effectiveness of irregular immigration policies from domestic actors towards the EU' (Carrera and Allsopp 2018; Carrera, Allsopp and Vosyliūtė forthcoming 2018). The 'ineffectiveness conundrum' (Carrera and Allsopp 2017) characterising the implementation of EU and national migration management policies may well be among the main reasons why critical CSAs are being subjected to increasing policing modalities in their activities seeking humanitarian assistance and access to justice and rights for irregular immigrants and asylum-seekers in need.

As with mistrust of the effectiveness of policies to control irregular migration, mistrust of policies' fairness or democratic legitimacy has also emerged from across the political spectrum over the course of the European refugee crisis. It is important to stress this has led to civil society mobilisation to open and close borders and both to welcome and deter migrants. In a context where the EU is increasingly joining individual nation states' efforts to determine and reframe the boundaries of inclusion and exclusion, and where civil society is witnessing and affected by such processes and their enforcement, the development of a pan-European civil society movement is crucial to holding EU and Member State institutions to account in accordance with a democratic rule of law and human rights-compliant agenda. The debate poses new questions in an increasingly interconnected world about what a European civil society looks like. Some initial observations are clear.

First, the state of 'emergency' introduced in parts of the EU in response to the 'European refugee crisis' has brought in a raft of illiberal policies and allowed for unprecedented restrictions on civil society in a number of Member States, including the four under investigation in this book: Greece, Hungary, Italy and the UK. Where CSAs were often the first to respond to humanitarian needs and gaps, they are now being 'forced out', often through a combination of various modes of policing. In this context, it is crucial that civil society remains connected to preserve the important monitoring and service space it occupies in the national and Europe-wide spaces.

Secondly, the nature of CSAs and the work of non-governmental actors in the EU has changed during the European refugee crisis. Our research suggests that the main concerns of practitioners continues to be how to deliver their assistance tasks and responsibilities without being penalised, and how to avoid social exclusion, maintain social cohesion and cater to the needs of all these populations. Meanwhile, organisations used to providing shelter and food have leant into new areas such as legal assistance in recognition of shortcomings in avenues for justice.

The spaces for CSAs supporting migrants and refugees in Europe has also gradually expanded and remains ever-evolving, so as to include more informal and loose networks and activist groups which are increasingly connected across borders. This very much follows and corresponds with the trend, previously identified by Neier (2012: 9), concerning the increasing international linkages of human rights movements and activists who 'feel a kinship and seek ties to others within the movement' across borders or globally in international rights efforts. In these emerging spaces of pan-European civil society activism and mobilisation, a caution approach must be taken to recognising the specificity of each national and local context. It is at the regional and local levels that various modes of policing and different manifestations of civic mobilisation react, adapt or respond to the former in peculiar and characteristic forms.

Many CSA groups and citizens are working for the first time with migrants and refugees as a result of the common EU external (Schengen) border. It is yet to be seen how these new arrangements will develop and the diverse threads work together. More research is needed to explore how different types of CSA position themselves strategically according to different frames and policing modalities – international humanitarian law, religious values, national ethics, political stances and personal ethics and views which must all be accommodated for civil society to operate independently from government and law enforcement interference. This is particularly so with respect to the ways in which they 'mobilise' and carry out their monitoring activities in relation or response to the increasing 'Europeanisation' of migration, border and asylum policies.

Thirdly, it is important to note that the stakes of maintaining an independent civil society have impacts far beyond the responses to the European refugee crisis. The impacts of policies which criminalise migration have been shown to have broader impacts on the population as a whole, including making life more difficult for other minority groups in society and impairing social trust in society. Policies that police contact with irregular migrants in different ways may lead to widespread feelings of subjective insecurity as well as stigma, distrust and prejudice towards immigrants and refugees.[8]

[8] See, eg, Webber (2008); Fundamental Rights Agency (2014) 'Criminalisation of migrants in an irregular situation and of persons engaging with them'; and the 2010 report on the *Criminalisation of Migration in Europe: Human Rights Implications* by the Council of Europe Commissioner for Human Rights, on the risk of hate crime and xenophobia.

# 9

# Conclusions

The data gathered via 89 interviews as well as field research trips, online questionnaires, focus group discussions with civil society actors and closed-door events with coastguards, law enforcement and judicial actors show that policing mobility society is indeed a complex phenomenon in the EU. The research covered the cases of Italy, Greece, Hungary and the UK, where new types of policies emerged in the context of the so-called 'European refugee humanitarian crisis' that began in 2015.

The book has examined how EU policies aimed at countering migrant-smuggling have affected civil society actors' activities in the provision of humanitarian assistance and access to rights for undocumented migrants and asylum-seekers. It explored and showcased the effects of EU laws, policies and agencies' operations in countering migrant-smuggling and their implementation, ranging from mere suspicion, intimidation or harassment, disciplining to formal criminalisation.

The book has demonstrated that the EU's Facilitators Package and EU Member States' national criminal law is not in line with the standards set by the UN Migrant Smuggling Protocol. At the moment, it is not mandatory for the criterion of 'financial gain or other material benefit' to be met in order to establish a base crime in terms of facilitation of entry (in Greece, Hungary, Italy, the UK and the majority of EU Member States); it is merely an aggravating circumstance. This is also the case for the facilitation of stay (in Greece, the UK and half of EU Member States). This in turn creates legal uncertainty, as a broad range of not-for-profit acts of compassion can be criminalised, without criminal intent.

The book has also examined the political pressures and practical challenges arising for national border and coastguards and judicial authorities in effectively implementing anti-migrant-smuggling policies. Political salience and prioritisation of the issue of migrant-smuggling has gained momentum among the EU's Justice and Home Affairs agencies. Frontex, Europol, Eurojust, and even EASO are gathering intelligence and information and sharing it in order to predict and prevent migrant-smuggling. At the height of the EU migration management crisis, even military actors, such as EUNAVFOR MED Operation Sophia, were engaged to combat migrant-smuggling on the high seas.

The effects of EU and national policies that criminalise the facilitation of entry and residence of irregular immigrants extend beyond cases where civil society actors have faced actual prosecutions or administrative penalties when assisting irregular immigrants and asylum-seekers. The book captures 'policing the mobility society' – a wider set of punitive and restrictive dynamics that directly or indirectly follow EU anti-smuggling policies. We have elaborated how EU anti-migrant-smuggling policies are (un)intentionally translated into the policing of civil society actors and citizens' movements, especially those engaged in monitoring states' performance in implementing migration practices and in mobilising for migrants' access to their fundamental rights. We therefore conclude that the stakes are high not only for civil society actors (section I) but also for society as a whole (section II).

## I. Impacts on Civil Society Actors

'Migrant-smuggling' is by definition a very politically charged concept in Europe. The embeddedness of 'anti-smuggling laws' in national migration laws and not in criminal codes confirms they are tools of migration management. A closed-door discussion also confirmed that initiatives to counter migrant-smuggling are intended to 'curb and prevent' migration. Efforts to include or subjugate the activities of humanitarians in the fight against migrant-smuggling are against the ethos and the very mandate of various CSAs, which base their mission on human rights, including the rights of undocumented migrants. The example of CSAs conducting search and rescue being asked to take pictures of migrants on the ship, destroy the engines or take police officers on board are some of the difficult situations where humanitarian actors face the dilemma of whether to continue their live-saving operations, as happened in the central Mediterranean Sea (see chapter 5.I).

This explains why the calls by ministries of the interior, police and prosecutors, for more information about the humanitarian actors, service providers and anyone coming into contact with those presumed to be undocumented can be abused and misused. This applies not only to those who are facilitating the entry of migrants and refugees without any material benefit, but also to those which provide or aim to help them with food, shelter and access to justice.

Here the concept of the 'firewall' becomes useful to explain and resolve clashes between different mandates. The concept was first proposed by François Crépeau (2013), at that time the UN Special Rapporteur on the Human Rights of Migrants. The firewall has been broadly defined as 'a separation between immigration enforcement activities and public service provision' (Crépeau and Hastie 2015: 157). The firewall aims in particular to cover those provisions that preserve the basic rights applicable to 'everyone' within the jurisdiction of the country, regardless of their migration status. Such rights include prohibitions against torture, slavery and servitude, discrimination, the right to health, education, fair labour conditions and remuneration (including for undeclared work), and legal redress – under both national, international and European regional standards.

As Crépeau and Hastie highlight, '[r]eponses in the legal, political and social arenas have focused significantly on deterring, controlling and criminalising migration, with little attention paid to the situation of irregular migrants already settled in destination countries' (2015: 157–58). This statement was also confirmed during the field trips to the four selected countries for this research, where various reporting obligations or prohibitions on the provision of basic services were seen as making external border countries and the EU as a whole less attractive for migrant and asylum-seekers. Chapters four to seven illustrate that implicitly EU external borders and points of arrival are intended to become 'less attractive' not only for those who move, but also for those who mobilise on behalf of refugees, asylum-seekers and undocumented migrants: CSAs providing various kinds of basic needs that are all too commonly neglected by the public sector.

As showcased in chapter four, the lack of legal certainty stemming from overly broad interpretations of anti-smuggling laws combined with political pressures is serving to deter, police, control and criminalise humanitarian assistance. There is a worrying trend, on the part of both EU and national actors, of portraying various humanitarian actors as 'colluding' or 'enabling' migrant-smuggling. These law enforcement actors sometimes implicitly and sometimes quite directly ask CSAs to choose sides – 'to cooperate with us or with smugglers', when for example requiring SAR NGOs to take and share pictures, or to sign a code of conduct (see chapter 5.I).

In addition, as has been noted previously, 'Basic services, such a healthcare, are becoming increasingly difficult for irregular migrants who have reason to suspect and fear detection and deportation in attempting to access such services' (Crépeau and Hastie 2015: 158–59). This book has documented that CSAs providing humanitarian assistance to migrants and refugees experience fears in relation to their work which run on a spectrum from damage to their public reputation and losing their clients' trust, to being charged with aiding and abetting smuggling and forced to discontinue their activities.

CSAs are placed between society and the group whom they are serving or representing. Faced with the effects of intimidation, disciplining and criminalisation, their main preoccupation is to uphold their clients' trust, but negative public opinion is the greatest preoccupation for CSAs in Italy, Greece and, most obviously, Hungary (see the Figure 9.1).

Yet the humanitarian actors who participated in focus group discussions for this research revealed that the picture of law enforcement and civil society as being inextricably at odds with one another is a misconception. Civil society discussants highlighted that they are willing to collaborate with law enforcement officials under certain conditions, namely, if their independent mandate is respected.[1] Several discussants representing national CSOs echoed that not only are they

[1] Focus group with CSAs providing humanitarian assistance, 11 May 2017, Brussels, Belgium.

**Figure 9.1** Comparison of perception of the costs of increased humanitarian assistance

**QAP. In your opinion, what is most at stake for your organisation, when thinking about increased policing of humanitarian assistance? Rank from 5 (most important) to 1 (least important).**

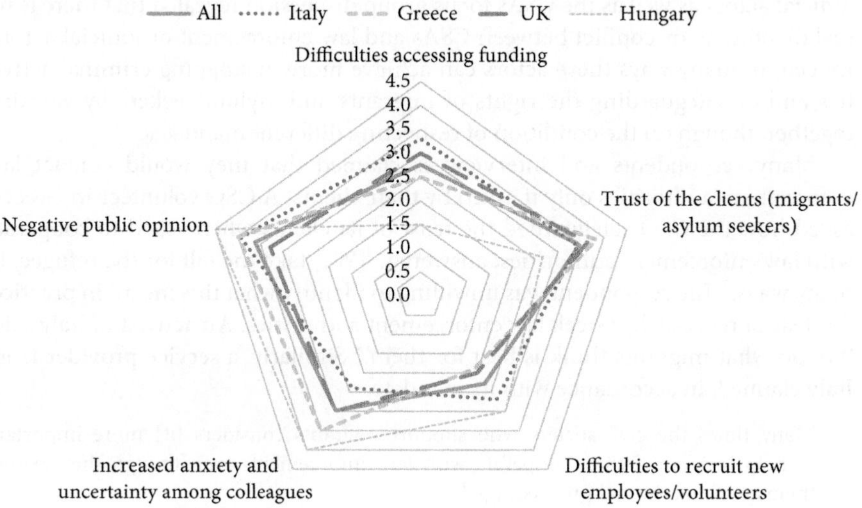


Source: CSA Online Survey (2017).

willing, but that it is essential for them to cooperate with law enforcement in order to fulfil their mission and ensure the safety of their clients and their own activities.[2] A discussant from a Hungarian CSO explained that its assistance to migrants and asylum-seekers was 'driving smugglers out of business'.[3] Indeed, because they were receiving some threats from smugglers, they stressed that it 'is essential to have good relations with the police to protect our activities'.[4] A CSO working at the EU-level mentioned the lawless situation in Calais, where the lack of law enforcement presence led to many CSAs leaving the area as it 'became too dangerous for NGOs' due to the increased number of various criminals trying to take advantage of the hopeless situation of migrants.[5]

In addition, several interviewees, CSA focus group discussants and online survey respondents stressed the importance of having a good working relationship with law enforcement officers, particularly when CSOs need to protect their clients from ongoing abuse, violence, rape and other crimes. These could be literally questions of life and death. For example, a survey respondent volunteering for a CSO in Greece mentioned reporting '[a] suicide note to the police to

[2] Focus group with CSAs providing humanitarian assistance, 11 May 2017, Brussels, Belgium.
[3] Focus group with CSAs providing humanitarian assistance, 11 May 2017, Brussels, Belgium.
[4] Focus group with CSAs providing humanitarian assistance, 11 May 2017, Brussels, Belgium.
[5] Focus group with CSAs providing humanitarian assistance, 11 May 2017, Brussels, Belgium.

follow up on'.[6] It would be counterproductive if such a CSO were to have little or no faith in law enforcement to act in the interest of migrants.

Both the closed-door discussion with coastguards, law enforcement and judicial actors as well as the CSAs focus group discussion revealed that there is no real dichotomy or conflict between CSAs and law enforcement or judicial actors. Indeed, in many ways these actors can achieve more in stopping criminal activities and/or safeguarding the rights of migrants and asylum-seekers by working together, though on the condition of respecting different mandates.

Many respondents and interviewees claimed that they would contact law enforcement authorities only if asked by their clients. A CSO volunteer in Greece, asked how the CSO safeguarded the trust of its clients when asked to cooperate with law enforcement authorities, answered, '[We] take the fall for the refugee, in many ways'.[7] The respondent was unwilling to identify what this meant in practice, for 'fear of reprisal' by Greek law enforcement authorities. An activist in Italy said, 'We do what migrants think is best for them'.[8] Similarly, a service provider from Italy claimed, in accordance with its mandate,

> Many times the civil society who support migrants considers [it] more important to help [migrants] than cooperate with law enforcement, even though they expose themselves to criminal proceedings.[9]

Many CSAs outlined certain conditions on what could and could not be shared. Discussion participants from CSAs, for example, agreed that personal data should not be shared with law enforcement agencies, unless there was some imminent risk to their clients or own staff. In line with this logic, some organisations established clear guidelines for their staff. For example, a respondent working for a CSO in Hungary stressed:

> Our services are anonymous and confidential: we don't give out personal data, and users of the services are not required to disclose their identity and residence status.[10]

An Italian volunteer said, 'The civil society safeguards the trust of irregular migrants protecting them, giving assistance and information'. This respondent also acknowledged that this is not always possible when interacting with public service providers, since 'certain administrative proceedings and services cannot take place without this [identity and residence status]'.[11] A respondent from Italy highlighted the ethical and practical difficulties for service providers:

> Working in the reception system you can't refuse to cooperate because there is a contract with the Ministry of the Interior. In my job, I try to be honest and transparent,

[6] A respondent volunteering for a CSO in Greece, CSA Online Survey (2017).
[7] A respondent volunteering for a CSO in Greece, CSA Online Survey (2017).
[8] A respondent belonging to an activist group in Italy, CSA Online Survey (2017).
[9] A respondent providing services in Italy, CSA Online Survey (2017).
[10] A respondent working for a CSO in Hungary, CSA Online Survey (2017).
[11] A respondent working for a CSO in Hungary, CSA Online Survey (2017).

> especially when it's about the enforcement of decisions or laws that I can't change or refuse to respect. Even if most of the time I don't agree with them.[12]

CSOs which were less targeted by policing activities and criminalisation and felt that their mandate was respected were more likely to cooperate with law enforcement than were individuals and activists. For example, a respondent who was an individual, volunteering in Greece, unaffiliated with any CSO and personally knew of cases of police intimidation and harassment, claimed that non-cooperation is the only solution:

> I think the only way is avoiding cooperation with those authorities *at all cost* and if they're unavoidable – trying to protect people without papers from deportation and trying to create pressure on the authorities so that their position of power is threatened. [Emphasis added.][13]

Similarly, an activist from Italy highlighted the modes of ideological resistance, such as 'protesting and doing political activism'.[14] CSOs working in a highly pressured field, such as SAR, also became reluctant to cooperate with law enforcement by taking pictures for the identification of migrants or asylum-seekers who were steering the boat or holding a compass. A respondent working for a CSO in Italy confirmed that some 'Search and Rescue civil society NGO vessels … are not willing to cooperate with the police (for the identification [of suspect smugglers among migrants]).[15]

The two examples above indicate a lack of trust among some CSAs that law enforcement will actually respect their humanitarian mandate or acts of solidarity. However, an interviewee from the CSO conducting SAR in the central Mediterranean stressed the very good cooperation and understanding between it and the Italian Coast Guard, the authority responsible for the coordination of SAR operations.[16] Nevertheless, the same interviewee highlighted numerous misunderstandings with other law enforcement branches which are tasked with borders controls and investigation in smuggling.

All in all, the picture is mixed. CSAs are more willing to cooperate with law enforcement when there is mutual understanding and respect for differences in their mandates. CSAs providing assistance, services and access to rights for refugees and asylum seekers feel it is important that the social trust and ethos of various humanitarian organisations and other civil society actors are not undermined.[17]

[12] A respondent providing services in Italy, CSA Online Survey (2017).

[13] A respondent, an individual volunteer in Greece (not affiliated with any CSO), CSA Online Survey (2017).

[14] A respondent belonging to an activist group in Italy, CSA Online Survey (2017).

[15] A respondent working for a CSO in Italy, CSA Online Survey (2017).

[16] Interview with CSO conducting SAR, 10 November 2016, Rome, Italy.

[17] Focus group with CSAs providing humanitarian assistance, 11 May 2017, Brussels, Belgium.

## II. Impact on Society as a Whole: Liberal Democracy, Refugees and the Crisis of Exclusion

In the context of the recent so-called 'European humanitarian refugee crisis', we are starting to see the emergence of immanent critiques of policy at the EU level. Several civil society groups have appropriated the frame of European values to justify their actions in solidarity with migrants and refugees, appealing – as with the WeMove.eu petition – to a common sense European citizenship. Many anti-Brexit civil society 'Remain' groups in the UK also made the case for staying in the EU on the basis of common enlightenment values of human rights, for example. Indeed, it was a common sight at UK Remain rallies to see 'Refugees Welcome' placards alongside EU flags, as part of a progressive narrative about staying in Europe. Other civil society actors have argued that the EU community's 'basic principles' include assisting vulnerable migrants based on its common history of receiving refugees (and a common shame regarding the episodes in European history when states did not 'do their bit') (see Allsopp 2017).

UK efforts to resettle children from Calais to the UK were framed, for example, as a modern-day equivalent of the *Kindertransport* which sought to honour Europe's past tradition and learn from mistakes. Lord Alf Dubs, a former *Kindertransport* refugee himself and former British Member of Parliament, lent his own name to the Bill seeking to facilitate the safe passage to more unaccompanied minors from Europe to Britain. As Heidi Allen, the Conservative MP that tabled the amendment, stressed in Parliament, the amendment was not just about helping child refugees, but also about the principle of 'European solidarity'.

Significantly, thousands upon thousands of EU citizens voted with their feet, exercising their Schengen privilege to travel freely across EU Member States to volunteer at the height of the crisis. Some European citizen activists and volunteers stated that being a European citizen helped them in their work, meaning that they could mobilise their own 'citizen privilege' to assist less fortunate migrants.[18] Other civil society volunteers claim that they were targeted regardless, or specifically because, of their European citizenship by way of 'being made an example' to dissuade others.[19] This includes a group of five Spanish and Danish volunteers facing trial for migrant-smuggling in the Aegean Sea for their work with the search and rescue NGOs PROEM-AID and Team Humanity;[20] Jugend Rettet SAR operations in the central Mediterranean, pending in the Court of Trapani; and

[18] Interview with civil society activist providing social assistance in Ventimiglia, Italy, via Skype, 20 February 2017.

[19] Interview with civil society activist providing social assistance in Ventimiglia, Italy, via Skype, 20 February 2017. See also G Gulia 'Chronology of Incidents against migrants and activists in Ventimiglia 2015–2016' (2016) *Q Code Magazine*, www.qcodemag.it/2016/12/09/ventimiglia-migranti-repressione/.

[20] Discussion with Spanish firefighter on trial for migrant-smuggling, 21 November 2016, European Parliament. For more information on the event see: www.socialplatform.org/blog/round-table-meeting-in-the-european-parliament-on-the-eu-facilitation-directive/.

some European activists in Ventimiglia who were banned from the border territory (see chapter 6.I).

The CSA online survey conducted for the purposes of this research confirms that general reporting obligations in national laws had no significant effect on respondents. Political pressures to 'curb migration' and particular experiences of increased policing of humanitarian actors were nevertheless shown to make organisations change and adapt their practices. The respondents who reported that they knew personally of cases of intimidation, disciplining and criminalisation were more likely to change their practices than those who knew about it from media.

This rooting of universal values and obligations towards outsiders within the European tradition expands the breadth of the movement to a broader spectrum of citizens. The adopted frame exemplifies a combination of ideology and strategy theorised by Westby (2002), whereby framing 'strategically appropriates hegemonic ideology'. This strategy, common in democratic polities and among social movements involving civil disobedience, 'displays the ideology and its lived contradictions in collective actions that affirm rather than deny the basic legitimacy of the system'. Matringe (2009: 13) has commented that the same logic was used by French protesters who used the frame of *fraternité* to defend their right to assist irregular migrants. In doing so, they sought 'the modification of the rule or institution, not the throwing into doubt of the entire system'.

In some areas of civil society – particularly among the newer, more informal civil society groups – European citizens have thus replicated and sought to transform the solidarity dynamics at the EU institutional level through activism and volunteering: just as EU institutions have positioned themselves in regional solidarity, such as posting Frontex officers pooled from EU Member States at certain EU external borders, EU civil society actors and activists are also present at these borders serving a protective, safeguarding and monitoring function.

As Allsopp (2017b) argued, the phenomenon of increased policing and criminalisation of NGOs that has accompanied the EU response to the European humanitarian refugee crisis can be understood as part of a fundamental tension of liberal democracy and nation states writ large at the EU level. This tension is encapsulated by the three-part question: (i) who has the power to include and to exclude; (ii) under what conditions; and (iii) how is this power policed? What is the role of European civil society in providing humanitarian assistance and monitoring the human rights effects of anti-smuggling legislation and operations?

It is recognised in international humanitarian law that we all have a duty to act to save fellow human beings in need, and that human rights are universal. Other protections are included, for example, in the 1999 UN Declaration on Human Rights Defenders. Yet the boundaries of where this duty begins and ends are often contested. Meanwhile, as Feldman and Ticktin (2012: 12) have argued, and as this book has documented, 'human rights and humanitarian perspectives on how best to protect human life can mandate conflicting courses of action'. We have seen that in the fight against migrant-smuggling in the EU, the rhetoric of 'humanitarian reason' (Fassin 2010) has been used by states and EU agencies to justify stringent anti-smuggling laws and the increased policing of NGOs in the Mediterranean and across the EU to avoid the risk of 'collaboration' or 'pull factors'.

Anti-smuggling operations are justified as necessary to protect EU Member States from terrorism and organised crime, but also as a form of 'saving migrants from themselves' by deterring them from taking unsafe journeys and risking their lives. The ongoing deaths of migrants seeking safe passage both to and within the EU in real time is a price that many statutory actors appear willing to pay to deter future migrants. Meanwhile, NGOs assert the humanitarian nature of their acts as justification for critiquing and, in some cases, disobeying increased policing and new anti-smuggling regulations and laws. To repeat the words of the NGO worker in Calais cited in chapter five, 'No child should die to deter others from coming'.

The unprecedented new concentration of powers to deter migrants and control the actions of civil society actors at the level of the EU, coupled with a lack of clear protection for citizens to provide humanitarian assistance to irregular migrants and asylum-seekers at the same level, has made the EU for the first times an arena of democratic deliberation. Parts of civil society have awoken across borders to contest policies and laws that they believe to be contrary to the 'core principles' of both the EU and its Member States, as well as to broader humanitarian or political principles (Allsopp 2017).

Carrera and Allsopp have argued elsewhere that 'the increasing involvement of the EU and its actors in irregular immigration is likely to displace mistrust on the effectiveness of irregular immigration policies from domestic actors towards the EU' (Carrera and Allsopp 2018: 79). As with mistrust of the effectiveness of policies to control irregular migration, mistrust of policies' fairness or democratic legitimacy has also emerged from across the political spectrum over the course of the refugee crisis. It is important to stress that this has led to civil society mobilisation to open and close borders and both to welcome and deter migrants. It is beyond the scope of this volume to explore civil society actors' mobilisations to close borders and exclude migrants and refugees, but it must be noted that anti-migrant and xenophobic movements are also on the rise in the EU. In 2017, for example, a group of activists crowdfunded more than £67,000 to hire a boat as part of a mission to 'Defend Europe' (Roberts 2017). Still, efforts to include migrants and asylum-seekers have largely been the domain of parts of European civil society, while, with some exceptions, for example, Germany's 2015 commitment to assisting Syrian refugees (Hall and Lichfield 2015), the policies and activities of the EU, its Home Affairs agencies and Member States, have largely followed the populist logic of exclusion.

In a context where the EU is increasingly joining individual nation states' efforts to determine the boundaries of inclusion and exclusion and where civil society – the natural counterpart in such discussions – is increasingly the subject of such boundaries and their enforcement, the development of a pan-European civil society is more important than ever for holding EU and Member State institutions to account in accordance with a liberal, democratic and humanitarian agenda.

The debate poses new questions in an increasingly interconnected world as to what a European civil society looks like.

First, the state of 'emergency' introduced in parts of the EU in response to the European humanitarian 'refugee crisis' has brought in a raft of illiberal measures and allowed for unprecedented restrictions on civil society in a number of Member States including Italy, Greece, Hungary and the UK. Where civil society actors were often the first to respond to the refugee crisis, they are now being forced out, often through measures of policing including intimidation, disciplining and criminalisation (Carrera et al 2018).

Secondly, the nature of civil society groups and the work of NGOs in the EU has changed over the course of the migration management crisis. Our ongoing research suggests that the main concerns of practitioners continues to be how to deliver their assistance tasks and responsibilities without being penalised, and how to avoid social exclusion and cater to the needs of these populations. Meanwhile, organisations used to providing shelter and food have leant into new areas such as legal assistance in recognition of shortcomings in avenues for justice.[21] The space for civil society groups supporting migrants and refugees in Europe has also expanded to include more informal and loose networks and activist groups which are increasingly connected across borders. We propose the term 'mobility society' to capture the demographic of those who move and those who mobilise to support migrants in the EU (Carrera et al 2018). Many such groups are working with migrants and refugees for the first time. It is yet to be seen how this new arrangement will develop and how these diverse threads will work together, although current research suggests there are examples of tensions as well as fruitful collaborations.

More research is needed to explore how different types of civil society groups position themselves strategically according to different frames – international humanitarian law, religious values, national ethics, political stances and personal ethics, which must all be accommodated for civil society actors to operate (Allsopp 2012; 2017a). And also, how this changes due to the experiences of policing – whether they become more 'political' and 'activist', or more wary and self-censor their statements. Interviews in all four countries surveyed for this research confirmed evidence of both: while some parts of civil society are '(self)-shrinking', others are becoming more vocal and articulating their concerns alongside broader political issues of fundamental rights, democracy and rule of law.

Thirdly, it is important to note that the stakes of maintaining an independent civil society have impacts far beyond the response to the European humanitarian refugee crisis. Policies which criminalise migration have been shown to have broader impacts on the population as a whole, including making life more difficult for other minority groups in society and negatively impacting social trust in society (Allsopp 2016; Jones et al 2017).

[21] Interview with international civil society organisation, London, via Skype, 13 July 2017.

It is hypothesised that policies that criminalise contact with irregular migrants may lead to widespread feelings of subjective insecurity as well as stigma, distrust and prejudice towards migrants (Webber 2008; Council of Europe 2010; FRA 2014; Fekete, Webber and Edmond-Pettitt 2017). Speaking of the deployment of 3,000 new 'border hunters' and enhanced policing and reports of violence at the external Schengen border between Hungary and Serbia, one civil society interviewee commented,

> I wonder what is going to happen in a few years' time, when those officers who have taken part in these acts of violence will go back to their original postings and community … if it will normalise that violence? … [I]t's a very serious issue, not to do with migrants and asylum seekers. These police officers will be the ones who stop me on the road or anyone else so that's very problematic.[22]

Fourthly, in this emerging arena of pan-European civil society activism, caution must be taken in recognising the specificity of each national context. One Hungarian civil society volunteer highlighted the problems that arose in this regard when activists came to show solidarity with migrants in Szeged at the external Schengen border with Serbia in 2015:

> No Borders struggles in the West have a strong anti-capitalist focus, but you don't say that here [in Central Eastern Europe] because of the past traumas of communism. So this new European solidarity is great, we were calling people ahead in different countries and coordinating between service providers and activist groups … [B]ut there's also a problem in this idea of facilitating only the transit of migrants from East to West, not challenging ideas of East and West within the Union.[23]

Greece, is another example, where European citizens who came to Greek islands to volunteer individually or as a part of international CSOs were greeted with suspicion and labelled as 'foreigners'.

Fifthly and finally, it is crucial that civil society creates and maintains a space for the voices of affected migrants themselves. As François Crépeau (2013) has stressed in one of his speeches on the structural limitations of democracy:

> Only 'we the people' are represented. Migrants are not and will not, in the foreseeable future, be significantly represented politically. All human rights battles have been won through political mobilisation and judicial battles, but irregular and vulnerable migrants don't vote, rarely mobilise and mostly don't protest.

An important body of research is emerging which documents migrant-led activism and rights-claiming in Europe (see, eg, Ataç et al 2016 and the special issue of *Citizenship Studies* to which it marks the introduction).

This research has shown the diverse ways in which those who seek to act as a voice for the 'voiceless' or who mobilise for migrants' mobility and fundamental

[22] Interview with representative of a civil society organisation providing legal services, Budapest, Hungary, via Skype, 16 August 2017.

[23] Interview with representative of a civil society organisation providing social services, Budapest, 30 August 2017.

rights are affected by the EU's anti-migrant-smuggling policies, practices and grand narratives. The impacts go far beyond individual cases of criminalisation: within civil society seeds of mistrust are being sown; we are moving towards a society where mere contact with a refugee or other migrant becomes a reason for heightened policing. Such a phenomenon is all too well documented in the darkest pages of European history, how the prohibition of human compassion and solidarity can result in crimes against humanity, genocides and ethnic cleansing. The rich evidence presented in this book calls on readers to stop and critically reflect on what is happening and on where the EU's anti-smuggling priority is heading.

# ANNEX 1

# Anonymised Lists of Interviews

**Field trip to Italy and related preparatory/follow-up interviews**

| No | Type | Date | Place |
|---|---|---|---|
| 1. | Preparation interview with EU agencies | 4 October 2016 | via Skype |
| 2. | Preparation interview with CSO conducting SAR | 7 October 2016 | via Skype |
| 3. | Preparation interview with CSO conducting SAR | 7 October 2016 | via Skype |
| 4. | Interview with non-formal group (volunteers & activists) | 7 November 2016 | Rome, Italy |
| 5. | Interview with CSO providing social and medical assistance | 8 November 2016 | Rome, Italy |
| 6. | Interview with national border/ coastguard authorities | 8 November 2016 | Rome, Italy |
| 7. | Interview with EU agencies | 8 November 2016 | Rome, Italy |
| 8. | Interview with CSO providing social assistance | 9 November 2016 | Rome, Italy |
| 9. | Interview with the UN actor | 9 November 2016 | Rome, Italy |
| 10. | Interview with EU agencies | 9 November 2016 | Rome, Italy |
| 11. | Interview with national border/ coastguard authorities | 9 November 2016 | Rome, Italy |
| 12. | Interview with CSO conducting SAR | 10 November 2016 | Rome, Italy |
| 13. | Interview with the UN actor | 10 November 2016 | Catania, Italy |
| 14. | Interview with CSO providing legal and social assistance | 11 of November, 2016 | Catania, Italy |
| 15. | Interview with the UN actor | 11 November 2016 | Catania, Italy |
| 16. | Interview with non-formal group (activists) | 11 November 2016 | Catania, Italy |
| 17. | Interview win national judicial authorities | 12 November 2016 | Catania, Italy |
| 18. | Interview with CSO providing medical assistance (volunteers) | 12 November 2016 | Syracuse, Italy |
| 19. | Interview with EU agencies/officials (a) | 13 November 2016 | Catania, Italy |

| No | Type | Date | Place |
|---|---|---|---|
| 20. | Interview with EU agencies/officials (b) | 13 November 2016 | Catania, Italy |
| 21. | Interview with CSA providing social assistance (volunteers) | 31 January 2017 | Rome, Italy |
| 22. | Interview with non-formal group (activists) in Ventimiglia | 20 February 2017 | via Skype |
| 23. | Interview with national border/coastguard authorities | 27 of June 2017 | via Skype |
| 24. | Follow-up interview with CSO conducting SAR | 3 of July 2017 | via Skype |
| 25. | Follow-up interview with CSO conducting SAR | 22 August 2017 | via Skype |
| 26. | Follow-up interview with CSA providing social assistance (volunteers) in Rome | 23 September 2017 | via Skype |

## Field trip to Greece and related follow-up interviews

| No | Type | Date | Place |
|---|---|---|---|
| 27. | Interview with CSO enabling integration | 6 June 2017 | Athens, Greece |
| 28. | Interview with EU agency | 6 June 2017 | Athens, Greece |
| 29. | Interview with CSO providing legal assistance | 6 June 2017 | Athens, Greece |
| 30. | Interview with CSO providing social assistance | 6 June 2017 | Athens, Greece |
| 31. | Interview with national border/ coastguard authorities | 7 June 2017 | Athens, Greece |
| 32. | Interview with EU agency (a) | 7 June 2017 | Athens, Greece |
| 33. | Interview with EU agency (b) | 7 June 2017 | Athens, Greece |
| 34. | Interview with CSO providing social assistance | 7 June 2017 | Athens, Greece |
| 35. | Interview with CSO providing legal assistance | 8 June 2017 | Lesvos island, Greece |
| 36. | Interview with EU agencies/officials | 8 June 2017 | Lesvos island, Greece |
| 37. | Interview with national border/ coastguard authorities | 9 June 2017 | Lesvos island, Greece |
| 38. | Interview with UN actor (a) | 9 June 2017 | Lesvos island, Greece |
| 39. | Interview with UN actor (b) | 9 June 2017 | Lesvos island, Greece |
| 40. | Interview with EU agencies/officials | 9 June 2017 | Lesvos island, Greece |

| No | Type | Date | Place |
|---|---|---|---|
| 41. | Interview with expert on national border/ coastguard authorities | 12 June 2017 | Athens, Greece |
| 42. | Follow-up interview with CSO providing social assistance in Lesvos island | 14 July 2017 | via Skype |

**Field trip to UK and related follow-up interviews**

| No | Type | Date | Place |
|---|---|---|---|
| 43. | Interview with UK Member of European Parliament | 7 June 2017 | via Skype |
| 44. | Interview with CSO providing social and legal assistance | 3 July,2017 | London, UK |
| 45. | Interview with professional body representing the private sector | 4 July 2017 | London, UK |
| 46. | Interview with CSO providing social and legal assistance | 4 July 2017 | London, UK |
| 47. | Interview with CSO providing social and legal assistance | 5 July 2017 | London, UK |
| 48. | Interview with CSO providing social assistance | 5 July 2017 | via Skype |
| 49. | Interview with CSO providing medical assistance | 6 July 2017 | London, UK |
| 50. | Interview with national welfare authorities providing social assistance | 6 July 2017 | London, UK |
| 51. | Interview with CSO providing social and legal assistance | 7 July 2017 | London, UK |
| 52. | Interview with CSO providing social and legal assistance | 7 July 2017 | London, UK |
| 53. | Interview with CSO providing medical assistance | 7 July 2017 | Via Skype |
| 54. | Interview with non-formal group (activists) | 7 July 2017 | London, UK |
| 55. | Interview with CSO providing legal assistance | 7 July 2017 | London, UK |
| 56. | Interview with CSO providing social assistance | 11 July 2017 | London, UK |
| 57. | Interview with professional body representing the private sector | 11 July 2017 | London, UK |
| 58. | Interview with national welfare authority providing social and medical assistance | 12 July 2017 | London, UK |
| 59. | Interview with CSO providing legal and social assistance | 13 July 2017 | Oxford, UK |
| 60. | Interview with CSO providing social and legal assistance | 16 August 2017 | London, UK |
| 61. | Interview with UN actor | 17 August 2017 | via Skype |
| 62. | Interview with UN actor | 22 August 2017 | via Skype |

**Field trip to Hungary and related follow-up interviews**

| No | Type | Date | Place |
|---|---|---|---|
| 63. | Interview with CSO providing legal assistance | 16 August | via Skype |
| 64. | Interview with legal expert | 18 August | via Skype |
| 65. | Interview with CSO providing medical assistance | 22 August | via Skype |
| 66. | Interview with legal expert | 28 August 2017 | Budapest, Hungary |
| 67. | Interview with CSO providing legal assistance | 28 August 2017 | Budapest, Hungary |
| 68. | Interview with UN actor | 29 August 2017 | Budapest, Hungary |
| 69. | Interview with CSO providing social and legal assistance | 29 August 2017 | Budapest, Hungary |
| 70. | Interview with UN actor | 29 August 2017 | Budapest, Hungary |
| 71. | Interview with CSO providing social assistance | 29 August 2017 | Budapest, Hungary |
| 72. | Interview with CSO providing social assistance | 29 August 2017 | Budapest, Hungary |
| 73. | Interview with CSO providing social assistance | 30 August 2017 | Budapest, Hungary |
| 74. | Interview with EU agencies/officials | 30 August 2017 | Budapest, Hungary |
| 75. | Interview with CSO providing social and medical assistance | 30 August 2017 | Budapest, Hungary |
| 76. | Interview with government-affiliated think tank | 30 August 2017 | Budapest, Hungary |
| 77. | Interview with non-formal group (activists) providing social assistance | 30 August 2017 | Budapest, Hungary |
| 78. | Interview with legal expert | 30 August 2017 | Budapest, Hungary |
| 79. | Interview with UN actor | 31 August 2017 | Szeged, Hungary |
| 80. | Interview with lawyer | 31 August 2017 | Szeged, Hungary |
| 81. | Interview with non-formal group (activists) providing social assistance | 31 August 2017 | Szeged, Hungary |
| 82. | Interview with non-formal group (activists) providing social assistance | 31 August 2017 | Subotica, Serbia |
| 83. | Interview with national welfare authority providing social and medical assistance | 31 August 2017 | Subotica, Serbia |

**Visit to EU's JHA agencies**

| No | Type | Date | Place |
|---|---|---|---|
| 84. | Interview with EU agencies | 24 August 2017 | Hague, the Netherlands |
| 85. | Interview with national border/ law enforcement authorities (a) | 24 August 2017 | Hague, the Netherlands |
| 86. | Interview with national border/ law enforcement authorities (b) | 24 August 2017 | Hague, the Netherlands |
| 87. | Interview with national border/ law enforcement authorities (c) | 24 August 2017 | Hague, the Netherlands |
| 88. | Interview with national border/ law enforcement authorities (d) | 24 August 2017 | Hague, the Netherlands |
| 89. | Interview with national judicial authorities | 24 August 2017 | Hague, the Netherlands |

# ANNEX 2

# Coding Framework for Semi-Structured Interviews

| Substantive codes | Sub-codes |
|---|---|
| **A priori codes** | |
| National policies | Entry, transit, residence, other |
| The role of the EU | EU Home Affairs agencies (FRONTEX, Europol, Eurojust, EASO), other |
| Civil society organisation activities | Legal assistance, healthcare, education, housing, food, other |
| Impact on work of civil society organisation | 'chilling effect'/'self-censorship', funding, existential threat, psychological pressure, shift towards political activism, leaving the site/abandoning activities, making concessions, other |
| Social trust | Trust of their clients (migrants, refugees and asylum seekers), trust with the society (negative public opinion), trust with law enforcement and asylum authorities (co-operation) |
| Effective ways to fight smuggling | Criteria for effectiveness, impact, intel v. evidence, other |
| Criminalisation of migrants | Criminal sanctions, administrative fines, other |
| Criminalisation of humanitarian assistance | Criminal sanctions, administrative fines, other |
| Policing of humanitarian assistance | Suspicion, intimidation and harassment, disciplining, other |
| Search and rescue | EU-led operations (EUNAVFOR MED Sophia, JO Triton, JO Poseidon), NATO, SAR NGOs, SAR zones (Turkish Coast Guard, Libyan Coast Guard), other |
| Hotspots approach | Access for CSAs to monitor situation in hotspots, provision of services, access to clients in order to defend their rights, excessive use of force by the law enforcement, other |

| Substantive codes | Sub-codes |
|---|---|
| Access to residence and rights | Informal settlements, squats |
| Visions for best practice or better policies/working together | Fire wall protections, role of local authorities, other |
| **Emerging codes** | |
| 'Hostile environment' | Political discourses, media, social media attacks, counter-movements, lack of policing v. over-policing. |

# ANNEX 3

# Mapping Key Actors Involved in Search and Rescue and Anti-Smuggling Activities in Italy

**Figure A3.1** EU and national actors in combating smuggling and conducting SAR operations

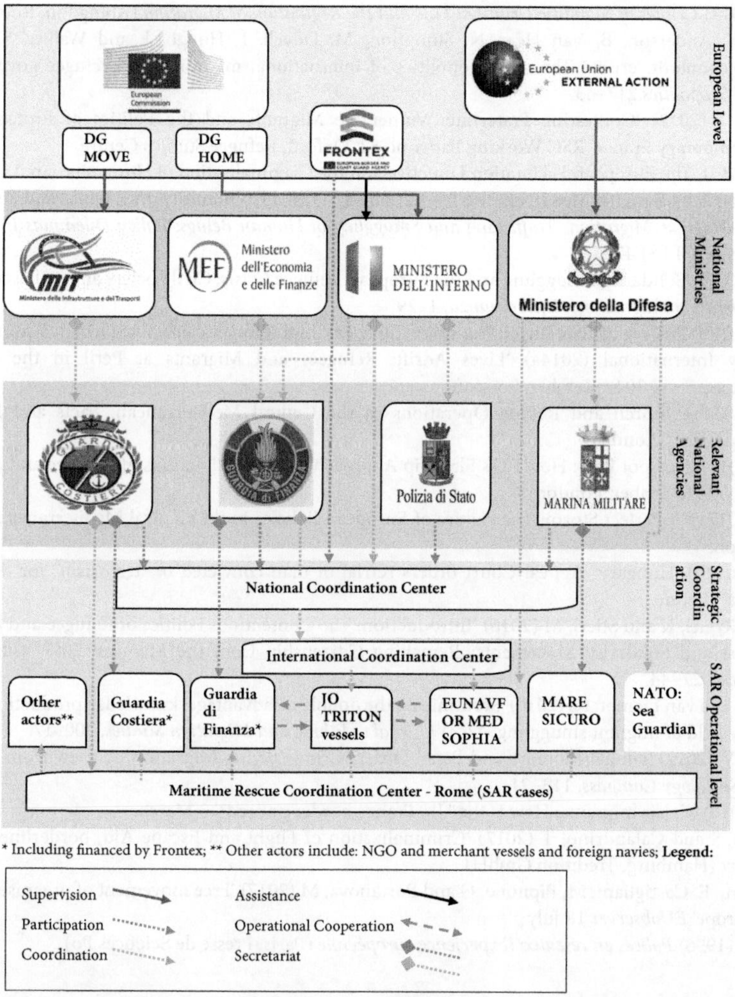


* Including financed by Frontex; ** Other actors include: NGO and merchant vessels and foreign navies; **Legend:**

# BIBLIOGRAPHY


Addley, E (2014) 'Border police arrest cleaner at heart of Mark Harper immigration row' *The Guardian* 18 July.

Aitkenhead, D and Wintour, P (2013) 'Lib Dem MP Attacks Coalition's Plans for Immigration Reform' *The Guardian* 13 July.

ALB (2012) 'All eyes on Orbán' *The Economist* 30 December.

Albanese, F 'Abbiamo le prove dei contatti tra scafisti e alcuni soccorritori' (2017) *La Stampa* 23 April.

Aliverti, A (2012) 'Making People Criminal: The Role of the Criminal Law in Immigration Enforcement' 16(4) *Theoretical Criminology* 417–34.

—— (2013) *Crimes of Mobility: Criminal Law and the Regulation of Migration* (Abingdon, Routledge).

Allen, W, Anderson, B, Van Hear, N, Sumption, M, Düvell, F, Hough, J, and Walker, S (2018) 'Who counts in crises? The new geopolitics of international migration and refugee governance' 23(1) *Geopolitics* 217–43.

Allsopp, J (2012) 'Contesting Fraternité: Vulnerable Migrants and the Politics of Protection in Contemporary France' RSC Working Paper no 82, Oxford, Refugee Studies Centre.

—— (2016) 'The European Facilitation Directive and the Criminalisation of Humanitarian Assistance to Irregular Migrants: Measuring the Impact on the Whole Community' in E Guild and S Carrera (eds) *Irregular Migration, Trafficking and Smuggling of Human Beings: Policy Dilemmas in the EU* (Brussels, CEPS) 47–57.

—— (2017a) 'Solidarity, Smuggling and the European Refugee Crisis: Civil Society and its Discontents' (3) *Diritto, Immigrazione, Cittadinanza*, 1–29.

—— (2017b) 'A Very British Tug of War Over Europe's Child Refugees', *openDemocracy*, 9 March.

Amnesty International (2014a) 'Lives Adrift: Refugees and Migrants at Peril in the Central Mediterranean', 30 September, London.

—— (2014b) 'Search and Rescue Operations in the Central Mediterranean: Facts and Figures', 30 September, London.

—— (2016) 'Hotspot Italy: How EU's Flagship Approach Leads to Violations of Refugee and Migrant Rights', 3 November, London.

—— (2017a) 'A Perfect Storm: The Failure of European Policies in the Central Mediterranean', 6 July, London.

—— (2017b) 'Hungary: Appeal Court orders retrial of man convicted of "terrorism" for throwing stones' 15 June.

Ataç, I, Rygiel, K and Stierl, M (2016) 'Introduction: The Contentious Politics of Refugee and Migrant Protest and Solidarity Movements: Remaking Citizenship from the Margins' 20(5) *Citizenship Studies*, 527–44.

Baird, T and van Liempt, IC (2016) 'Scrutinising the double disadvantage: knowledge production in the messy field of migrant smuggling' 42(3) *Journal of Ethnic and Migration Studies*, 400–17.

Barker, V (2012) 'Global Mobility and Penal Order: Criminalizing Migration, A View from Europe' 6(2) *Sociology Compass*, 113–21.

BBC (2016) 'Calais migrants: How is the UK-France border policed?' 3 March.

Bellezza, S and Calandrino, T (2017) 'Criminalization of Flight and Escape Aid', borderline-europe Report (Hamburg, Tredition GmbH).

Bianchini, E, Castigliani, M, Pipitone, G and Portanova, M (2017) 'Free movement of organised crime in Europe' *EUobserver* 18 July.

Bigo, D (1996) *Polices en réseaux: l'expérience européenne* (Paris, Presse de Sciences Po).

—— (2005) 'Frontier Controls in the European Union: Who Is in Control?' in D Bigo and E Guild (eds) *Controlling Frontiers: Free Movement into and within Europe* (Aldershot, Ashgate Publishing) 49–99.

—— (2014) 'The (In)securitization Practices of the Three Universes of EU Border Control: Military/Navy-Border Guards/Police-Database Analysts' 45 *Security Dialogue*.

Bigo, D and Guild, E (eds) (2005) *Controlling Frontiers: Free Movement into and within Europe* (Aldershot, Ashgate Publishing).

Bloch, A and McKay, S (2015) 'Sanctioning employers does not prevent exploitation and unfree labour', *openDemocracy*, 8 December.

Block, L and Bonjour, S (2013) 'Fortress Europe or Europe of Rights? The Europeanisation of Family Migration Policies in France, Germany and the Netherlands' 15(2) *European Journal of Migration and Law* 203–24.

Bonjour, S and Vink, M (2014) 'When Europeanisation Backfires: The Normalisation of European Migration Politics' 38 *Acta Política* 389–407.

Brassard-Boureau, C and Hubert, D (2010) 'Shrinking Humanitarian Space? Trends and Prospects on Security and Access' *The Journal of Humanitarian Assistance*, November.

Butler, G and Ratcovich, M (2016) 'Operation Sophia in Uncharted Waters: European and International Law Challenges for the EU Naval Mission in the Mediterranean Sea' 85 *Nordic Journal of International Law*.

Camilli, A (2017) 'Sgomberare gli sgomberati, il fallimento dell'accoglienza a Roma', *Internazionale* 24 August.

Carrera, S (2016) 'Implementation of EU Readmission Agreements: Identity Determination Dilemmas and the Blurring of Rights', *Springer Briefs in Law*, Springer International Publishers.

Carrera, S and Allsopp, J (2017) 'The irregular immigration policy conundrum: problematizing "effectiveness" as a frame for EU criminalization and expulsion policies', in F Trauner and A Ripoll (eds) *Routledge Handbook of Justice and Home Affairs Research* (London, Routledge).

Carrera, S and Guild, E (eds) (2016) *Irregular Migration, Trafficking and Smuggling of Human Beings: Policy Dilemmas in the EU* (Brussels, CEPS).

Carrera, S and Hernanz, N (2016) 'Re-Imagining Mobility and Identity Controls: The Next Generation of the EU Migration Management Toolkit' *Journal of Borderlands Studies*.

Carrera, S, Allsopp, J and Vosyliūtė, L (forthcoming, 2018) 'Policing the Mobility Society: The Effects of Anti-Human Smuggling Policies on Humanitarian Assistance in the EU' *International Journal of Migration and Border Studies*.

Carrera, S, Blockmans, S, Gros, D, and Guild, E (2015) 'The EU's Response to the Refugee Crisis: Taking Stock and Setting Policy Priorities', *CEPS Essay*, No 20/16 December.

Carrera, S, den Hertog, L and Parkin, J (2013) 'The Peculiar Nature of EU Home Affairs Agencies in Migration Control: Beyond Accountability versus Autonomy?' 4 *European Journal of Migration and Law*.

Carrera, S, Guild, E, Aliverti, A, Allsopp, J, Manieri, M-G and Levoy, M (2016a). 'Fit for purpose? The Facilitation Directive and the criminalisation of humanitarian assistance to irregular migrants', report commissioned by the Policy Department for Citizens' Rights and Constitutional Affairs at the request of the LIBE Committee, European Parliament, February, European Parliament, Brussels.

Carrera, S, Guild, E, Vosyliūtė, L, Scherrer, A and Mitsilegas, V (2016b) 'The Cost of Non-Europe in the Area of Organised Crime', report commissioned by the European Parliamentary Research Service at the request of LIBE Committee, European Parliament, April.

Chazan, D (2014) 'Calais migrants "becoming more violent" in attempts to reach Britain', *The Telegraph*, 12 September.

Cholewinski, R (2012) 'The EU Acquis on Irregular Migration Ten Years On' in E Guild and P Minderhoud (eds) *The First Decade of EU Migration and Asylum Law* (Leiden, Martinus Nijhoff) 127–78.

Council of Europe (2010) 'Criminalisation of Migration in Europe: Human Rights Implications', Issue Paper, Commissioner for Human Rights. URL.

—— (2017) 'Alarming developments in Hungary: draft NGO law restricting civil society and possible closure of the European Central University', Doc 14298, 25 April.

Council of Europe Venice Commission (2017a) 'Hungary – Preliminary Opinion on the Draft Law on the Transparency of Organisations receiving support from abroad', Opinion 889, 2 June.

—— (2017b) 'Hungary – Opinion on the Draft Law on the Transparency of Organisations receiving support from abroad', Opinion 889, 2 June.

Council of the EU (2015a) Council Conclusions 'Migration crisis: aspects of judicial cooperation and fight against xenophobia – progress report', 14716/15, Brussels, 1 December.

—— (2015b) Decision (CFSP) 2015/778 of 18 May 2015 on a European Union military operation in the Southern Central Mediterranean (EUNAVFOR MED) [2015] OJ L122/31.

—— (2015c) Council Decision (CFSP) 2015/972 of 22 June 2015 launching the European Union military operation in the southern Central Mediterranean (EUNAVFOR MED) [2015] OJ L 157/51.

—— (2015d) Council Decision (CFSP) 2015/1772 of 28 September 2015 concerning the transition by EUNAVFOR MED to the second phase of the operation, as laid down in point (b)(i) of Article 2(2) of Decision (CFSP) 2015/778 on a European Union military operation in the Southern Central Mediterranean (EUNAVFOR MED) (EUNAVFOR MED/2/2015) [2015] OJ L 258/5.

—— (2015e) Council Decision (CFSP) 2015/1926 of 26 October 2015 amending Decision (CFSP) 2015/778 on a European Union military operation in the Southern Central Mediterranean (EUNAVFOR MED) [2015] OJ L281/13, Article 1.

—— (2015f) 'Measures to handle the refugee and migration crisis – Council Conclusions (9 November 2015)', 13880/15, Brussels, 9 November 2015.

Council of the EU (2016a) 'EU-Turkey statement', Press Release, 18 March.

—— (2016b) Draft Council conclusions on migrant smuggling, Brussels, 26 January.

—— (2016c) Council Decision (CFSP) 2016/118 of 20 January 2016 concerning the implementation by EUNAVFOR MED operation SOPHIA of United Nations Security Council Resolution 2240 (2015) (EUNAVFOR MED operation SOPHIA/1/2016) [2016] OJ L 23/63.

—— (2016d) Council Decision (CFSP) 2016/993 of 20 June 2016 amending Decision (CFSP) 2015/778 on a European Union military operation in the Southern Central Mediterranean (EUNAVFOR MED operation SOPHIA) [2016] OJ L162/18.

—— (2016e) Council Decision (CFSP) 2016/1635 of 30 August 2016 on the commencement of the capacity building and training of the Libyan Coast Guard and Navy by the European Union military operation in the Southern Central Mediterranean (EUNAVFOR MED operation SOPHIA) (EUNAVFOR MED/3/2016) [2016] OJ L 243/11.

—— (2016f) Council Decision (CFSP) 2016/2314 of 19 December 2016 amending Decision (CFSP) 2015/778 on a European Union military operation in the Southern Central Mediterranean (EUNAVFOR MED operation SOPHIA) [2016] OJ L345/62.

—— (2017a) Council conclusions on setting the EU's priorities for the fight against organised and serious international crime between 2018 and 2021 – Council conclusions (18 May 2017) 9450/17, Brussels, 19 May 2017.

—— (2017b) Strategic Review on EUBAM Libya, EUNAVFOR MED Op Sophia & EU. Liaison and Planning Cell, Working document of the European External Action Service of 15 May 2017 (leaked by Statewatch).

—— (2017c) Council Decision (CFSP) 2017/1385 of 25 July 2017 amending Decision (CFSP) 2015/778 on a European Union military operation in the Southern Central Mediterranean (EUNAVFOR MED operation SOPHIA) L 194/61.

Crépeau, F (2013) 'UN Special Rapporteur on the Human Rights of Migrants Concluding Remarks', Speech, FRA-ECtHR Seminar on European Law on Asylum, borders and immigration, 11 June.

Crépeau, F and Hastie, B (2015) 'The Case for 'Firewall' Protections for Irregular Migrants: Safeguarding Fundamental Rights' 2–3 *European Journal of Migration and Law (EMIL)* 157–83.

Dearden, L (2017a) 'UN condemns Hungary's new law targeting foreign-funded NGOs for "chilling effect" on freedoms and scrutiny' *The Independent*, 16 May.

—— (2017b) 'Italy seizes refugee rescue ship accused of having contact with Libyan smugglers' *The Independent*, 3 August.
DNAA (2015) Statement of the Italian National Anti-Mafia and Counterterrorism (DNAA) Prosecutor, Rome, 1 October.
*The Economist* (2016) 'Calais Capers: Threats to move Britain's border back from Calais to Dover are mostly empty' 1 September.
Edwards, M (2004) *Civil Society* (Cambridge, Policy Press).
—— (ed) (2011) *The Oxford Handbook of Civil Society* (New York, Oxford University Press).
Elbagir, N, Razek, R, Platt, A and Jones, B (2017) 'People for Sale: Where lives are auctioned for $400' CNN Exclusive Report, 14 November.
Eurojust (2015) 'Eurojust signs letter of understanding with EUNAVFOR MED', The Hague, 1 October.
—— (2016a) Outcome document of the 'Tactical meeting on judicial challenges in illegal migrant smuggling [*sic*]', Eurojust, The Hague, 4–5 February.
—— (2016b) EUROJUST 2016 Annual Report, The Hague, April.
European Commission (2014a) 'Statement by Commissioner Malmström after the meeting with Italian Interior Minister Alfano', Brussels, 27 August.
—— (2014b) 'Frontex Joint Operation "Triton" – Concerted efforts to manage migration in the Central Mediterranean', Memo, Brussels, 7 October.
—— (2015a) A European Agenda on Migration, Communication, COM(2015) 240 final, 13 May, Brussels.
—— (2015b) Communication, EU Action Plan against migrant smuggling (2015–2020) COM(2015) 285 final, 27 May 2017.
—— (2015c) Annex 2 of Communication on 'Managing the refugees crisis: immediate operational, budgetary and legal measures under the European Agenda on Migration' of 23 September 2015, COM(2015) 490 final, Brussels, 29 September.
—— (2015d) The European Agenda on Security, Communication, COM(2015) 185 final, 28 April 2015, Strasbourg.
—— (2016a) The State of Play of Implementation of the Priority Actions under the European Agenda, COM(2016) 85 final, Brussels, 10 February; and its Annex 3, 'Italy – State of Play Report', Brussels, 10 February.
—— (2016b) Next Operational Steps in EU-Turkey Cooperation in the Field of Migration, COM(2016) 166 final, Brussels, 16 March.
—— (2016c) 'Joint action plan on the implementation of the EU-Turkey Statement'.
—— (2016d) 'EU Operations in The Mediterranean Sea', Factsheet updated on 4 October.
—— (2017a) Seventh Report on the on the progress made in the Implementation of the EU-Turkey Statement, COM(2017) 470 final, Brussels, 6 September.
—— (2017b) 'Operational implementation of the EU-Turkey Statement', Brussels, 22 September.
—— (2017c) 'Irregular Migration via the Central Mediterranean', EPSC Strategic Notes, Issue 22, 2 February.
—— (2017d) REFIT Evaluation of the EU legal framework against facilitation of unauthorised entry, transit and residence: the Facilitators Package (Directive 2002/90/EC and Framework Decision 2002/946/JHA) SWD(2017) 117 final Commission Staff Working Document, Brussels, 22 March.
—— (2017e) 'Hungary: Commission launches infringement procedure for law on foreign-funded NGOs', Press Release, 13 July.
European Council (2017) Document EUCO 8/17 (23 June).
European Court of Auditors (ECA) (2017) Special Report 'EU response to the refugee crisis: the "hotspot' approach" (pursuant to Article 287(4) second subparagraph, TFEU) Luxembourg.
European Union (2002a) Directive 2002/90 of 28 November 2002 defining the facilitation of unauthorised entry, transit and residence, OJ L 328, 5.12.2002.
—— (2002b) Framework Decision 2002/946 of 28 November 2002 on the strengthening of the penal framework to prevent the facilitation of unauthorized entry, transit and residence, 5 December.
—— (2013) Regulation No 1052/2013 of the European Parliament and of the Council of 22 October 2013 establishing the European Border Surveillance System (Eurosur) OJ L 295/11, 6.11.2013.

—— (2016a) European Border and Coast Guard Regulation (EU/2016/1624) on the European Border and Coast Guard, 14 September, OJ L 251/1, 16.9.2016.
—— (2016b) Regulation (EU) 2016/794 of the European Parliament and of the Council of 11 May 2016 on the European Union Agency for Law Enforcement Cooperation (Europol) and replacing and repealing Council Decisions 2009/371/JHA, 2009/934/JHA, 2009/935/JHA, 2009/936/JHA and 2009/968/JHA, OJ L 135/53, 24.05.2016.
European Union Agency for Fundamental Rights (FRA) (2014) 'Criminalisation of Migrants in an Irregular Situation and of persons engaging with them', March, Vienna.
Europol (2015a) About Europol.
—— (2015b) EU Policy Cycle – EMPACT.
—— (2016a) European Migrant Smuggling Centre Infographic.
—— (2016b) 'Europol Launches the European Migrant Smuggling Centre', Press Release, The Hague, 22 February.
—— (2016c) Report 'Migrant smuggling in the EU', The Hague, February.
—— (2016d) 'Europol Supports Hungarian-Slovakian Team in Dismantling Migrant Smuggling Network', Press Release, The Hague, 2 June.
—— (2017a) EPMT No 300/2 Year special edition, The Hague.
—— (2017b) 'Operation Taurus – Greece and Europol Dismantle an Organized Crime Group', Press Release, The Hague, 6 November.
—— (2017c) 'European Migrant Smuggling Centre – First Year Activity Report: January 2016–January 2017', The Hague.
Fassin, D (2011) *Humanitarian Reason: A Moral History of the Present* (Berkeley and Los Angeles, University of California Press).
Fekete, L, Webber, F and Edmond-Pettitt, A (2017) 'Humanitarianism: the unacceptable face of solidarity', London, Institute of Race Relations.
Feldman, I and Ticktin, M (eds) (2010) *In the Name of Humanity: The Government of Threat and Care* (Durham and London, Duke University Press).
Ford, P (2017) 'Priest Named "Guardian Angel of Refugees" Under Investigation in Italy', *News Deeply*, 4 September.
Foucault (1980) *Power/Knowledge: Selected Interviews and Other Writings, 1972–1977* (New York, Pantheon Books).
Frayer, L (2015) 'Risking Arrest, Thousands of Hungarians Offer Help to Refugees', National Public Radio, npr.org, 29 September.
Freedom House (2017) 'Hungary: Freedom of the Press 2016'.
Frontex (2016a) 'The role of Frontex in search and rescue', 7 July.
—— (2016b) 'Joint Operation Poseidon (Greece)', 10 October.
—— (2016c) 'Joint Operation Triton (Italy)', 10 October.
—— (2017) Annual Risk Analysis of 2017.
Giannoli, V and Lucente, S (2015) 'Blitz nel centro di accoglienza "Baobab" a Roma: migranti perquisiti e identificati' *Repubblica* 24 November.
Gkliati, M (2016) 'Proud to Aid and Abet Refugees: The Criminalization of "Flight Helpers" in Greece', Border Criminologies Blog, University of Oxford, Faculty of Law, 24 May.
Global Detention Project (2016) 'The UK Profile 2016'.
Guild, E (2006a) 'Conclusions: The Variable Political and Legal Geography of People Smuggling and Trafficking in Europe' in E Guild and P Minderhoud (eds) *Immigration and Criminal Law in the European Union: The Legal Measures and Social Consequences of Criminal Law in Member States on Trafficking and Smuggling in Human Beings* (Leiden, Martinus Nijhoff Publishers) 407.
—— (2006b) 'Danger – Borders under Construction: Assessing the First Five Years of Border Policy in an Area of Freedom, Security and Justice' in J de Zwaan and FANJ Goudappel (eds) *Freedom, Security and Justice in the European Union: Implementation of the Hague Programme* (The Hague: TMC Asser Press) 62–67.
—— (2010) 'The Criminalisation of Migration in Europe: Human Rights Implications', Issue Paper, Council of Europe, Strasbourg.

Guild, E and Minderhoud, P (eds) (2006) *Immigration and Criminal Law in the European Union: The Legal Measures and Social Consequences of Criminal Law in Member States on Trafficking and Smuggling in Human Beings* (Leiden, Martinus Nijhoff Publishers).

Guiraudon, V (2000) 'European Integration and Migration Policy: Vertical Policy Making as Venue Shopping' 38 *Journal of Common Market Studies*, 251–71.

Gulia, G (2016) 'Chronology of Incidents against migrants and activists in Ventimiglia 2015–2016' *Q Code Magazine* 9 December.

Hall, A and Lichfield, J (2015) 'Germany opens its gates: Berlin says all Syrian asylum-seekers are welcome to remain, as Britain is urged to make a "similar statement"' *The Independent* 24 August.

Held, D (2006) *Models of Democracy*, 2nd edn (Cambridge, Polity Press).

Howden, D and Bode, K (2017) 'Expert Opinion: Should Search and Rescue NGOs Sign Mediterranean Code of Conduct?' News Deeply, 16 August.

Human Rights at Sea (2017) 'Voluntary NGO Code of Conduct', March.

—— (2017) 'World Report 2017: Events of 2016'.

Hungarian Helsinki Committee (2015) *No Country for Refugees – New asylum rules deny protection to refugees and lead to unprecedented human rights violations in Hungary*, 18 September.

—— (2016) 'Destitute but Waiting: Report on the visit to the Tompa and Röszke "Pre-Transit Zone" Area on the Serbian-Hungarian border', 22 April.

—— (2017a) 'Best Interest Out of Sight – The Treatment of Asylum Seeking Children in Hungary', 17 May.

—— (2017 b) 'Unidentified and Unattended: The Response of Eastern EU Member States to the Special Needs of Torture Survivor and Traumatised Asylum Seekers', May 2017.

Iqbal, N (2017) 'Eritrean priest in Italy denies "people smuggling"' BBC 17 August.

Italian Ministry of the Interior (2016) Standard Operating Procedures Applicable in Italian Hotspots.

Italian Navy (2014) Mare Nostrum Operation.

Jackson, J (2017) 'Home Office decision to end Dubs scheme "not backed by evidence"' *The Guardian* 6 March.

Jeandesboz, J 'Beyond the Tartar Steppe: EUROSUR and the Ethics of European Border Control Practices' in JP Burgess and S Gurtwith (eds) *A Threat Against Europe? Security, Migration and Integration* (Brussels, VUB Press, 2011) 111–32.

Jones, H, Gunaratnam, Y, Bhattacharyya, G, Davies, W, Dhaliwal, S, Forkert, K, Jackson, E and Saltus, R (2017) *Go home?: The Politics of Immigration Controversies* (Manchester, Manchester University Press).

Jordan, L and Van Tuijl, P (eds) (2006) *NGO Accountability: Politics, Principles and Innovation* (London, Earthscan).

Juncker, JC (2017) 'Letter to Victor Orban' *Politico* 5 September.

Kent Online (2015) 'Fines for Lorry Drivers Caught with Illegal Immigrants Triples', 5 August.

Krugman, P (2012) 'The Unconstitutional Constitution' *The New York Times* 2 January.

Lusher, A (2016) 'Rob Lawrie: Ex-soldier who smuggled Afghan girl out of Calais refugee camp spared jail', *The Independent*, 14 January.

Mason, R (2014) 'David Cameron criticised for PR stunt in home of suspected illegal immigrants' *The Guardian*, 30 July.

Matringe, J (2009) 'Le délit de solidarité et la résistance à l'oppression', paper delivered at the Observatoire Juridique de la vie politique on 24 September.

Médecins Sans Frontières (2017) 'MSF denounces widespread violence against migrants and refugees at the Serbia-Hungary border', msn.org, 8 March.

Meret, S and Goffredo, S (2017) 'Solidarity under attack', *openDemocracy*, 18 October.

Middle East Eye (2016) 'UN Agency slams New Greek Refugee Detention Facilities', 22 March.

Miller, T (2003) 'Citizenship & Severity: Recent Immigration Reforms and the New Penology' 10 *Georgetown Immigration Law Review*, 611–13.

Mitsilegas, V (2015) 'The Criminalisation of Migration in Europe: Challenges for Human Rights and the Rule of Law', *Springer Briefs in Law*, London, Springer.

—— (2016) *EU Criminal Law after Lisbon: Rights, Trust and the Transformation of Justice in Europe* (Oxford, Hart Publishing).
—— (2018, forthcoming) 'Extraterritorial Immigration Control, Preventive Justice and the Rule of Law in Turbulent Times' in Santos Vara, J, S Carrera and T Strik (eds) *Constitutionalising the External Dimension of EU Migration Policies in Times of Crisis: Legality, Rule of Law and Fundamental Rights Reconsidered* (Cheltenham, Edward Elgar, 2018).
Mitsilegas, V and N Vavoula (2015) 'Criminal Law: Institutional Rebalancing and Judicialisation as Drivers of Policy Change' in *Policy change in the Area of Freedom, Security and Justice*, Abingdon, Routledge, 149–166.
Moreno-Lax, V (2017) *Accessing Asylum in Europe. Extraterritorial Border Controls. Oxford Scholarship Online*, Oxford, Oxford University Press.
Morris, L (2009), 'Civic stratification and the cosmopolitan ideal: the case of welfare and asylum' 11(4) *European Societies* 603–24.
NATO (2016) 'Factsheet: NATO's Deployment in the Aegean Sea', October.
Neier, A (2012) *The International Human Rights Movement: A History* (Princeton, Princeton University Press).
Nielsen, N (2016) 'Amnesty: Italian police tortured migrants to meet EU target' *EUobserver* 3 November.
Nobel Peace Prize Committee (2017) 'The Righteous of the Mediterranean Sea', 2018 nominations.
O'Carroll, L (2016) 'Immigration raid on Byron Hamburgers rounds up 35 workers' *The Guardian*, 27 July.
*Open Migration* (2017) 'The 10 Best Articles on Refugees and Migration 16/2017', 25 April.
Open the Islands Campaign (2017) Statement, 22 October.
Orbán, V (2014) 'Full text of Viktor Orbán's speech at Băile Tuşnad (Tusnádfürdő) of 26 July 2014' *The Budapest Beacon* 29 July.
Papastavridis, E (2016) 'EUNAVFOR MED Operation Sophia and the question of jurisdiction over transnational organized crime at sea' *Questions of International Law* 5 August.
Parkin, J (2013) 'The Criminalisation of Migration in Europe: A State of the Art of the Academic Literature and Research', CEPS Papers in Liberty and Security in Europe, No 61, October, CEPS, Brussels.
PICUM (2017) 'Help Is No Crime: People Share their Stories of Being Accused, Intimidated and Punished for Helping Migrants', testimonies website.
Provera, M (2015) 'The Criminalisation of Irregular Migration in the European Union', CEPS Papers on Liberty and Security in Europe, No 80, February, CEPS, Brussels.
Ragazzi, S (2016) 'New experiences in investigating and prosecuting the migrants' smuggling: from the national dimension to a European approach', presented at seminar 'Europe's crisis: What future for immigration and asylum law and policy?', Queen Mary University London, 27–28 June, London.
Rantsiou, F (2017) 'Winterization in Kara Tepe camp, Lesvos', *openDemocracy*, 4 October.
Refugee Action (2013) 'Petition calls for Home Office to give asylum seekers the right to volunteer', Press release, 26 July.
Roberts, R (2017) 'Mayor aims to stop "vigilante" anti-immigrant activists from docking in Sicily' *The Independent* 22 July.
Robinson, D (2016) 'EU border force flags concerns over charities' interaction with migrant smugglers' *Financial Times* 15 December.
Ruetenik, D (2016) 'Keeping the Lights On for Migrants in Rome' (multimedia) *The New York Times* 21 December.
Safdar, A (2016) 'NGOs decry charges against volunteers in Greece' *Al Jazeera* 16 January.
Safe Passage (2017) 'Briefing: Calais and unaccompanied child refugees in Europe', 1 November.
Sandru, M (2017) 'In FRA, 10–18 April, European Union Agency for Fundamental Rights', European legal affairs blog, 10 April.
Schengen acquis (2000) Convention implementing the Schengen Agreement of 14 June 1985 between the Governments of the States of the Benelux Economic Union, the Federal Republic of Germany and the French Republic on the gradual abolition of checks at their common borders, OJ L 239, 22/09/2000 P. 0019–0062.

Sea Watch (2017) '"Nonsensical", "Dishonest", "Illegal": the "Code of Conduct"', Interview with Dr Violeta Moreno-Lax, 24 July.
Sharman, A (2017) 'Over 50 charities write to political parties over Lobbying Act concerns' *Civil Society*, 6 June.
Smalemay, A (2017) 'Hungary Indicts 11 in Truck Suffocation of 71 Refugees' *The New York Times* 4 May.
SOS Méditerranée (2017) 'SOS Méditerannée Signs Amended Version of the Code of Conduct During Meeting in Rome', Press Release, 11 August.
Squat.net (2017) 'Athens: Today City Plaza is one and half years old – October 21st, 2017', 21 October.
Statewatch (2016) 'Refugee crisis: Council proposals on migrant smuggling would criminalise humanitarian assistance by civil society, local people and volunteers – Greece: NGOs and volunteers have to "register" with the police and be vetted', 28 January.
—— (2017) 'Migrant smuggling tops EU crime priorities – restricted document shows extent of police operations', 11 October.
Stumpf, J (2006) 'The Crimmigration Crisis: Immigrants, Crime and Sovereign Power' 56(2) *American University Law Review*, 367–419.
Taylor, M, X. Raufer, M. Den Boer, A. Sinn, M. Levi, L.Paoli, E. Savona (SOCTA Academic Advisory Group) SOCTA 2017: Comments by Academic Advisors, Europol, 2017.
*The Telegraph* (2012) 'London Metropolitan University to launch legal action against UK Border Agency', 4 September.
Triandafyllidou, A (2017) 'Governing migrant smuggling' in P Bourbeau (ed) *Handbook on Migration and Security* (Cheltenham, Edward Elgar Publishing) 210–31.
UK Anti-Slavery Commissioner (2018) Official Website of the Anti-Slavery Commissioner.
UK Crown Prosecution Service (2013) The Code for Crown Prosecutors, London, January.
—— (2017) 'Immigration: Legal Guidance', online guidance.
UK Home Office (2016) Code of practice on illegal immigrants and private rented accommodation, updated 25 May.
—— (2017) Modern Slavery Collection, updated 17 October.
UK House of Lords (2017) European Union Committee, 'Operation Sophia: a failed mission', 2nd Report of Session 2017–19 HL Paper 5, London, 12 July.
—— (2016) European Union Committee, 'Children in crisis: unaccompanied migrant children in the EU' 26 July 2016.
UK Government (1971) Immigration Act 1971, Chapter 77, 28 October.
—— (2017) Penalties for employing illegal workers, guidance on government website.
UN High Commissioner for Human Rights (2016) 'UN expert urges Hungary not to stigmatise and intimidate human rights defenders', UN OHCHR website, Geneva, 16 February.
—— (2017) 'UN human rights chief: Suffering of migrants in Libya outrage to conscience of humanity', UN OHCHR website, Geneva, 14 November.
—— (UNHCR) (2017) 'Donors for the Greek operation: Donors for 2017', UNHCR website.
United Nations (2000a) Protocol against the Smuggling of Migrants by Land, Sea and Air, Supplementing the United Nations Convention against Transnational Organized Crime, 15 November.
—— (2000b) Protocol to Prevent, Suppress and Punish Trafficking in Persons, especially Women and Children, Supplementing The United Nations Convention Against Transnational Organized Crime.
United Nations Office on Drugs and Crime (2004) Legislative Guides for the Implementation of the United Nations Convention against Transnational Organized Crime and the Protocols thereto, UN Sales No E05V2, 2004, p 333, para 19, as quoted in United Nations Office on Drugs and Crime, 'The Concept of "Financial or Other Material Benefit" in the Smuggling of Migrants Protocol', UNODC Issue Paper, UN Office, Vienna, 2017, p 10.
—— (2017) 'The Concept of "Financial or Other Material Benefit" in the Smuggling of Migrants Protocol', UNODC Issue Paper, UN Office, Vienna.
UN Security Council (2015) Resolution 2240 (2015) 9 October.
—— (2016) Resolution 2292 (2016) 14 June.

—— (2017a) Resolution 2357 (2017) 12 June.
—— (2017b) Resolution 2380 (2017) adopted by the Security Council at its 8061st meeting, 5 October.
UN Special rapporteur on human rights defenders (2016) 'UN expert urges Hungary not to stigmatise and intimidate human rights defenders', UN OHCHR website, Geneva, 16 February.
Van der Borgh, C and Terwindt, C (2012) 'Shrinking Operational Space of NGOs – A Framework of Analysis' 22(8) *Development in Practice* 1065–1081, 1068.
Van der Ploeg, T (2017) *Civil Society in Europe* (Cambridge, Cambridge University Press).
'Volunteer lifeguards: "In jail we were treated like terrorists"' (2016) *The Local*, 18 January.
Voynov, G, H Franková, A Bakonyi, M Górczyńska and M Nabergoj (2017) *Pushed Back at the Door: Denial of Access to Asylum in Eastern EU Member States* (Hungarian Helsinki Committee).
Webber, F (2008) *Border Wars and Asylum Crimes* (London, Institute of Race Relations).
Westby, L (2002) 'Strategic imperative, ideology, and frame' 7(3) *Mobilization: An International Quarterly*, 287–304.
Wilding, M (2016) 'European Governments Are Arresting Refugee Crisis Volunteers', *Vice*, 3 May.
Yeo, C (2016) 'Home Office imposes illegal working fines of £14 million on small businesses in 3 month period', Freedom of Movement blog, 6 September.
—— (2017) 'The Hostile Environment: What Is It and Who Does it Affect?', Freedom of Movement blog, 29 May.
Youngs, R and Echagüe, A (2017) 'Shrinking Space for Civil Society: The EU Response', paper requested by European Parliament Subcommittee on Human Rights, Brussels, 5.
Zhang, X, Sanchez G, Achilli L (2018) 'Crimes of Solidarity in Mobility: Alternative Views on Migrant Smuggling' 676(1) *The Annals*, 6–15, Article first published online.

# INDEX